RULERS AND RULED
IN THE US EMPIRE

RULERS
AND RULED
IN THE US
EMPIRE

BANKERS, ZIONISTS, MILITANTS

JAMES PETRAS

CLARITY PRESS, INC.

ISBN: 0-932863-54-X
    978-0932863-54-6

In-house editor: Diana G. Collier
Cover: Mona Dovina Prodaniuk

Library of Congress Cataloging-in-Publication Data

Petras, James F., 1937-
    Rulers and ruled in the US Empire : bankers, zionists and militants /
    James Petras.
        p. cm.
    ISBN 0-932863-54-X (978-932863-54-6)
1. Elite (Social sciences)—United States. 2. Power (Social sciences)—
United States. 3. United States—Politics and government. I. Title.
HN90.E4P48 2007
306.20973—dc22

                    2007016468

Clarity Press, Inc.
Ste. 469, 3277 Roswell Rd. NE
Atlanta, GA. 30305
USA
http://www.claritypress.com

TO MY FRIENDS, COLLEAGUES AND COMRADES

Michael, Morris
Antonio and Carmen, Lucio and Waldir
John and Teresa
Luciano and Rita
Irene, Henry, Miguel
Manuel, Chury

ACKNOWLEDGMENTS

Robin Eastman Abaya for our continual discussions, her editorial and substantive critique. Diana G. Collier for her excellent editorial assistance.

TABLE OF CONTENTS

PART I

THE US EMPIRE
AS A SYSTEM

CHAPTER 1

WHO RULES AMERICA?

*"We make the rules—the news, war, peace, famine, upheaval,
the cost of a paper clip... you're not naive enough to think
we're living in a democracy are you? It's the free market."*
Michael Douglas in **Wall Street**

Introduction

In the broadest and deepest sense, understanding how the US political
system functions, how the decisions of war and peace are taken, who gets
what, how and why, requires that we address the question of 'Who rules
America?' In tackling the question of 'ruling' one needs to clarify a great
number of misunderstandings, particularly the confusion between those who
make governmental decisions and the socio-economic institutional parameters
which define the interests to be served. Ruling is exacting: it concerns
setting the rules to be followed by the political and administrative decision-
makers in formulating budgetary expenditures, taxes, labor and social
legislation, trade policy, military and strategic questions of war and peace.

*The high school textbook version of American politics is that the
major political parties and candidates present ideas to the American people
on public policy, and the people choose which ideas will rule the country. In
this textbook version of things, the politicians take interest groups into
account in formulating their ideas. These interests groups include business,
labor, religious, civic and other organizations. No one of them is dominant.
This is the 'pluralist' view of American politics.*

*In actuality, something very different happens. The people in key
positions in financial, corporate and other business institutions establish the
parameters within which the politicians, parties and media discuss ideas.
These people constitute a ruling class. Their composition changes according
to which sector of these business institutions is dominant at a given point in
history. The rules are established, modified and adjusted according to the
specific composition of the leading sectors of a ruling class. Rules change
with shifts in power within the ruling class. Shifts in power can reflect the
internal dynamics of an economy or the changing position of economic sectors
in the world economy, particularly the rise and decline of economic competitors.*

To illustrate how the ruling class operates, take the control of public
power utilities. While many studies demonstrate that publicly controlled

utilities offer cheaper power to consumers and a better revenue source for public services, there has been no serious challenge to privatized 'investor-owned' utilities in most of the US. Not even liberal San Francisco can appropriate funds for a feasibility study of public utilities,[1] which is dismissed as 'socialistic' and not even covered in the mass media. On the other hand, utilities are public in Nyack, New York where the energy-intensive aluminum industry has benefited from the cheaper electricity and teamed up with its labor union to ensure that power stays public.

The rules imposed by one economic sector of the ruling class at a time of favorable conditions in the world economy will be altered as new dominant economic sectors emerge and unfavorable external conditions weaken the former dominant economic sectors. As we shall describe below, the relative and absolute decline of the US manufacturing sector is directly related to the rise of a multidimensional 'financial sector' and to the greater competitiveness of other manufacturing countries. The result is an accelerating process of liberalization of the economy favored by the ascending financial sectors even though this is to the detriment of the manufacturing sector. Liberalization in pursuit of unregulated flows of investments, buyouts, acquisitions and trade increases the financial sector's profits, commissions, incomes and bonuses. Liberalization facilitates the financial sector's acquisition of assets. The declining competitiveness of the older ruling class manufacturing sector dependent on statist protectionism and subsidies leads to 'rear-guard' policies, attempting to fashion an unwieldy policy of liberalization abroad and protectionism at home.

The question of *who rules* requires that we specify the historical moment and place in the world economy. The answer is complicated by the fact that shifts among sectors of the ruling class involve a prolonged transitional period. During this period declining and ascending sectors may intermingle and the class members of declining sectors convert to the rising sector. Hence while power between *economic sectors* may change, the leading *class groupings* may not lose out or decline. They merely shift their investments and adapt to the new and more lucrative opportunities created by the ascending sector.

For example, while the US manufacturing sector has declined relative to finance capital, many of the major investment institutions have shifted to the new financial growth sectors. Concomitantly, the converted sectors of the ruling class shift their policies toward greater liberalization and deregulation, thus severely weakening the rear-guard demands of the uncompetitive manufacturing sector. Equally important, within the declining economic sectors of the ruling class, drastic structural changes may ensue, reflecting efforts to regain profitable returns and retain influence and power. Foremost of these changes is *relocation* of production overseas to low wage, low tax, non-union locations, the *introduction of IT* technology designed to reduce labor costs and increase productivity, and *diversification* of economic activity to incorporate lucrative financial services.

As an instance, General Electric has moved from manufacturing toward financial services, relocated labor-intensive activity offshore and computerized operations. Through moves such as these occurring across the manufacturing sector, the distinction between manufacturing and financial capital has been made obsolete in describing the ruling class.

To the degree that older manufacturing capitalists retain any economic and political weight in the ruling class, they have done so via sub-contracting overseas to Asia and Mexico (General Motors/Ford), investing in overseas plants to capture foreign markets, or converting in large part into *commercial and importing* operations (shoes, textiles, toys, electronics and computer chips).

Locally based manufacturers which remain in the ruling class are largely military contractors living off the largesse of state spending and depending on the political support of congressional and trade union officials, eager to secure employment for a shrinking manufacturing labor force.

During a transitional period of rapid and all-encompassing changes in the ruling class, enormous financial opportunities have opened throughout the world. As a result of political tensions within the governing class, key policymakers are drawn directly from the most representative institutions of Wall Street. Key economic policies, especially those which are most relevant to the ruling class, tend to be overwhelmingly in the hands of tried and experienced top leaders from Wall Street.

Despite the ascendancy of various sectors of financial capital in the ruling class, reflected in their capacity to institute their agreements through a host of 'liberalizing' economic policies, they are not homogeneous in all of their political outlooks, party affiliations, or their foreign policy orientation. Most of these political differences are questions of small matter—except on one issue where there is a major and growing rift, namely the Middle East. A sector of the ruling class strongly aligned with the state of Israel supports a bellicose policy toward the Jewish state's adversaries (Iran, Syria, Hezbollah and Palestine) while another sector of the ruling class favors a diplomatic approach, directed toward securing closer ties with Arab and Persian elites. Given the highly militarized turn in US foreign policy (largely due to the ascendancy of neo-conservative ideologues, the strong influence of the Zionist Lobby,[2] and the instability and failures of their policies in the Middle East and China), the new/newly dominant financial sector of the ruling class has pressed for and secured direct control by inserting Wall Street executives into senior executive offices making foreign economic policy.

The tensions and conflicts within this ruling class—especially between the *Zioncons* and the 'free marketeers'—have been papered over by the enormous economic benefits accruing to all sectors. All ruling class financial sectors have been enriched by White House and Congressional policies. All have benefited from the ascendancy of liberalizing regimes throughout the world. They all have reaped the gains of the expansionary phase of the international economy. While the entire ruling financial, real estate and trading sectors have been the main beneficiaries, it has been the financial groups, particularly the investment banks, that have led the way and provide the political leadership.

The Ascendancy of Financial Capital

'Finance capital' has many faces and cannot be understood without reference to specific sectors. Investment banks, pension funds, hedge funds, savings and loan banks, and investment funds are only a few of the operative managers of a multi-trillion dollar economy. Moreover each of these sectors has specialized departments engaged in particular types of speculative-financial activity including commodity and currency trading, consulting and managing acquisitions and mergers. Despite a few exposés, court cases, fines and an occasional jailing, the financial sector writes its rules, controls its regulators and has secured license to speculate on everything, everywhere and all the time. They have created the framework or universe in which most other economic activities (manufacturing, retail sales and real estate) take place.

Finance capital is not an isolated sector and cannot be counter-posed to the productive economy except in the most marginal local activity. In large part finance capital interacts with and is the essential driving force in real estate speculation, agro-business, commodity production and manufacturing activity. To a large degree market prices are as influenced by speculative intervention as they are by supply and demand. Equally important, the entire architecture of the 'paper empire' (the entire complex of inter-related financial investments) is ultimately dependent on the production of goods and services.

The structure of power and wealth takes the form of an inverted triangle in which a vast army of workers, peasants and salary employees produce value which becomes the basis for near and remote, simple and exotic, lucrative and speculative financial instruments. The transfer of value from the productive activities of labor up through the trunk and branches of financial instruments is carried out through various vehicles: direct financial ownership of enterprises, credit, debt leveraging, buyouts and mergers. The tendency of productive capitalists is to start-up an enterprise, innovate, exploit labor, capture markets and then sell out or go public (stock offerings). The financial sector acts as combined intermediary, manager, proxy-purchaser and consultant, capturing substantial fees, expanding their economic empires and preparing the way to higher levels of acquisitions and mergers. Finance capital is the midwife of the concentration and centralization of wealth and capital as well as the direct owner of the means of production and distribution. Finance capital has moved from exacting a larger and larger 'tribute' or 'rent' (commission or fee) on each large-scale capital transaction, toward penetrating and controlling an enormous array of economic activities, transferring capital across national and sectoral boundaries, extracting profits and dumping shares according to the business, product and profit cycle.

Within the ruling class, the financial elite is the most parasitical component and exceeds the corporate bosses (CEOs) and most entrepreneurs in wealth and annual payments, though it falls short of the annual income and assets of the super-rich entrepreneurs like William Gates and Michael Dell.

The financial ruling class is internally stratified into three sub-groups: at the top are big private equity bankers and hedge-fund managers, followed by the Wall Street chief executives, who in turn are above the next rung of senior associates or vice-presidents of big private equity funds who are followed by their counterparts at Wall Street's public equity funds. Top hedge fund managers and executive have made $1 billion dollars or more a year—several times what the CEOs make at publicly traded investment houses. For example in 2006 Lloyd Blankfein, CEO of Goldman Sachs, was paid $53.4 million in cash and stock, while Dan Ochs, executive of the hedge fund Och-Ziff Capital, paid himself $220 million dollars. That same year the Morgan Stanley CEO, John Mack, received $40 million dollars in stock and options, while the chief executive of the hedge fund Citadel was paid over $300 million dollars.[3] According to the *Financial Times* of April 2, 2007, "The combined earnings of the world's top 25 hedge fund managers exceeded $15 billion USD. Jim Simons of Renaissance Technologies gained 1.7 billion, Ken Griffin of Citadel Investment Group, $1.4 billion, and Ed Lampbert of ESL Investment, $1.3 billion."

While the hedge fund speculators receive the highest *annual salaries*, the private equity executives can equal their hundreds of millions payments through deal fees and special dividend payments from portfolio companies. This was especially true in 2006 when buyouts reached a record $710 billion dollars.[4] The big bucks for the private equity bosses comes from the accumulating stake executives have in portfolio companies. They typically skim twenty percent of profits, which are realized when a group sells or lists a portfolio company. At that time, the payday runs into the hundreds of millions of dollars.

The subset of the financial ruling class is the 'junior bankers' of private equity firms who take about $500,000 a year. At the bottom rung are the junior bankers of publicly traded investment houses (Wall Street) who average $350,000 a year. The financial ruling class is made up of these multi-billionaire elites from the hedge funds, private and public equity bankers and their associates in big prestigious corporate legal and accounting firms.

They in turn are linked to the judicial and regulatory authorities, through political appointments and contributions, and by their central position in the national economy.

Within the financial ruling class, *political leadership* does not usually come from the richest hedge fund speculators, even less from among the junior bankers. Political leaders come from the public and private equity banks, namely Wall Street—especially Goldman Sachs, Blackstone, the Carlyle Group and others. They organize and fund both major parties and their electoral campaigns. They pressure, negotiate and draw up the most comprehensive and favorable legislation on global strategies (liberalization and deregulation) and sectoral policies (reductions in taxes, government pressure on countries like China to 'open' their financial services to foreign penetration and so on). They pressure the government to bail out bankrupt and failed speculative firms and to balance the budget by lowering social expenditures instead of raising taxes on speculative 'windfall' profits.

The Dance of the Billions:
Finance Capital Reaps the Profits from Their Power

Speculators of the world had a spectacular year in 2006 as global equities hit double digit gains in the US, European and Asian markets. China, Brazil, Russia and India were centers of speculative profiteering as the China FTSE index rose 94 percent, Russia's stock market rose sixty percent, Brazil's Bovespa was up 32.9 percent and India's Sensex climbed 46.7 percent.[5] In large part the stock markets rose because of cheap credit (enabling speculation), strong liquidity (huge financial, petrol and commodity profits and rents) and so-called reforms which gave foreign investors greater access to markets in China, India and Brazil. The biggest profits in stock market speculation occurred under putative 'center-left' regimes (Brazil and India) and 'Communist' China, which have realigned themselves with the most retrograde and 'leading' sectors of their financial ruling class.

Russia's booming stock market reflects a different process involving the re-nationalization of gas and petroleum sectors, at the expense of the gangster-oligarchs of the Yeltsin era and the giveaway contracts to European/ US oil and gas companies (Shell, Texaco). As a result huge windfall profits have been recycled internally among the new Putin-era millionaires who have been engaged in conspicuous consumption, speculation and investment in joint ventures with foreign manufacturers in transport and energy related industries.

The shift toward foreign-controlled speculative capital emerging in China, India and Brazil as opposed to national- and state-funded investment in Russia accounts for the seemingly irrational and undoubtedly vitriolic hostility exhibited by the western financial press to President Putin.

One of the major sources of profit making is in the area of mergers and acquisitions (M&A)—the buying and selling of multinational conglomerates, with $3,900 billion in deals for 2006. Investment banks took $18.8 billion dollars in 'fees' leading to multi-million dollar bonuses for M&A bankers. M&A, hostile or benign, are largely speculative activity fueled by cheap debt and leading to the greater concentration of ownership and profits. Today, the richest two percent of adults own more than half of the world's wealth,[6] while according to *Times* writer, David Brown, the richest tenth own 85 percent of the world's assets.[7] Within this small elite, a fraction embedded in financial capital owns and controls the bulk of the world's assets and organizes and facilitates further concentration of conglomerates. In 2006 the value of speculative M&A on a world scale was 16 percent higher than at the height of the DOTCOM speculative boom of 2000. In the US alone over $400 billion dollars worth of private equity deals were struck in 2005, three times higher than the previous year; by 2006, the value of such deals had increased to over $550 billion (see table below). To understand who are the leading members of the financial ruling class one need only look at the ten leading private equity banks and the value and number of M&A deals in which they were engaged:

Private equity rankings by M&A deals (Year to Dec 20 2006)

US	Value $bn	Number
Blackstone	85.3	12
Texas Pacific	81.9	11
Bain Capital Partners	74.7	9
Thomas H Lee Partners	53.4	6
Goldman Sachs	51.2	5
Carlyle	50.0	14
Apollo Management	44.9	7
Kohlberg Kravis Roberts	44.5	3
Merrill Lynch	35.9	3
Cerberus Capital Management	28.6	4
Industry Total	**550.4**	**74**

Financial Times 12/27/2006 p. 13 - FT montage: Bob Haslett

The crucial fact is that these private equity banks are involved in every sector of the US economy, in every region of the world economy and increasingly speculate in the conglomerates which are acquired.

In the era of the ascendancy of speculative finance capital it is not surprising that the three leading investment banks, Goldman Sachs, Lehman Brothers and Bear Stearns, reported record annual profits based on their expansion in Europe and Asia, and their transfer of profits from manufacturing and services to the financial sector. For the year 2006, Goldman Sachs

(GS) recorded the most profitable year ever for a Wall Street investment bank, on the basis of big (speculative) 'trading gains and lucrative investments' in the world's worst sweatshops in Asia. GS reported a 69 percent jump in annual earnings to $9.54 billion dollars. Lehman Brothers (LB) and Bear Stearns (BS) equity banks also recorded record earnings. LB earned a record $4 billion for the year. BS earned a record $2.1 billion dollars. For the year Lehman set aside about $334,000 dollars per junior banker, while top speculators and bankers earned a big multiple of that amount. For the year 2006 investment banking revenue reached nearly $38 billion dollars compared to $25 billion dollars in 2004—an increase of 34 percent.[8]

The dominance of finance capital has been nurtured by the speculative activity of the controllers and directors of state-owned companies. *'State ownership'* is an ambiguous term since it raises a further more precise question: *'Who owns the state'?* In the Middle East there are seven state-owned oil and gas companies. In six of those companies the principal beneficiaries are a small ruling elite. They recycle their revenues and profits through US and EU investment banks largely into bonds, real estate and other speculative financial instruments.[9] State ownership and speculative capital, in the context of the closed 'Gulf-State' type of ruling classes, are complementary, not contradictory, activities. The ruling regime in Dubai converts oil rents into building a regional financial center. Many Jewish-American-led Wall Street investment banks work with new self-designated Islamic banking and investment houses,[10] both reaping speculative returns.

Much of the investment funds now in the hands of US investment banks, hedge funds and other sectors of the financial ruling class originated in profits extracted from workers in the manufacturing and service sector. Two interrelated processes led to the growth and dominance of finance capital: the transfer of capital and profits from the 'productive' to the financial and speculative sector and the transfer of finance capital overseas,[11] in the form of takeovers of foreign assets, now equivalent to around eighty percent of the US GDP. The roots of finance capital are embedded in three types of intensified exploitation: 1) labor (via extended hours, transfer of pension and health costs from capital to labor, frozen minimum wages, stagnant and declining real wages and salaries); 2) manufacturing profits (through higher rents, inter-sectoral transfers to financial instruments, interest payments and fees and commissions for mergers and acquisitions); and 3) state fiscal policies (by lowering capital gains taxes, increasing tax write-offs and tax incentives for overseas investments and imposing regressive local, state and federal taxes).

The result is increasing inequality between, on the one hand, senior and junior bankers, public, private equity, investment and hedge fund directors, and their entourage of lawyers and accountants, and, on the other hand, wage and salaried workers. Income ratios ranging between 400 to one and

1,000 to one between the ruling class and median wage and salary workers is the norm.

Crisis of the Working and Middle Class
(Inequalities Begin to Worry the Ruling Class)

Living standards for the working and middle classes and the urban poor have declined substantially over the past thirty years (1978-2006) to a point where one can point to a burgeoning crisis. While real hourly wages in constant 2005 dollars have stagnated, health, pension, energy and educational costs (increasingly borne by wage and salary workers) have skyrocketed. If extensions in work time and intensification of workplace production (increases in productivity) are included in the equation, it is clear that living (including working) conditions have declined sharply. Even the financial press is writing articles such as that entitled: "Why Ordinary Americans have Missed Out on the Benefits of Growth".[12]

Financial and investment banks are in charge of advising and directing the 'restructuring' of enterprises for mergers and acquisitions by downsizing, outsourcing, give-backs and other cost-cutting measures. This has led to downward mobility for the wage and salaried workers who retain their jobs even as their tenure is more precarious. In other words, the greater the salaries, bonuses, profits and rents for the financial ruling class engaged in 'restructuring' for M&A, the greater the decline in living standards for the working and middle classes.

One measure of the enormous influence of the financial ruling class in heightening the exploitation of labor is found in the enormous disparity between productivity and wages. Between 2000 and 2005, the US economy grew 12 percent, and productivity (measured by output per hour worked in the business sector) rose 17 percent while hourly wages rose only 3 percent. Real *family* income fell during the same period.[13] According to a poll in November 2006, three quarters of Americans say they are either worse off or no better off than they were six years ago.[14]

The impact of the policies of the financial ruling class on both the manufacturing and service sectors transcends their profit skimming, credit leverage on business operations and management practices. It embraces the entire architecture of the income, investment and class structure. The growth of vast inequalities between the yearly payments of the financial ruling class and the medium salary of workers has reached unprecedented levels.

Members of the financial ruling class have noted these vast and growing inequalities and express some concern over their possible social and political repercussions. According to the *Financial Times,* billionaire Stephen Schwartzman, CEO of the private equity group Blackstone, warned "that the widening gap between Wall Street's lavish pay packages and middle America's stagnating wages risks causing a political and social backlash against the US's 'New Rich'".[15] Treasury Secretary and former CEO of Goldman Sachs, Hank Paulson, admitted that median wage stagnation was a problem and that amidst "strong economic expansion many Americans simply are not feeling [*sic!*] the benefits".[16]

Ben Bernanke, Chairman of the Federal Reserve Bank, testified before the Senate that "inequality is potentially a concern for the US economy…to the extent that incomes and wealth are spreading apart. I think that is not a good trend."[17] In 2005 the proportion of national income to GDP going to profits, rents and other non-wage and salary sources was at record levels—43 percent. Inequality in the distribution of national income in the US is the worst in the entire developed capitalist world. Moreover studies of time series data reveal that in the US, the inequality increase was far greater and intergenerational social mobility was far more difficult than in any country in Western Europe. The growth of monstrous and rigid class inequalities reflects the narrow social base of an economy dominated by finance capital, its ingrown intergenerational linkages and the exorbitant entry fees (ranging around $50,000 per annum tuition with room and board) to elite private universities and post-graduate business schools. Equally important, finance capital and its associated conglomerates wield uncontested political power in the US in comparison to their counterparts in any country in Europe. As a result the US government redistributes far less through the tax and social security, health and educational system than other countries.[18]

While some financial rulers express some anxiety about a 'backlash' from the deepening class divide, not a single one publicly supports any tax or other redistributive measures. Instead they call for increases in educational upgrading and job retraining—though it is precisely the educated middle class which is suffering salary stagnation—and greater geographical mobility.

Neither the Democratic Party majority in Congress nor the Republican-controlled Executive offer any proposals to challenge the financial ruling class's dominance nor are there any significant proposals to reverse retrograde policies causing the growing inequalities, wage stagnation and the increasing rigidity of the class structure. In fact, it even proved impossible to get a proposed $1 increase in the federal hourly minimum wage through the Senate. The reason has been reported in the *Wall Street Journal* and the *Financial Times*: an overwhelming chunk of the funds that Democrats raise nationally for election campaigns comes either from Wall Street financiers or Silicon Valley software entrepreneurs.[19] The Democratic congressional electoral campaign was tightly controlled by two of Wall Street's favorite Democrats, Senator Charles 'Israel First' Schumer and Congressman Rahm Emanuel,[20] who selectively funded candidates who were pro-war, pro-

Wall Street and unconditionally pro-Israel.[21] Democrats slated to head strategic Congressional committees like Zionlib[22] Barney Frank have already announced they have 'good working relations' with Wall Street.

Now the Financial Ruling Class Also Governs

Ruling classes rule the economy, are at the top of the social structure and establish the parameters and rules within which politicians operate. However, more often than not, few of their members actually engage directly and personally in congressional politics, preferring to build economic empires while channeling money toward candidates prepared to do their bidding. Only when an apparent division occurs, especially within the Executive, between the interests of the ruling class and the policies of the regime, will elite members of the ruling class intervene directly or take a senior executive position to 'rectify' policy.

Ruling Class Political Power: Paulson Takes Over Treasury

Several sharp divergences occurred during the Bush regime between finance capital and policymakers. These policies prejudiced or threatened to seriously damage important sectors of the financial ruling class. These include: 1) the aggressive militarist and protectionist policies pursued by senior Pentagon officials and Zioncon Senators toward China; 2) the political veto by Congress of the sale of US port management to a Gulf State-owned company[23] and its successful blockage of the sale of Unocal, a US oil company, to China;[24] 3) the failure of the Bush regime to secure the privatization of social security and to weaken the regulatory measures introduced in the aftermath of the massive corporate (Enron and World Com) and Wall Street swindles; and 4) the uncontrolled growth of fiscal deficits resulting from the Middle East wars, the ballooning trade deficits and the weakening dollar.

The headlines of the financial press[25] spell out finance capital's direct intervention into key White House policymaking: "Goldman Sachs Top Alumni Wield Clout in White House" and "Former Bank Executives Hold Unprecedented Power within a US Administration"

US financial and manufacturing ruling classes have long influenced, advised and formulated policy for US presidents. But given the stakes, the risks and the opportunities facing the financial ruling class, its representatives have moved directly into key government posts. What is especially unprecedented is the dominant presence of members from one investment bank—Goldman Sachs (GS). In late November 2006, GS senior executive William Dudley took over the Federal Reserve Bank of New York's markets group. Hank Paulson, ex-CEO of GS, is Treasury Secretary—explicitly anointed by President Bush as undisputed czar of all economic policies. Reuben Jeffrey, a former GS managing partner is the chief regulator of commodity futures and options trading. Joshua Bolten, White House Chief of Staff (he decides who Bush sees, when and for how long—in other words arranges Bush's agenda) served as GS executive director. Robert Steel, former GS vice chairman, advises Paulson on domestic finance. Randall Fort, ex-GS director of global security, advises Secretary of State Rice. The ex-GS officials also dominate Bush's working group on financial markets and financial crisis management. The investment bankers wielding state power will control the Bush regime's biggest housing giants (Fannie Mae and Freddie Mac), tax policy, and energy markets—all of which directly affect the investment banks. In other words, the financial banks will be 'regulated' by their own executives. The degree of finance capital's stranglehold on political power is evidenced by the total lack of criticism by either party. As one financial newspaper noted:

> Neither Mr. Bush nor Goldman have been criticized by Democrats for holding too many powerful jobs in part because the investment bank (GS) also has deep ties to Democrats. Goldman represented the biggest single donor base to the Democrats ahead of this (2006) year's mid-term election.[26]

Among Paulson's first moves was to organize a top level delegation to China and a working group to formulate a 'strategic partnership'. Its task is to accelerate the 'opening' of China's financial markets to penetration and majority takeovers by US-operated investment funds. This represents a potential multi-trillion-dollar window of opportunity. By seizing the initiative Paulson hopes to undercut the anti-China cohort of neo-con, Pentagon and White House militarists, as well as backwater backers of Taiwanese independence and Congressional protectionist opponents such as Senator Schumer who threaten to undermine lucrative US-Chinese economic relations.

To lower the fiscal deficit, Paulson proposes to 'reform' entitlements—to reduce spending on Medicare and Medicaid and to work out a deal with the Democrats to privatize Social Security piecemeal.

Where finance capital has not been able to fashion a coherent economic strategy is with regard to Washington's Middle East wars. Because of the pull of the Zionist Lobby on many of leading lights of Wall Street, including its unofficial mouthpieces, the *Wall Street Journal* and the *New York Times*, Paulson has failed to formulate a strategy. He did not even pay lip service to the Baker Iraq Study Group's proposal to gradually draw down troops for fear of alienating some key senior executives of Goldman Sachs, Bear Stearns, Lehman Brothers, et al who follow the Israel First line.

As a result, Paulson has to work around the Lobby by focusing on dealing with the Gulf city-state monarchies and Saudi Arabia in order to avoid another disastrous repetition of the Dubai Port management sale. Paulson above all wants to avoid Zionist political interference with the two-way flow of finance capital between the petrol-financial-banking complexes in the Gulf States and Wall Street. He wants to facilitate US finance capital's access to the large dollar surpluses in the region. It is not surprising that the Israeli regime has accommodated their wealthy and influential financial backers on Wall Street by drawing a distinction between 'moderates' (Gulf States) with whom they claim common interests and 'Islamic extremists'. Israeli Prime Minister Olmert has directed his zealots in the US-Jewish Lobby to take heed of the refinements in the Party Line in dealing with US-Arab relations.

Nevertheless with all its concentrated political power and its enormous wealth and economic leverage over the economy, Wall Street cannot control or avoid serious economic vulnerabilities or possible catastrophic military-political events initiated elsewhere with the support of its pro-Zionist wing.

The Future of the Financial Ruling Class

What is abundantly clear is that one of the main threats to world markets—and the health of the financial ruling class—is an Israeli and/or US military attack on Iran. This will extend warfare throughout Asia and the Islamic world, drive energy prices beyond levels heretofore known, and cause a major recession and likely a crash in financial markets. But as in the case of the relationships between Israel and the US, the Zionist Lobby calls the shots and its Wall Street acolytes acquiesce. As matters now stand, the Jewish Lobby supports the escalation of the Iraq war and the savaging of Palestine, Somalia and Afghanistan. It has neutralized the biggest and most concerted efforts by big name centrist political figures to alter White House policy. Baker, Carter, and protesting former military commanders of US forces in Iraq have all been savaged by Zionist ideologues. Under their influence the White House is putting into practice the war strategy presented by the 'American' Enterprise Institute (a Zioncon thinktank). As a result, parallel to his appointment of Paulson and Wall Streeters to run imperial economic policy, Bush has appointed an entire new pro-war civilian military-security apparatus to escalate and extend the Middle East wars to Africa (Somalia) and Latin America (Venezuela).

Sooner or later a break between Wall Street and the militarists may occur. The additional costs of an escalating war, the continual ballooning debt payments, huge imbalances in the balance of payments and decreasing inflows of capital as multinationals repatriate profits and overseas central banks diversify their currency reserves may force the issue. The enormous and growing inequalities within America, the massive concentration of wealth and capital at a time of declining living standards and stagnant income for the vast majority, gives the financial ruling class little political capital or credibility if and when an economic and financial crisis breaks.

With foreign investors owning 47 percent of all marketable US Treasury bonds in 2006 compared to 33 percent in 2001 and foreign holdings of US corporate debt up to thirty percent today from 23 percent just five years ago, a rapid sell-off would totally destabilize US financial markets and the economic system as well as the world economy. A rapid sell-off of dollars with catastrophic consequences cannot be ruled out if US-Zionist militarism continues to run amuck, creating conditions of extended and prolonged warfare.

The paradox is that some of the most wealthy and powerful beneficiaries of the ascendancy of finance capital are precisely the same class of people who are financing their own self-destruction. While cheap finance fuels multi-billion dollar mergers, acquisitions, commissions and executive payoffs, heightened militarism operates on a budget plagued by tax reductions, exemptions and evasions for the financial ruling class and ever greater squeezing of the overburdened wage and salary classes. Something has to break the cohabitation between ruling class financiers and political militarists. They are running in opposite directions. One is investing capital abroad and the other spending borrowed funds at home. For the moment there are no signs of any serious clashes at the top, and in the middle and working classes there are no signs of any political break with the two Wall Street parties or any serious challenge to the militarist-Zionist stranglehold on Congress. Likely it will take a catastrophe, like a White House-backed Israeli (nuclear) air attack on Iran, to detonate the kind of crisis which will provoke a deep and widespread popular backlash of all things military, financial and made in Israel.

CHAPTER 2

CRISIS OF US CAPITALISM OR CRISES OF US WORKERS?

Introduction

Progressive, leftist, radical and even a few 'Bearish' Wall Street pundits have been arguing for years about the coming collapse, decline or demise of US capitalism. No amount of continued growth in the number of billionaires, millionaires and multimillionaires, or record earnings by investment houses and double digit profit growth of major corporations can convince our doom optimists to rethink their prophecies. Nothing has discredited the Anglo-American left more than its apocalyptic visions of the Big Crash in the face of robust growth. Given the 'long term' or imprecise time frame and their ritualistic litany of profound structural weaknesses, their predictions have been swallowed and regurgitated in the progressive media, websites and blogs where they are spread to a dubious public.

While the Left preaches 'the crisis and end' of US capitalism, most workers are complaining about the bigger take of their bosses, their intensified exploitation that has generated rising productivity, and extensions to their work day and work year because of cuts in vacation, sick time and holidays.

For too many years, the Left's whole premise for an awakening and presumably a shift to the left by the working and middle classes is the '*collapse of capitalism*'. In fact this argument has ignored several crucial issues.

The collapse of capitalism has not taken place because business, banking and the government have shifted the entire burden of adapting US capitalism to the demands of the market onto the back of the wage and salaried workers. What is called the 'crisis of capitalism' is in reality the 'crisis of labor', by which I mean the relative and absolute decline in living standards—evident in (a) the elimination of corporate-funded pension plans and the increase in worker payments; (b) the elimination or reduction in employer payments to health plans and the increased deductions for same from workers wages; (c) the double-digit growth in the costs for energy, health, education and medicines which are not calculated in the consumer price index, used as a marker to estimate wage, social security and pension payments; and (d) the rising tide of *give backs* by sclerotic, overpaid (six-digit) trade union executives, which decrease living standards and increase profits for the corporations.

The deregulation of environmental, workplace and consumer protection agencies has led to greater health problems and loss of income for wage workers but greater profits for the corporate beneficiaries.

The correct focus for a radical revival is in discussing the *intensification and extension of the exploitation* of labor, the environment and consumers by corporate capital, which enables the US corporate economy to continue to grow and overcome any momentary downturn or crisis. Predictions of US capital's collapse are built on a specious set of arguments, which are easily turned on their head and which misdirect our attention from the real tasks of joining the struggle at the workplace, on the environment, at the sites of consumption and in the legislative arena.

Myths about the End of US Capitalism

Several arguments have been circulating for over a decade predicting the coming collapse of US capitalism. They include the following:

1. The US budget deficit—annual and cumulative
2. The US balance of trade deficit
3. The speculative nature of the US economy
4. The weakness of the US dollar
5. The energy crisis—the high price of energy resources (Big Oil)
6. The unsustainability of the US model
7. The 'export' of skilled jobs overseas

Combined and separately, the proponents of the coming collapse have cited one or more of these arguments. While these problems are not to be dismissed out of hand, they are not as serious as their proponents argue for a number of reasons.

The Budget Deficit

While the prophets of the crisis of capitalism were breathlessly pointing to the 'ballooning budget deficits' leading to an economic implosion, the data for 2006 indicate a declining deficit from 3.2 percent of GDP predicted in February to 2.3 percent by the end of the year, according to the US Office of Management and Budget. The reason is that tax revenues rose by 11 percent over the year—largely derived from owners of capital and high earners whose profits, salaries, rents and royalty payments extracted from labor are at record levels. In other words, the budget deficit is declining because the exploitation of labor is intensifying—earning greater wealth for the rich which, even with the big tax cuts, has led to increased tax revenues by nineteen percent.[1] Individual income tax revenue has increased by fifteen percent largely due to the profits accruing to small business owners who file tax in profits under the individual code.

While the deficit may increase after 2006, the point is that its financing via intensifying labor exploitation is the key issue, not some self-induced collapse.

In the meantime, the concentration and centralization of capital and the robust fees of investment banks proceed on their merry way: mergers and acquisitions during 2006 hit $4 trillion dollars, with a record number of billion-dollar deals. The driving force of this capitalist bonanza is the capacity of capitalists to cut labor costs and relocate to low wage areas, as well as the high liquidity in capital markets and low interest rates. The mergers and acquisitions all take place because there is no resistance by the trade unions to any of management's plant closures and demands for increased productivity and higher profits. Buyouts are hardly likely to take place where workers have a role in plant decisions, and/or resist intensified speedups and cutbacks in wages and benefits.

No doubt in the next year or two there will be a sharp rise in the number of bankruptcies resulting from over-indebted firms engaging in speculative acquisitions which fail to achieve sufficient returns to pay the corporate debt contracted in the buyouts. This is likely to lead to another chorus of the 'imminent collapse of capitalism'… when in fact it will merely serve to enrich the bankruptcy billionaires who look to the process as an opportunity to snap up undervalued assets.

Conservatives, especially bankers and the IMF, have traditionally argued against budget deficits because of their alleged tendency to stimulate inflation, and devaluate the currency, resulting in the paying down of debts with devalued currency—though indeed it seems likely that their concerns related more to payments to be received from indebted third world states than to the repayment of US debts with a declining US currency. Keynesians and leftists on the other hand have not opposed deficits, particularly if they finance employment and increase mass consumption. The joining of the Left with the conservatives in focusing on the deficit as a catastrophic event, is thus anomalous and out of keeping with the Left's concern with demand side economics. The real issue is not the deficit but the way the deficit *is structured*—based on tax cuts for the rich, and investments in capital-intensive, high tech military programs and financial instruments.

The use of deficit spending to stimulate growth has its limits, as the late 1930s (1936-1940—prior to wartime deficit spending) demonstrated. However to think that reducing a deficit which has sustained US growth will benefit the Left or avoid an economic downturn (recession/depression) is simply voodoo economics. The question of the deficit is a political question in the first instance—*what classes will finance the budget and what classes will benefit from state expenditures.* More generally, the key political question is *what social configuration will exercise control over the budgetary process, taxes, public investments and expenditures.*

As long as the working and salaried classes are willing to suffer cuts in state social expenditures, the privatization of pension and health plans, and the extra expenditures of energy and time to increase capitalist productivity, profit and growth, the deficit is manageable. The deficit will become a problem when the class struggle from below reverses the distribution of taxes and expenditures and lowers the rate of exploitation (productivity).

The Balance of Trade Deficit

Another of the discoveries of the Left—echoing the monetarist pundits of the extreme right—is the balance of trade deficit.

For over a decade the US has had a balance of trade deficit with no visible ill-effects despite yearly predictions from the apocalyptic left that 'it's coming'. There are many reasons for the failure of the prophecies. For one, the US dollar remains the principal currency of reserve, despite constant warnings of its imminent abandonment. As long as the US can print dollars to pay its deficits and as long as it remains and is seen by governments and overseas investors as the safest and most stable bastion of capitalist security, the dollar and US Treasury Bonds will remain the currency of last resort. Secondly, the Asian countries with whom the US has the greatest trade deficit are highly dependent on sales to the US market and have demonstrated for over fifteen years a willingness to buy and hold dollars in order to continue their dynamic export-based growth model. Despite the decline in the relative value of the US dollar to the Euro, none of the Asian countries, least of all China, have dumped their dollars. On the contrary, they *increased* their holdings by over $300 billion US dollars net over the period of the three-year slide (2004-2006) in the value of the dollar.

The rationale for this behavior can be understood if we look at the class dynamics of the Chinese growth model, which is based on highly unequal control of the dynamic export sectors. Between local Chinese billionaires, Western and Japanese multinationals and overseas Chinese conglomerates, the export industries concentrate the vast proportion of wealth, capital and profits, resulting from the most savage exploitation and inequalities in the modern world. The result is that China's growth and the perpetuation and expansion of the Chinese ruling classes' profits depends first and foremost on securing *export* markets, since the domestic purchasing power of 800 million Chinese peasants, workers and unemployed is desperately weak.

Changing the Chinese growth model would require a social revolution—vast shifts in political and social power to permit the imposition of progressive taxation on non-paying billionaires and millionaires, the wholesale arrest of most of the corrupt leading public and private officials for extortion and pillage of public property, and a redistribution of wealth, budget expenditures and property. The Chinese elite naturally prefers to stay with the export model and sit comfortably on an ever-increasing pile of US dollars.

A Speculative Economy

The US economy obviously has a strong and growing speculative sector that has produced substantial commodity and stock market volatility that has a negative—but not catastrophic—effect on US workers, retail investors and would-be pensioners. Speculation has spawned an entire class of high-end corporate kleptocrats such as World Com, Enron, and lesser-known entities. However there are several problems with the 'speculative roads to doomsday' theory. First of all the US economy is not entirely speculative. The US is still a major manufacturer and exporter of high tech products. It led in productivity gains for six of the last seven years among the advanced capitalist countries. It still leads in innovations measured by the number of patents incorporated each year. Moreover there is not a hard and fast distinction between speculative and productive capital—they are intertwined, with capital moving between each sector, depending on where the risk is lower and profits higher.

The real crisis is not speculator capital per se but how the movements of capital affect the working class. More precisely, the question is whether the workers will secure the social power and capacity to influence or control investments in order to lower the rates of exploitation and to secure job stability and security. Speculative activity has led to temporary crises in a number of instances over the past twenty years without causing the collapse of capitalism. These crises in large part prejudiced workers' pension funds and retail investors, and led to bankruptcies and layoffs. But labor has played no role as the millionaire trade union CEOs (all top trade union officials receive between $200,000 and $1 million dollars in salaries plus perks and other benefits) have largely refrained from trying to cushion the effects on the workers.

The Weakness of the Dollar

Another variant of the collapse of capitalism theorizing focuses on the weakness of the dollar, usually thrown in with the balance of trade deficit. The dollar, over the past 20 years, has weakened and strengthened in accordance with the ups and downs of US interest rates, political events and the strengths and weaknesses of the US economy. The weak dollar has traditionally favored US exporters and produced trade surpluses or held down deficits. To call for a stronger dollar while criticizing the trade deficit is more voodoo economics, promoted by potshot critics. The weak dollar allows the US to penetrate export markets without affecting its capacity to import a whole host of low-priced consumer imports (clothes, shoes and electronics) from countries where US multinationals super-exploit local labor. The weak dollar is a result of interest rates far below the historic levels, allowing US consumers to purchase homes, furnishings and other essential and non-essential goods on credit, which they otherwise could not afford. The 'weak dollar' forces US tourists overseas to pay more, it increases the cost of imports but it also makes US made goods more competitive in the domestic market, especially industries that do not depend on imported inputs. The real problem is that local capitalists have not invested in large-scale, long-term export industries here, or upgraded local plants to increase the US share of world markets. Instead, they have transferred capital returns to investments in cheap low wage plants overseas with a view to realizing even higher profits, while lowering labor costs at home. In other words, the question is not the 'weak dollar' per se, but how the virtues of a weak dollar are not taken advantage of by the capitalist class to promote domestic well being, due to the absence of any leftist or progressive political movement, which envisions or fights for an alternative.

The Energy Crisis

The energy crisis is generally seen in partial terms: the high prices charged by Big Oil, the lack of government investment in public transport and alternative non-fossil fuels, the influence of the automobile industry, the greed of the Arab sheiks, and so on. The balance of trade deficit tends to be attributed to energy imports when the finger is not being pointed at the exploitation of cheap labor in Asia.

Obviously energy prices have adversely affected household budgets and the depletion of fossil fuel reserves in the coming decades is a fact of life. But to predict the 'collapse of capitalism' from energy cost increases is a real stretch of unimaginative minds. First, over half of petrol earnings in the Middle East, Africa and most of Latin America are recycled to US or European banks, leading to greater liquidity (for local lending) and greater profits. Secondly, most petrol and gas foreign exchange reserves are held in US dollars or Euros in US or European banks. Most of the marketing and retail sales of the oil (which is the most lucrative part of the oil industry) is through European or US companies. In other words, the 'balance of trade deficit' is countered by the positive balances (or inflows) of recycled profits to the US and EU from the sales of oil.

The real problem is the class problem: how are the prices determined and profits from oil production distributed? Supply and demand is only part of the story. The other side is the potential of administered prices based on government priorities, oil company investment policies, and the political configuration in the oil-producing states. In Venezuela, oil prices are a fraction of world market prices; profits of overseas sales are reinvested in social programs for the poor, and prices of overseas sales are adjusted to buyer country and poor peoples' needs. In Iran, the government is investing in alternative sources of energy (nuclear). In other words, if we see the energy issue as a political/class issue related to achieving social benefits instead of as a precipitant to a 'collapse of capitalism' we can begin to pursue strategies to lower the costs of energy to consumers and to invest in alternative sources of energy.

The 'Unsustainability' of US Capitalism

The unsustainability of US capitalism adds up all of the above arguments in favor of the 'collapsist' theorizing. Apart from underplaying the potentialities of new technologies and the possibility of social-political action in sustaining capitalism for the near to middle future, it ignores the key political factor: All the factors cited as undermining sustainability are dependent on one premise—that the current configuration of socio-political power is not forever sustainable. In other words, that the current capitalist ruling class cannot sustain and/or expand the current budgetary injustices, that US capital cannot successfully count on the Asian export elites (who recycle US dollars) to rule unhindered by super-exploited workers, that the Middle East ruling rentiers will be affected by the popular resistance to Western wars and Israeli ethnocide.

In other words the prophets of the collapse of capitalism assume the self-destruction of capitalism by overestimating the economic weakness of the system and by underestimating the degree to which the system depends on the subordination and exploitation of the US (and EU) working classes and the billions of super-exploited workers and peasants in Asia, Latin America and Africa.

Is US Capitalism in Crisis?

Capitalism, especially US capitalism, will not collapse because it causes harm to the majority of Americans—in fact the stock valuations perversely rise with massive layoffs and salary and benefit reductions. Nor will it decline by academic fiat deduced from general theory; nor will it inevitably decline because knowledgeable historians point to previous decaying empires. Capitalism or any other mode of production can survive numerous 'crises' unless new social forces arise to overthrow it and replace it with another, presumably socialist, system. In the meantime, in the US today, neither the internal mechanisms of capitalism are in fatal disrepair nor are the supporting cast of workers, consumers, taxpayers showing any signs of political organization, let alone rebellion.

The Facts Against the Collapse of Capitalism Theory

"Currently [July 2006] US companies remain on track to achieve the longest ever stretch of double digit profit growth," reads the *Financial Times*.[2] For twelve consecutive quarters, profits at US companies have grown by at least ten percent. The projection is for this profit rate to continue through 2007. Profits are what sustain, not collapse, capital. Double-digit profits over several years are not indicators of declining capitalism. What it does strongly suggest is that the corporate 'slash and burn' policies toward worker pay and benefits turns up record profit runs. It means that by facilitating give-backs, impotent and ineffectual trade union bureaucrats have established a pattern of exploitation, which consolidates high returns for capital.

Far from a world of collapsing capitalism, recent history has witnessed a virulent growth of capitalist billionaires and millionaires particularly in the regions of commodity booms and high growth rates. Between 2004 and 2005, the number of millionaires (including billionaires) in Africa increased by nearly twelve percent, in the Middle East and Latin America by nearly ten percent and Asia-Pacific by seven percent.[3] There are now 8.7 million millionaires in the global capitalist system, an increase of 6.5 percent since 2004. The super rich are becoming richer with their total assets rising 8.5 percent in 2005 to an estimated $33 trillion USD.[4] Over eighty percent of these million-billionaires are from North America, Europe and Asia. Their rising wealth is the result of capitalist growth—based on rising rates of exploitation of labor, raw materials and the environment.

The inequalities in pay between the US capitalist ruling class and workers increased fourfold between 1990 and 2004. In 1990 the average CEO pay at 367 big corporations was 100 times that of a worker; by 2004, the AFL-CIO reports, the ratio was approximately 430 times. It is abundantly clear that the key problem of capitalism is the increasing inequalities resulting from heightened exploitation—not its imminent collapse or decline.

If speculation is leading to the eventual collapse of the US economy, it is difficult to understand the enormous and sustained number of record-setting transactions mainly consummated and funded by US investment banks. Between May 2005 to May 2006, all five of the top five financial advisers engaged in mergers and acquisitions were US-based (Goldman Sachs, JP Morgan, Citigroup, Morgan Stanley and Merrill Lynch), the same investment banks that predominated in 2004-2005. A similar pattern of increasing US financial dominance is evident from examining the top ten investment banks in relation to global debt capital markets and global equity markets. While some refer to this type of economic activity as 'casino capitalism' they forget that the House never or rarely loses; it's the players, not the banks that lose. What this means is that as the world's banker, US finance capital is in a position to skim off lucrative fees throughout the world, highly parasitical in one sense, but hardly indicative of a coming collapse.

The point that needs emphasizing is that the dynamic expansion of the US financial sector is not a sign of decline but of a highly effective form of direct and indirect exploitation. For example, multinational corporations frequently consult the banks on strategies for acquisitions, mergers and sell-offs. The banks advise cuts in labor costs to make the firm more profitable and raise stock valuations; then the banks arrange loans to finance the transaction, leading to corporate indebtedness and subsequent cuts in wages and benefits. The banks up front collect hundreds of millions of dollars in fees for their advice and 'deal making' —putting pressure on the corporations to squeeze labor to pay the dealmakers. *The key issue is not whether financial capital is 'viable' or 'sustainable' but what are the capital/labor relations or more precisely the increased rates of exploitation, which allow the transactions even to take place.*

Luxury goods industries are booming as profits of the ruling classes of the five continents are expanding. In the US alone, sales of luxury goods enjoy a compound annual growth of twelve percent.[5] In contrast, the numbers of workers covered by company-financed health plans and pensions declined by the same percentage or greater every year. Rising inequality is providing the great motor force for capitalist accumulation—a clear consequence of rising profits based on greater exploitation.

Rising profits are clearly a sign that capitalism is expanding, not declining and that consolidation and not collapse defines reality. The conservative financial press has it right—not the Leftist doomsday pundits. "The rise and rise of US corporate profits", reads the *Financial Times* editorial.[6] US capitalism is experiencing a "historically unprecedented share of profits as a proportion of US gross domestic product...from 7% of GDP...in mid 2001 to 12.2% at the start of this year (Jan 2006)".[7] In direct contrast and *a direct cause of rising profits*, "the median US household income is three percent lower in 2006 than in 2000, according to the US census bureau".[8]

Profits have climbed by 123 percent over the past five years, jumping from $714.5 billion to $1.6 trillion. Moreover official data show that manufacturing profits have outstripped the rest of the economy—calling into question the notion that US industry is being 'hollowed out' or disappearing. Despite rising costs of raw materials—petroleum, copper, zinc, nickel and iron—profits rose because labor costs which represent seventy percent of corporate expenses are declining due to greater exploitation of workers, both legal and illegal, reflected in declining total wage and benefit packets.

It is time to get off our hands waiting for the coming collapse (or decline) of capitalism. The real issue is the declining living standards of US wage and salaried workers, the collapse of the welfare state, the extended work life and working hours, the job speed ups, the frequent firing and hiring of workers, giving rise to the tension and insecurity of working families which accompanies the unprecedented growth rates of profits.

Conclusion

Ninety-one percent of US private sector workers are unorganized and totally subject to the commands of their employers. The nine percent of US private sector workers organized into trade unions are led by six-digit salaried bureaucrats who specialize in giving back workers' rights to employers and remain captive to the pro-business Democratic Party. Given these conditions there is no reason to expect any serious challenge to the status quo. As is likely to happen with a turn in the business cycle, when the economy slows or even goes into recession and profit margins decrease, capitalism will simply turn the screw even tighter on working class and salaried workers' wages, impose more of the costs of recovery on their backs, and pressure the Democrats and Republicans for greater Federal handouts, tax rebates and cuts in their pursuit of recovery.

Only if new social and political movements, leaders and activists stop pandering to the soothsayers of a coming 'collapse of capitalism' and a future 'systemic decline' and start engaging in a deeper and more profound analysis of Marx's "dirty secret" and Adam Smith's source of the 'wealth of all nations' as lying in the *exploitation of labor* and the class struggle can a beginning be made toward detonating the foundations of capitalism and bringing about its collapse and replacement.

CHAPTER 3

MARKET LIBERALIZATION AND FORCED EMIGRATION

Introduction: Micro-Analysis

Most writers who discuss international migration focus largely on the individual micro decision-making process, the family networks in the receiving country and the so-called 'push-pull factors' which motivate it. While these approaches provide some data at the level of individual behavior, they fail to explain several fundamental questions.

While the focus on individual micro decision-making provides data on the social background of the individual migrant (relatively more ambitious, better educated and more risk-taking than those within their class who do not immigrate), data on individual decision-making indicates that most migrate for economic reasons, and secondarily to flee political conditions (thereby obtaining refugee status).

Family network analysis tells us that international migrants are likely to locate in countries where they have family or relatives. It also describes the support networks, which operate in the receiving country by providing housing and job contacts. Push-pull theory examines some of the general 'macro structural factors' such as overpopulation, underdevelopment and underemployment in the sender country as well as the employment needs of the receiving country to explain international migration. However useful the data these approaches provide may be, its value is overshadowed by their serious methodological, theoretical, conceptual and empirical flaws.

A Marxist Critique and Alternative Approach

Our macro-analysis is historical and structural in the sense that we begin by examining the dynamic inequalities and exploitative relations between 'sender countries' and 'receiver countries' in order to determine the socio-economic conditions which lead to individual decisions to migrate and to explain *why* masses of immigrants depart when they do, and why not before. Historical and structural analyses provide a global map of the flows of profits, interest payments, rents and royalties and superimpose that map on the immigration flow to argue the hypothesis that *global flows of capital determine the direction and flows of immigration.*

In other words, rather than merely describing family networks, our historical-structural approach addresses the deeper question of *where* family networks emerge and *why* in one country or region rather than in another.

'Push-pull' explanations cannot explain *why* jobs are scarce in the sender countries and available in the receiver countries. In other works, they fail to address the fact that the receiver countries structurally *eliminates* peasant farming in the sender country and do so through exports of subsidized agricultural products which in turn creates low paying agricultural jobs in the receiving country. Moreover the 'push-pull' explanation fails to examine the central role of the imperialist state (the 'receiver nation') in determining the regulations, rules and policies for immigration. In other words, the 'push' factors—low pay, high unemployment—in the sending countries are dependent on the imperialist policies establishing how many and which immigrants enter at what time period and under what conditions.

All the orthodox explanations of international migration fail to examine the social structure of the political economy of the 'people-exporting' countries and 'people-importing' countries. To do so, it is obligatory to put forth an economic model which encompasses the historical relations between the imperialist nations and semi-colonies of the Third World.

The Imperialist-Centered Model of Capitalist Accumulation

To understand the dynamics of international migration, we have to examine how the imperialist-centered model of capitalist accumulation functions. Through multinational corporations (MNCs) and banks, it exports capital in the form of investments in stocks and bonds, and lends money to public and private enterprises. Through these loans and investments it captures control over productive and financial sectors of the target economies, via buyouts of privatized and de-nationalized enterprises. Through the IMF and World Bank, which work in concert with and for the interests of private financial institutions, they *condition* loans to the borrower country. These 'conditions' result in the lowering of protective barriers and the subsequent penetration and domination of local markets by subsidized agriculture exporters and large-scale manufacturers.

The IMF was a big factor when commodity prices were low and financial liquidity was a problem. Since 2002, however, the high commodity prices, especially for Latin American agro-mineral exports, have led to huge trade surpluses and allowed countries to pay off IMF debts and either self-finance or go to commercial private financing, avoiding IMF conditional borrowing. Nevertheless, many Latin American regimes like that of Brazil's Lula da Silva follow IMF policies on their own without signing IMF agreements, as it suits their development strategies tied to finance capital.

As a result of their strategic control over lucrative sectors of the economy, perpetual interest payments and monopoly trade positions, the capital export or imperial countries reap a large-scale transfer of profits and interest payments from the dominated nations. The imperialist-centered model of capitalist accumulation results in the destruction of millions of small peasant plots and medium size farms, which can neither compete with the subsidized agricultural imports from first world countries nor be assisted or protected by their states, which are hamstrung by IMF conditionalities. Large numbers of agricultural workers are replaced by machinery and specialized production. In the cities, foreign-owned large-scale enterprises in retail trade (shopping centers and supermarkets), manufacturing and high tech services displace hundreds of thousands of small but labor-intensive businesses, further increasing unemployment and underemployment. In order to meet the debt demands of the banks and the conditions of the IMF, major cuts in public spending are required, resulting in tens of thousands of skilled public sector professional and skilled workers losing their jobs. The inflows of capital and loans undermine job opportunities in the agricultural sector and public services while the capital-intensive 'new industries' provide few opportunities for livable employment for the millions of dispossessed. This dire employment and income situation is exacerbated by the repatriation of the bulk of profits and interest back to the home office in the imperial countries, leading to little or no 'multiplier effect' of the initial investment, especially where most of inputs to businesses are imported from other countries.

The *de-structuring* of labor (delinking the development of industry and infrastructure from the local population) and the relocation of profits to the receiving country creates a permanent mass surplus labor population in the dominated country. The imperialist-centered model of capitalist accumulation (ICMCA) further weakens the employment generating potentialities of the dominated 'people-exporting' countries by capturing local savings—they do not risk their own capital. Local banks prefer to lend to large foreign MNCs because they believe there is less risk than in lending to local manufacturers, farmers or service enterprises. By 'crowding out' local borrowers from the credit market and forcing them to borrow at higher rates in the informal credit market, the MNCs increase the local bankruptcy rates among the locally owned, labor-intensive enterprises.

The ICMCA is not simply an imposition from the outside by the IMF and MNCs. It is also in large part a model imposed from the *inside* by imperial *hegemonized economists* whose higher education has been financed by imperial foundations and institutions. Through the people-exporting countries, the local policy elites linked by business interests, bribes and ideology to the imperial countries impose and implement the ICMCA. Financial and economic ministers, central bankers, and trade and agricultural officials trained by, and identifying and identified with the ICMCA, execute the 'neo-liberal' policies, which are an integral part of the empire-centered model.

In order to sustain the employment- and income-destroying policies of the ICMCA, the imperialist state and its local collaborators engage in destabilizing activities against those governments that promote national and social development-oriented domestic policies of benefit to domestic workers, peasants and employees.

It is interesting to note that when a leftist government implements 'inward' egalitarian policies, there is a different class of international immigrants, namely big business people, wealthy private professionals, and affluent politicians and generals.

The key purpose of counterinsurgency is to destroy alternatives to the ICMCA, to defend its political clients and to retain market dominance and total control over resource exploitation and cheap labor. In other words, adverse economic and social conditions in the labor exporting nations are not a natural or given condition as some of the micro-theorists argue but a consequence of the imperial centered model of capital accumulation, just as the job opportunities in the imperial centers are a product of the reinvestment of the profits and interest payments in the home country.

Imperialism and the Regulation of Immigration

Contrary to orthodox neoclassical economic theory or what is now called neo-liberalism, immigration is not simply a function of market 'push-pull' factors. Rather, political institutions play a major role in establishing the 'boundaries' or parameters of immigration. The imperial state regulates the inflow of and restrictions on labor immigration; it determines the scope (how many immigrants), the timing (when more or fewer immigrants can enter and when they will be expelled), the 'quality' of the immigrants (skill level and specific categories of professionals) and laws governing the longevity of the immigrants' work permits. Moreover the imperial state decides on the penalties for illegal entry and on repatriation and whether to bring criminal charges. The immigration policies of the imperial state are directly linked to the business cycle, to the tightness of the labor market and to the social strategies of the capitalist class. Historically imperial states pursued relatively open immigration policies during expansive phases of capitalist development and closed/expulsion policies in times of recession with a view to avoiding having to pay welfare benefits. Between 1950-1970 Europe and the US pursued 'open' policies coinciding with high growth, and repressive policies, especially with the crisis shortly after 1973.

Immigration policies have served the capitalist class by creating a reserve army of cheap labor to lower wages, undermine unionization and fill 'niches' in the domestic labor market in low-paid, unhealthy work. Equally significant, capitalists hire low wage immigrant workers to replace skilled and semi-skilled workers in higher paying jobs such as nurses, doctors, carpenters, plumbers, plasterers, painters, machinists, cooks, meat cutters and so on. Contrary to the argument of many 'progressives', immigrant labor is used to downgrade existing high-paying jobs with expensive health and safety protections into low-paying, degraded, unsafe and unhealthy work. For example, twenty years ago, the unionized US meatpacking and slaughterhouse workers received $20 an hour under relatively good working conditions. Today the bulk of the workers are non-unionized Mexican workers receiving from $6 to $10 an hour and suffering the highest accident rate among factory workers. In fact, as an Associated Press investigative report published in March 2004 revealed, Mexican workers in the United States are eighty percent more likely to die in the workplace than U.S.-born workers.[1]

Secondly the progressive defenders of foreign immigration who argued that immigrants are mostly 'unskilled' cheap labor engaged in work that the local workers reject are wrong, at least in part. While the 'first and second waves' of immigrants might have fit that profile during the 1950s and 1980s, it is not the story today. Capital now imports skilled labor in information technology, home and office specialty repairs, and medicine—in order to lower the costs to the state, employers and affluent homeowners. Specific capitalist sectors benefit from importing these skilled workers whose treatment in turn can be honed to their immigrant status rather than their level of skill: information technocrats work longer hours for less pay, have fewer vacations, with less interest in trade unions and less resistance to employers' demands. The importation of trained nurses to be employed as low-paid domestic care workers (for the elderly or infants) saves the state hundreds of millions in expenditures for public facilities (day care centers, public health centers and nursing homes). Real estate speculators and financiers benefit from the importation of low-paid electricians, plumbers and carpenters in the construction and repair of apartments and office towers. Hotels, restaurants, nightclubs and other tourist businesses benefit from the exploitation of non-unionized chefs, cooks, receptionists and not infrequently sex (slave) 'entertainers' imported by Eastern and Central European gangsters.

The capitalist class benefits from imported immigrant labor's payments into the pension system for local retirees, thus keeping state expenditures and thus taxes on the rich very low since many immigrant workers will never be able to benefit from their pension contributions. In brief, an open immigration policy lowers state expenditures, such as pension and health costs, allowing the Imperial state to channel resources to subsidize domestic agricultural interests and MNCs. Moreover the high rates of profits, derived directly from employing immigrant labor and indirectly from the depressed wages and salaries of local workers that result from this practice, facilitate overseas expansion. High sectoral concentrations of immigrant labor coincide with, indeed promote, low levels of labor militancy, unionization and political organization, not only among immigrants but also among local workers.

The major opponents of 'open' immigration among the capitalist class are small locally owned businesses, which depend on family labor and compete with new immigrant businesses and large-scale firms, which employ cheap immigrant labor. Local workers who must now compete in the labor market with low-paid immigrant workers are also opposed to open immigration. This is especially the case in a stagnant economy and where employers replace higher paid unionized workers with immigrants. The failure of the trade union bureaucracy to organize immigrant workers is a result of the labor contract system, the illegal status of immigrants and their dependence on employers' tolerance, and the dependence of trade union officials on social contracts with employers and state subsidies to protect unionized enclaves.

The inability and unwillingness of the trade unions to challenge capitalist hiring policies, to engage in major work stoppages to secure union contracts and to challenge immigration laws over deportation of militant immigrant workers, results in local workers being defenseless and their resistance deflected to largely futile and anti-racist immigrant movements for lack of a theoretical grip on the larger forces and processes that beset them.

US Imperial Practice and Mexican / Central American Immigration

Annually almost 500,000 Mexicans migrate to the United States, in addition to the estimated eleven million undocumented Mexican residing in the US 'illegally'.[2] While migration to the United States has existed for many decades, the large-scale, long-term migration exploded from the end of the 1980s and particularly after 1994 with the signing of the North American Free Trade Agreement (NAFTA). The massive expansion of Mexican migration in the 1980s was a result of the debt crisis or more accurately the debt *payment* crisis. High interest rates in the US forced Mexico's debt to grow geometrically at a time when the prices of its principal exports (gas and oil) were falling. As a result the IMF imposed harsh *debt payment conditions* and forced Mexico to liberalize its economy, discarding trade and investment barriers, which had protected its peasant farmers and national manufacturers. The result was a sharp rise in Mexican bankruptcies and millions of Mexican workers and peasants without a future. At the same time the liberal state under President de la Madrid sharply reduced transfers and loans to small businesses and agriculture. Many farmers rebelled and blocked bankruptcy auctions, later forming a militant debtors movement (Barzon), while others swelled the ranks of undocumented immigrants.

The most devastating blow to Mexican agriculture, industry and finance, however, took place between 1988-94 following the grotesque, fraudulent electoral theft that imposed 'President' Salinas in power. He proceeded to convert the *ejido*, a form of village common property, into private plots, setting the basis for massive land sales. Salinas signed NAFTA, leading to the vast importation of US subsidized agricultural products, especially corn, chickens, pork, rice and other basic crops previously produced by Mexican small farmers. He promoted Mexico as a capital-intensive agro-mineral export economy with foreign ownership of Mexican banks, retail sales, and other strategic sectors which undermined working class and small business income, jobs and opportunities.

The big winners were US and European capital. The big losers were the peasants, farmers, retailers and workers. The economic consequences of neo-liberalism, the social dislocation and disruption of the stable family and community, created the preconditions for massive immigration. In other words, as imperialism grows, the massive movement of dislocated workers toward the imperial center multiplies.

Imperial Militarism and Immigration as Refugee Flight

Imperialist expansion does not always take place through political-economic mechanisms, nor does the empire always defend its privileged place against popular rebellions through corrupt client politicians.

Immigration from Central America to the US, Europe, Mexico and Canada was steady, but relatively small-scale, until the early 1970s when millions of refugees fled the region. The reasons were not complicated. Immigration was not the first choice for the poor. When large-scale agro-export plantations forcibly evicted hundreds of thousands of peasants with the aid of gangsters and the military dictators, the peasant and urban workers organized and resisted. After suffering many killings, thousands joined or supported the guerrilla movements. A popular revolution took place in Nicaragua; a unified guerrilla and mass social movement of Indians, teachers, health workers and especially peasants gained hegemony over the popular classes in El Salvador, Guatemala and Honduras.

In turn, the US poured $1 million dollars a day in military aid and hundreds of military advisers into El Salvador; Washington gave total support to the genocidal regime of Rios Mont in Guatemala; and the CIA organized and directed the Nicaraguan Contra and 'civilian' bourgeois counter-revolution. The result was the murder of 300,000 people, the maiming and injury of twice that figure and the *forced exodus of over two million international migrants* to North America and Europe. Equally important, the US consolidated corrupt client regimes, which reversed the agrarian reforms in Nicaragua, exterminated 420 Indian villages in Guatemala and totally dislocated Salvadoran society. Under US-dominated regimes the Central American puppet rulers imposed free trade policies, which further destroyed local small-scale producers. Poverty levels rose from under forty percent under the Sandinistas to over eighty percent under pro-US rulers, second only to Haiti, also under US-EU control.

Imperial wars in Central America devastated the economies, terrorized the population and eliminated social reforms, which could have provided an alternative source of employment to international immigration. The poor, the ambitious worker or teacher no longer had a choice between domestic reform/ revolution or immigration. Faced with a clear vision of US willingness to exercise its seemingly overwhelming military power either overtly or covertly through counterinsurgency, those who sought improvement were driven from collective action to mass flight. European imperialism has functioned similarly, particularly (militarily) in Africa. Immigration decision making is first and foremost based on a rational diagnosis: since the US pillages the local economy and transfers wealth to the home of the empire...then the logical course is to follow the profits—move to the US or Europe or Canada.

There are several additional reasons for choosing imperial countries linked to national exploitation: the proximity of the border: Mexico/Central America/South America to the US; Africa/Eastern Europe to Western Europe. The exception is Japan: emigrants from the Asian countries are prevented by strict regulations to migrate to Japan, so they migrate to Australia, North America, the Middle East and to a lesser degree the European Union.

Localization of migrants is largely determined by the locus of capital demanding cheap labor. These sectors of capital become the sites for the relocation of migrant families who subsequently establish family networks to attract a second and third wave of migrants. In other words, when social scientists place importance on family ties in explaining the localization of migrants they forget to explain the original cause of family settlements— their proximity to sectors of capital which demand cheap, immigrant labor, namely agriculture and later low-paid service sectors, to serve as gardeners, sweatshop labor, hotel cleaners and kitchen staff. With the subsequent waves, new sectors of capital, like hospitals, elderly care and nursing homes, non-union manufacturers, and toxic clean-up industries seize upon the advantages of immigrant labor. In other words, as the reduction of labor costs becomes an essential element in the stock market's management evaluation of enterprises bought and sold, capitalists are encouraged to employ cheaper immigrant labor over existing unionized labor.

Who Supports and Who Opposes International Immigration

The principle opposition to international immigration is found in the following sectors:

1. Workers who compete with immigrants for jobs or who feel or actually are threatened by the downward pressure on their salaries by immigrants.
2. Small business people who feel threatened by increased local taxes to finance health and educational facilities for large influx of immigrants.
3. The middle class with school-age children who fear that large-scale entry of immigrant children would lower educational standards.
4. Lower middle class and working class neighborhoods in proximity to new immigrant neighborhoods that fear an increase in crime from immigrant gangs dealing in drugs, prostitution and robberies.
5. Communities whose identity is based on ethnic cultural homogeneity.
6. Bourgeois pseudo-populist politicians who exploit working class and middle class employment fears and cultural insecurities to deflect attention from the fact that immigration is driven by neo-liberal economic policies which devastate the economies of the states of origin, and that capitalists further benefit from the cutbacks in social benefits toward the immigrants—in other words, opportunists and politicians who seek to convert vertical conflicts (top against bottom) into horizontal conflicts (local workers against immigrants).

The supporters of international immigration are largely those capitalists in the highly exploitative competitive sectors (agriculture, restaurants, hotels and construction). The opponents are the local small business and property owners concerned with 'unfair competition', crime and local taxes which they attribute to low wage industries, immigrant gangs and high-welfare/social service demands.

In the United States the local government is responsible for education, welfare and health care for the very poor. Since the federal government has reduced transfer payments of federal revenues to local municipalities (as a consequence of the big tax-cuts for the top five percent of the wealthy), it is the local petit bourgeois and working class that are burdened with higher local taxes. In addition, because big corporations receive local tax exonerations in order to locate in cities and states, and hire both local and immigrant workers without providing for health benefits, the local governments are forced to increase taxes for the social services that these large corporations fail to provide.

The local petit bourgeois and many workers do not attack the federal government for shifting the tax burden to local government, and the organized trade unions do not challenge the non-unionized enterprises that do not pay health benefits, forcing local governments to provide emergency services. Instead, perversely, they blame the immigrants who are the *victims* of the discriminatory practices of the federal government and the miserable corporate labor contracts, which do not pay health insurance. Moreover, most immigrant workers pay taxes, including social security taxes—so it is false that they receive 'free benefits'.

The reasons many petit bourgeois and workers blame the victims is that the leaders of both political parties (Republican and Democrat) are tied to big business and support tax cuts for the rich, and thus encourage the criminalization of the immigrant—even as they seek to enjoy the benefits of their exploitation. Even as there is a conflict of economic interests between immigrant-exploiting industries and local businesses, for political reasons both sectors oppose giving immigrants citizenship and the right to vote because they fear the potential political power of the immigrant working class. In fact many immigrant-exploiting capitalists prefer employing undocumented workers because they can pay them lower wages and threaten to report them to federal immigration officials if they complain, protest or organize.

Despite this, in 2006, a powerful immigrant workers movement involving several million demonstrators organized massive marches and in some cases unprecedented 'general strikes', independently of the official trade unions, the two major political parties, and the petit bourgeois electoralist Latino organizations. The immigrant movement grew out of the regional, social, cultural and sports clubs organized in Latin, Asian and other immigrant communities. These activists communicated via local community-based radios, word of mouth, and other informal channels, including churches. The 'surprising militancy' was a product of previous experiences of class struggle in Central American and Mexican peasant and urban movements. The catalyst for the social explosion was Congressional legislation proposing to criminalize, imprison, uproot and deport eleven million immigrants, causing many to lose hundreds of millions in personal property. The 'compromise' proposed by the Bush Administration is to provide temporary work permits for immigrants living in the US for over three years—satisfying the immigrant-exploiting capitalist class, and criminal penalties and increased border police to repress new immigrants to satisfy the anti-immigrant petit bourgeois and working class.

Competing and conflicting segments of the capitalist class negotiate over the super-profits, which accrue to big capital via cheap labor and low-paid skilled workers, and the economic and political fears of declining property valuations and salaries of local workers.

Costs and Benefits of Second-Wave Immigration

Most orthodox neo-classical and neo-liberal economists (and not a few progressives) count the benefits of second-wave immigration as accruing to both sender countries and receiving countries, forgetting the great disparities in power that bring this about, especially the boundary-setting and regulatory power of the imperial receiving country. The historical and contemporary data on immigration provides ample evidence that out-migration is a tremendous loss for the labor-exporting countries' domestic economic capability, despite the rising inflows of immigrant remittances to the home country. And indeed, how long can these inflows be counted on to continue, as new American-born generations lose touch with their relatives over time and flux?

The Costs of Out-Migration

Almost all the costs of raising workers from childhood—educational, training and health costs—are borne by the 'sender' country. This means at least 25 years investment on the average, amounting to billions of dollars in expenditures by sender countries without their receiving the benefits of the productive years, which take place in the receiver country, and facing the possibility of the return of tapped-out workers once their usefulness has been exhausted. In other words, hundreds of billions of dollars in value added labor accrues to the overseas capitalist class and their states receive the tax revenues. What is remitted by the immigrants to their families in return is but a negligible percentage of the actual value produced.

Further, the overseas migration deprives the nation of its most innovative, skillful and ambitious workers who otherwise might have provided the basis for creating a diversified economy based on industry and services. What remains, as a result, is a client state dependent on agro-mineral exports, tourism and, of course, immigrant remittance.

Moreover, the flight overseas of skilled young workers and professionals deprives the urban and rural poor of potential social and political leaders capable of challenging the US client oligarchies. It is no surprise that the local ruling classes organize, encourage and promote out-migration not only for the remittances but as a political safety valve. The immigrant remittances help sustain a parasitical oligarchic ruling class which uses the hard currency remitted to pay illegal foreign debts, luxury imports and corrupt politicians. Without overseas remittances, many of the oligarchic regimes would collapse or enter into profound crises.

More specifically, the emigration of specialized professionals in health (doctors and nurses), education and engineering deepens the disastrous deterioration and scarcity of trained personnel to attend to the needs of the poor in the sender country. The resultant poor health conditions leading to millions of avoidable deaths and chronic illnesses further lowers national living standards and productivity. In contrast, the receiving country, especially the US, saves billions of dollars by receiving already trained professionals who provide important services that maintain and further develop a productive workforce in the imperial center.

This does not mean that the forcibly induced immigrant labor is fully utilized in the benefiting receiver country, however. In most cases immigrants are over-educated for the jobs they fill in the receiving country. Engineers drive taxis, trained nurses are domestic baby sitters or nursing home attendants or domestics, skilled farmers are dishwashers and electricians are busboys. In other words, the under-utilized educational capacity of immigrants means that the returns are far below their original time and energy spent in their education. The waste of this human talent is profound.

In any event, the increase in money income received by immigrant workers compared to that which might have been received in their country of origin may not lead to added wealth because of the high cost in rents, taxes, food, and travel to and from work in the receiver country. In addition while some immigrants may improve their financial situation compared to life in a peasant community, they are now at the bottom of the social and economic class hierarchy in the receiving country, and are exposed to discrimination additional to that related to poverty—disparagement of their culture and ethnicity.

The advocates of the 'positive role' of overseas immigration overlook the frequency with which immigrant labors are cheated of their salaries, subject to a kind of perpetual debt peonage, or abused by employers because of the lack of sender country protection or local trade union solidarity. The extreme case of unpaid immigrant labor is the multi-billion dollar sex-slavery economy, in which Third World officials and Western regimes are complicit. While aggregate remittance payments may be large, individual remittances are very low and based on extreme sacrifice to health, habitation and work safety. Moreover many immigrant workers cut ties to the sender country, especially if their elderly parents die, making reliance on remittances a short-term source of income.

A final cost exceeds measurement in economic terms. Immigrants' families, especially the elderly, do not receive personal support: remittances do not compensate them for the loss of affection and for the destruction of their families and indeed, their communities.

Remittances and Development

While many so-called development theorists might accept the above mentioned 'costs' but defend the positive contributions of immigration by citing the growth of overseas remittances as a contribution to the development of the sender countries. From the point of view of *development— the expansion of the productive forces*, namely investments in manufacturing, technology, skilled labor and scientific research—overseas remittances contribute very little. Most remittances are spent on personal consumption, survival and at best home improvements, taxis or private transport.

Educated family members usually follow the remitter overseas for employment. Moreover foreign remittances may create extended family dependency, lowering initiative and job seeking as family members develop a welfare cycle of poverty syndrome, living off the remittances instead of working in productive activities. Even where the foreign currency accrues to the government, very little is channeled into creating new productive employment for the subsequent generation. Since the advent of neo-liberalism, most sender countries have not advanced from labor exporting economies to diversified industrial societies, as happened with Spain in the 1970s. Mexico, Pakistan, the Philippines, Ecuador, Colombia, Peru and Central America are *increasingly* dependent or addicted to foreign remittances. The reason is that these countries see labor export as their role in the international division of labor, not as a 'transitory' phenomenon to a new development model. Entire states, then, become entrapped in a welfare/ cycle of poverty mentality.

Labor-exporting regimes use foreign earnings to pay off foreign debts incurred by corrupt local borrowers, by military weapon purchases and upper class luxury imports, while providing hard currency allowing local branch offices of MNCs to remit profits based on sales in the domestic market. Equally important, income from emigrant remittances has allowed their home states' regimes to pay the huge financial obligations of foreign financial institutions, which have engaged in massive fraud.

Conclusion

These are the real truths of international immigration and empire building:

1. The principal factor generating international migration is not 'globalization' but imperialism, which pillages nations and

creates conditions for the exploitation of labor in the imperial center.

2. Out-migration provides an escape valve for neo-colonial regimes, and a new source of foreign exchange for failed neo-liberal economies.

3. There is a correlation between intensified and expanded imperialist exploitation resulting in the increased transfer of profits and interest payments out of the neo-colonial countries and the increased flow of immigrant labor. Labor flows follow capital flows.

4. Imperial interventions, which block revolutions and profound structural changes and forcibly uproot families and labor, create a mass of potential international immigrants to the imperial country.

5. International migration is not simply an individual choice nor a reflection of market forces but is a consequence of the policies of the imperial state which establishes the time, place and extent of immigration. Immigration is not a result of internal conditions (people simply wanting to leave) but of capitalist demands in the imperial state.

6. Immigration policies are a product of contradictory capitalist policies. The capitalist class needs immigrant labor to reduce labor costs, to discipline local labor and to compensate for declining domestic birth rates in order to increase pension and health payments for the growing elderly population.

7. The cost of out-migration for the sender economy and people far exceeds the benefits they receive from remittances.

The alternative is for the young emigrant worker to stay in the home country and fight to change conditions, overthrow parasitical regimes and create a diversified economy with remunerative employment. For the working class in the imperial countries, the future lies not in attacking immigrants over low wages, high taxes and threats of job loss, but in integrating or unifying workers' movements against the capitalists and the state.

CHAPTER 4

ECONOMIC EMPIRE-BUILDING AND THE CENTRALITY OF CORRUPTION

Economic empire-building is the driving force of the US economy and became more central over the past five years. More than ever before in US economic history, the principal US banks, oil companies, manufacturers, investment houses, pension and mutual funds all depend on exploiting overseas nations and peoples to secure high rates of profit. Increasingly the majority of banking and corporate profits accrue from overseas plunder.

As economic empire-building becomes central to the viability of the entire US economy, competition with Europe and Asia for lucrative investment rates and economic resources intensifies. Because of heightened competition and the crucial importance of overseas profits, corporate corruption has become a decisive factor in determining which imperial center's MNCs and banks will capture lucrative profit-generating enterprises, resources and financial positions.

The centrality of corruption in imperial expansion and in securing privileged positions in the world market exemplifies the increasing importance of politics, in particular relations with states, in the imperial re-division of the world. Globalization, so-called, is a euphemism for the increasing importance of competing imperial powers intent on re-dividing the world. Corrupting overseas rulers is central to securing privileged access to lucrative resources, markets and enterprises.

The Imperial Necessity

Today everywhere you look, the central fact in the corporate and banking annual reports is the essential need for a strategy of overseas expansion in order to sustain profits. Citicorp, the largest banking enterprise in the world, announced a massive overseas expansion program to increase profits by 75 percent. "US institutional and retail investors have headed offshore in search of higher profits", writes the *Financial Times.*[1] For the year ending October 4, 2006, of the $124 billion dollars entering all the US equity mutual funds, $110 billion dollars went into funds investing in overseas companies. For the first eight months of 2006, 87 percent of total equity flows went offshore.

The drive for overseas profits is not a momentary preference but a secular shift. It will continue over the long term because of the higher rates of return overseas and the belief that the dollar will weaken because of high US fiscal and trade deficits. Oil and energy companies report record high profits. Exxon Mobil recorded a 26 percent increase in 2006 over the previous year, mostly resulting from exploiting overseas sites. IBM has shifted a substantial part of its research and design centers from New York to China, while retaining financial control and strategic decision-making in the US. Over sixty percent of China's exports are produced or subcontracted by US manufacturers. Ford and GM overseas profits, especially in Latin America and Asia, compensate in small part for their multi-billion dollar losses in the US.

The victory of the US imperial state in the Cold War and the subsequent ascent of US client regimes in the former Soviet Union, Eastern Europe, the Baltic and Balkan states, as well as China and Indochina's conversion to capitalism[2] have doubled the number of workers in the capitalist world economy from 1.5 billion to three billion. The growth of a billion-member reserve army of displaced peasants and factory workers led to an unprecedented forty percent decline in the capital-labor ratio. The massive growth of world wageworkers (especially in the ex-communist countries) has been fully exploited by the MNCs, both in increasing profits overseas and in exploiting immigrants in the home market. Adam Smith assumed that the labor surpluses in the poor, newly capitalized countries would be absorbed and competition for workers would drive living standards up. The current tendency is for money wages to grow while social wages (that part of wages taken in taxes but returned in benefits) decline in the so-called 'emerging countries' and both money and social wages to decline in the imperial centers. As an increasing number of occupations (even the highly skilled) are no longer safe from world competition, even better paid workers face declining living standards.

The significant fact about the flow of US capital abroad is that it takes place despite a 'rebound' in the domestic economy. In other words, the improved performance of the US stock market and domestic economy has failed to reverse the overseas profit-driven expansion of the US Empire. The principal new targets of MNCs, banks, pension funds and institutional investors are the 'BRIC' countries—Brazil, Russia, India and China. Russia is favored for its massive oil and gas wealth, and its market for transport and luxury goods, all of which yield high rates of profit. Brazil is an investor's paradise for its world record interest rates, raw materials and low labor costs in manufacturing, especially in the automobile sector. China attracts investors to its manufacturing sector and consumer market because of low labor costs. China also serves as an intermediary assembly and processing center for exports from other Asian countries prior to export (via US and EU MNCs) to the West. India attracts capital to its centers for low cost IT outsourcing, services and related activities.

What is striking about the 'BRIC' countries and their growing attraction for US and EU MNCs is their extremely poor rating with regard to corruption. There is a strong correlation between the 'attractiveness' of the 'BRIC' countries and the ease of doing business and having access to highly lucrative economic enterprises and sectors once the political leaders have been paid off.

Empire-building is going far beyond the traditional conquest of raw material and cheap labor exploitation. The empire builders are shoving their way into the new, extremely lucrative finance, insurance and real estate (FIRE) sectors. The hottest field of investment in China and Russia is real estate, with prices increasing by forty percent a year in most high growth metropolitan centers. Insurance and financial sectors in China and banking and finance in Brazil have returned billions of dollars over the past four years. US banking and MNCs have subcontracted billions in IT and service contracts to the new Indian business tycoons, who in turn subcontract to local employers.

Today, over fifty percent of the top 500 US MNCs earn over half their profits from overseas operations. A substantial minority earn over 75 percent of their profits from their overseas empires. This tendency will accentuate as US MNCs relocate almost all their operations, including manufacturing, design and execution. They will employ low tech and high tech employees in their pursuit for competitive advantages and high rates of profits.

Corruption as the Key to Success

While orthodox free market economists emphasize the role of innovation, managerial skills, leadership and organization in securing competitive advantages and increasing rates of profit ("market forces"), in real life these factors are frequently secondary to political factors, namely multiple forms of corruption in securing economic advantage. According to a six-country survey of 350 corporations published by the law firm, Control Risks, and Simmons and Simmons, "a third of international companies think they failed to win new business over the past year because of bribery by their competitors".[3] Moreover most MNCs and banks engage in corrupt practices through intermediaries. If we include direct and indirect forms of corporate corruption then it turns out that in some countries 9 out of 10 corporations engage in corruption. According to the survey, "about three quarters of the companies, including 94 percent in Germany and 90 percent in Britain think businesses from their countries use agents to circumvent anti-corruption laws".[4]

Market power is highly dependent on political relations with the state through a series of complex networks of 'intermediaries' who negotiate monetary and other payoffs in exchange for a range of highly profitable concessions. The MNCs are the basic unit of trade and investment in the world economy. In greasing the wheels of economic transactions through political corruption, they make a mockery of what orthodox economists tell us about global expansion.

Political corruption, not economic efficiency, is the driving force of economic empire-building. Its success is evident from the massive—trillion dollar—transfers of wealth, enterprises and resources from the state sector to US/EU MNCs which has taken place in Russia, Eastern Europe, the Balkans, Baltic countries and the Caucasus since the fall of communism. The scale and scope of Western pillage of the East is unprecedented in recent world history. In their European conquests, neither Stalin nor Hitler took over and profited from so many enterprises as have the Western MNCs over the past two decades. What is worse, the initial pillage set in motion an entire international political system embedded with kleptocratic pro-Western free market regimes, which constructed legislative frameworks that facilitated high rates of return. For example, legislation on reductions of wages, pensions, job tenure, work place safety and health regulations, and land use policies in the ex-communist countries were designed and enforced to maximize profits—and 'attract'[5] US and EU MNCs with their hard currencies. Pillage and political corruption created a mass of low paid, precarious, under-employed and unemployed workers who are available for exploitation by overseas US corporations and their partners, the overseas institutional investors looking for high return.

Corruption is especially prevalent in several sectors of MNCs' overseas operations. Arms sales, involving billions annually, is rampant with corruption as the military-industrial firms bribe state officials to purchase US weaponry. Military purchases, most with no real security value, deplete local treasuries of funds, while raising profit margins for the arms industries of a number of states, but mostly the US, and the institutional investors who engage in overseas investments.

Oil and energy companies secured exploration rights via corruption by buying out entire ministries in Russia, Nigeria, Angola, Bolivia and Venezuela in the 1990s. Securing a toehold in any economic sector of China to exploit cheap labor requires the MNC to payoff a small army of government officials. This is more than compensated by the regime's enforcement of a cheap labor regime, repression of labor discontent and the imposition of state-controlled pro-business 'labor unions'.

MNC bribery takes many forms: direct monetary payoffs to political officials, the awarding of positions in the enterprise for officials, family members, friends and/or cronies, paid excursions, partnerships, invitations to prestigious universities and scholarships for their children, etc. What is important is that bribery *works* for the MNCs, otherwise it would not be used so extensively and repeatedly.

On the other hand, MNC corruption more often than not has a prejudicial effect on the 'host' country. It reduces the regime's legitimacy and trustworthiness in the eyes of its people. It transfers wealth from national/ public use into private/foreign gain. It weakens the public authorities' leverage over policy and increases the decision-making power of the MNCs. It widens and deepens internal class inequalities and undermines 'good governance'. Finally it creates a culture of corruption which siphons public resources from social services and productive investment to personal wealth, and undermines the notion of collective well being.

Pervasive MNC corruption cannot take place without the knowledge of the imperial state. Despite anti-corruption legislation, corruption is endemic and becoming the norm in the expansion of competing MNCs and empires. Increasingly, corruption is seen by the corporate elite as the grease that keeps the wheels of 'globalization' rolling.

If the annexation of the former communist countries opened new opportunities for the imperial re-division of the world, and the pillage of post-communist countries opened vast new sources of capital accumulation, then ongoing and deepening corruption has become the mechanism through which rival capitals compete for global dominance. Economic empire-building cannot be seen strictly through the operation of 'market forces'—because market transactions are preceded by political corruption, accompanied by political influence, and followed by political realignments of power.

Conclusion

Whoever speaks today of the world economy by necessity must address the most salient aspect of that reality—the growth of economic empire-building. The entire network of MNCs criss-crossing the globe and forging political and economic compacts with corrupt political leaders forms the basis of contemporary economic empires.

The process of empire-building began with the privatization of publicly owned property, resources, banks and productive enterprises. It continues with deregulation of financial markets. It is legitimized by the election (and re-election) of pliable client politicians. The result is the creation of vast reserves of cheap labor and the elimination of protective social and labor legislation. The entire ensemble is based on political corruption at every level, in each and every country, including the imperial home states.

Electoral politics, moralizing anti-corruption rhetoric, lectures on corporate ethics and responsibility notwithstanding, corruption flows across boundaries and up and down the social structure, subordinating nations and workers to the emerging economic empires. While there are other imperial interests involved, it is the US that is the primary mainstay of this system, the primary ideological/political/military force which conditions/thwarts any systemic improvements whatsoever at every turn. This is *the US* Imperial System.

English Laborites, German Christian Democrats, Chinese Communists, Brazilian Worker Party officials, US Republicans and Democrats— in appearance from disparate ideological traditions—are all tightly enmeshed with long-term, large-scale MNC expansion through corruption. They encourage their MNCs to secure markets and wealth through whatever means necessary, including systematic corruption.

Despite tight labor markets, high profits, rising productivity and economic growth, living standards of workers in the West continue to decline, contrary to classical economic theory. This is in large part due to political intervention based on corrupt relations between corporate capital and the state, both in the imperial countries and overseas. Supply and demand of labor has had little effect on the price of labor because it has been superseded by the corrupt interventionist state, repressing labor, co-opting trade union bosses and setting wage targets below what a free labor movement would secure.

Corporate corruption is as integral a part of empire-building as overseas investments, buyouts and market penetration. It is not an incidental, isolated factor having to do with a lack of corporate ethical codes. It is a systemic factor built into the very harsh competitive conditions of contemporary empire-building. As markets are absorbed, as the surplus labor pools decline, as energy resources pass their peak, imperial competition will intensify and corruption will deepen.

Patchwork reforms have not and will not work. The OECD's anti-bribery convention came into force in 1999 and has had no impact. Over half of the MNCs claim to be "totally ignorant of their countries' laws on foreign corruption[6]. The other half simply "get round laws by using agents and intermediaries".[7] Only by ending the primary empire-building state's global dominance can the world move towards an international order on other bases than inter-state corruption, pillage and exploitation.

CHAPTER 5

THE SYSTEMIC APPLICATION OF FORCE: HIERARCHY, NETWORKS AND CLIENTS

Introduction

The imperial system is much more complex than what is commonly referred to as the "US Empire". The US Empire, with its vast network of financial investments, military bases, multinational corporations and client states, is the single most important component of the global imperial system.[1] Nevertheless, it is overly simplistic to overlook the complex hierarchies, networks, follower states and clients that define the contemporary imperial system.[2] To understand empire and imperialism today requires us to look at the complex and changing system of imperial stratification.

Hierarchy of Empire

The structure of power of the world imperial system can best be understood through a classification of countries according to their political, economic, diplomatic and military organization. The following is a schema of this system:

       I. Hierarchy of Empire (from top to bottom)
             A. Central Imperial Powers (CIP)
             B. Newly Emerging Imperial Powers (NEIP)
             C. Semi-autonomous Client Regimes (SACR)
             D. Client Collaborator Regimes (CCR)
       II. Independent States
             A. Revolutionary

Cuba and Venezuela
B. Nationalist
Sudan, Iran, Zimbabwe, North Korea
III. Contested Terrain and Regimes in Transition
Armed resistance, elected regimes, social movements

At the top of the imperial system are those imperial states whose power is projected on a world scale, whose ruling classes dominate investment and financial markets, and who penetrate the economies of the rest of the world. At the apex of the imperial system stand the US, the European Union (itself highly stratified) and Japan. Led by the US, they have established networks of 'follower imperial states' (largely regional hegemons) and client or vassal states which frequently act as surrogate military forces. Imperial states act in concert to break down barriers to penetration and takeovers, while at the same time competing to gain advantages for their own state and multinational interests.

Just below the central imperial states are newly emerging imperial powers (NEIP), namely China, India, Canada, Russia and Australia. The NEIP states are subject to imperial penetration, as well as expanding into neighboring and overseas underdeveloped states and countries rich in extractive resources. The NEIP are linked to the central imperial states (CIP) through joint ventures in their home states, while they increasingly compete for control over extractive resources in the underdeveloped countries. They frequently follow in the footsteps of the imperial powers, and in some cases take advantage of conflicts to better their own position. For example the overseas expansion of China and India focuses on investments in extractive mineral and energy sectors to fuel domestic industrialization, similar to the earlier (1880-1950s) imperial practices of the US and Europe. Similarly China invests in African countries, which are in conflict with the US and EU, just as the US developed ties with anti-colonial regimes (Algeria, Kenya and Francophone Africa) in conflict with their former European colonial rulers in the 1950s and 1960s.

Further down the hierarchy of the imperial system are the semi-autonomous client regimes (SACR). These include Brazil, South Korea, South Africa, Taiwan, Argentina, Saudi Arabia, Chile, and lately Bolivia. These states have a substantial national economic base of support through public or private ownership of key economic sectors. They are governed by regimes that pursue diversified markets, though highly dependent on exports to the emerging imperial states. On the other hand these states are highly dependent on imperial state military protection (Taiwan, South Korea and Saudi Arabia) and provide regional military bases for imperial operations. Many are resource-dependent exporters (Saudi Arabia, Chile, Nigeria and

Bolivia) who share revenues and profits with the multinationals of the imperial states. They include rapidly industrialized countries (Taiwan and South Korea), as well as relatively advanced agro-mineral export states (Brazil, Argentina and Chile).

The wealthy oil states have close ties with the financial ruling classes of the imperial countries and invest heavily in real estate, financial instruments and Treasury notes which finance the deficits in the US and England.

On key issues such as imperial wars in the Middle East, the invasion of Haiti, destabilizing regimes in Africa, global neo-liberal policies and imperial takeovers of strategic sectors, they collaborate with rulers from the CIP and the NEIP. Nevertheless, because of powerful elite interests and, in some cases, powerful national social movements, they come into limited conflicts with the imperial powers. For example, Brazil, Chile and Argentina disagree with the US efforts to undermine the nationalist Venezuelan government. They have lucrative trade, energy and investment relations with Venezuela. In addition they do not wish to legitimize military coups, which might threaten their own rule and legitimacy in the eyes of an electorate partial to President Chavez. While structurally deeply integrated into the imperial system, the SACR regimes retain a degree of autonomy in formulating foreign and domestic policy, which may even conflict or compete with imperial interests.

Despite their relative autonomy, the regimes also provide military and political mercenaries to serve the imperialist countries. This is best illustrated in the case of Haiti. Subsequent to the US invasion and overthrow of the elected Aristide Government in 2004, the US succeeded in securing an occupation force from its outright client and semi-autonomous client regimes. President Lula of Brazil sent a major contingent. A Brazilian general headed the entire mercenary military force. Chile's Gabriel Valdez headed the United Nations occupation administration as the senior official overseeing the bloody repression of Haitian resistance movements. Other semi-autonomous clients, such as Uruguay and Bolivia, added military contingents along with soldiers from client regimes such as Panama, Paraguay, Colombia and Peru. President Evo Morales justified Bolivia's continued military collaboration with the US in Haiti under his presidency by citing its 'peacekeeping role', knowing full well that between December 2006 and February 2007 scores of Haitian poor were slaughtered during a full-scale UN invasion of Haiti's poorest and most densely populated slums.

The key theoretical point is that given Washington's current state of being tied down in two wars in the Middle East and West Asia, it depends on its clients to police and repress anti-imperialist movements elsewhere. Somalia, as in Haiti, was invaded by mercenaries from Ethiopia, trained, financed, armed and directed by US military advisers. Subsequently, during the occupation, Washington succeeded in securing its African clients (via the African Union, according to the White House's stooge, Ugandan Army spokesman Captain Paddy Ankunda) to send a mercenary occupation army to prop up its unpopular Somali client warlord ruler. Despite opposition from its Parliament, Uganda sent 15,000 mercenaries.

At the bottom of the imperial hierarchy are the client collaborator regimes (CCR). These include Egypt, Jordan, the Gulf States, Central American and Caribbean Island states, the Axis of Sub-Saharan States (ASSS) (namely Kenya, Uganda, Ethiopia, Rwanda and Ghana), Colombia, Peru, Paraguay, Mexico, Eastern European states (in and out of the European Union), former states of the USSR (Georgia, Ukraine, Kazakhstan, Latvia, etc), the Philippines, Indonesia, North African states and Pakistan. These countries are governed by authoritarian political elites dependent on the imperial or NEIP states for arms, financing and political support. They provide vast opportunities for exploitation and export of raw materials. Unlike the SACR, exports from client regimes have little value added, as industrial processing of raw materials takes place in the imperial countries, particularly in the NEIP. Predator, rentier, comprador and kleptocratic elites who lack any entrepreneurial vocation rule the CCR. They frequently provide mercenary soldiers to service imperial countries intervening, conquering, occupying and imposing client regimes in imperial-targeted countries. The client regimes thus are subordinate collaborators of the imperial powers in the plunder of wealth, the displacement of peasants, the exploitation of billions of workers and the destruction of the environment.

The structure of the imperial system is based on the power of ruling classes to exercise and project state and market power, to retain control of exploitative class relations at home and abroad, and to organize mercenary armies from among their client states. Led and directed by imperial officials, mercenary armies collaborate in destroying autonomous popular nationalist movements and independent states.

Client regimes form a crucial link in sustaining the imperial powers. They complement imperial occupation forces, facilitating the extraction of raw materials. Without the 'mercenaries of color' the imperial powers would have to extend and over-stretch their own military forces, provoking high levels of internal opposition, and heightening overseas resistance to overt wars of re-colonization. Moreover client mercenaries are less costly to finance and their use reduces the loss of imperial soldiers while disguising imperial intervention. There are numerous euphemistic rubrics under which client mercenary forces operate: United Nations, Organization of American States and African Union 'peacekeepers'; various 'coalitions of the willing,' the Economic Community of West African States (ECOWAS), among others. In many cases a few white imperial senior officers command the lower officers and soldiers of color of the client mercenary armies.[3] The missions' executives are invariably drawn primarily from CIP states.

Independent States and Movements

While it straddles the globe and penetrates deeply into societies, economies and states, the imperial system is neither omnipotent nor omniscient. Challenges to the imperial system come from two sources: relatively independent states and powerful social and political movements.

The 'independent' states are largely regimes that are in opposition to and targeted by the imperial states. They include Venezuela, Cuba, Iran, North Korea, Sudan and Zimbabwe. What defines these regimes as 'independent' is their willingness to reject the policies of the imperial powers, particularly imperial military interventions. They also reject imperialist demands for unconditional access to markets, resources and military bases.

These regimes differ widely in terms of social policy, degree of popular support, secular-religious identities, economic development and consistency in opposing imperialist aggression. All face immediate military threats and /or destabilization programs, designed to replace the independent governments with client regimes.

Contested Terrain

The imperial hierarchy and networks are based on class and national power relations. This means that the maintenance of the entire system is based on ruling classes dominating the underlying populations—a very problematical situation given the unequal distribution of costs and benefits between the rulers and the ruled. Today massive armed resistance and social movements in numerous countries challenge the imperial system.

Contested terrain includes: Iraq, Afghanistan, Colombia, Somalia, Palestine, Sudan and Lebanon where armed resistance is intent on defeating imperial clients. Sites of mass confrontations include Bolivia, Ecuador, Venezuela and Iran where the imperial powers are intent on overthrowing new democratically elected independent regimes. Large-scale social movements organized to combat client regimes and the imperial patrons have recently emerged in Mexico, Palestine, Lebanon, China, Ecuador and elsewhere. Inside the imperial states themselves, there may be mass opposition to particular imperial wars and policies, but only small and weak anti-imperialist movements, per se.

The Anomaly: Israel in the Imperial System

Israel is clearly a colonialist power, with the fourth or fifth biggest nuclear arsenal and the fourth biggest arms exporter in the world.[4] Its population, territorial spread and economy, however, are puny in comparison with the imperial and newly emerging imperial powers. Despite these limitations Israel exercises supreme power in influencing the direction of United States war policy in the Middle East via a powerful internal Zionist political apparatus, which permeates the state, the mass media, elite economic sectors and civil society.[5] Through Israel's direct political influence in making US foreign policy, as well as through its overseas military collaboration with dictatorial imperial client regimes, Israel can be considered part of the imperial power configuration despite its demographic constraints, its near universal pariah diplomatic status, and its externally sustained economy.[6]

Regimes in Transition

The imperial system is highly asymmetrical, in constant disequilibrium and therefore in constant flux—as wars, class, and national struggles break out and economic crises bring down regimes and raise new political forces to power. In recent times we have seen the rapid conversion of Russia from a world hegemonic contender (prior to 1989) into an imperial client state subject to unprecedented pillage (1991-1999) to its current position as a newly emerging imperial state. While Russia is one of the most dramatic cases of rapid and profound changes in the world imperialist system, other historical experiences exemplify the importance of political and social changes in shaping countries' relationship to the world imperial system. China and Vietnam, former bulwarks as independent, anti-imperialist states, have seen the rise of liberal-capitalist elites, the dismantling of the socialized economy and their incorporation into the imperial system. China is a newly emerging imperialist power and Vietnam as a semi-autonomous client regime.

The major transitions during the 1980s–1990s involved the conversion of independent anti-imperialist states into imperial client regimes. In the Western hemisphere, these transitions include Nicaragua, Chile, Bolivia, Argentina, Jamaica and Grenada. In Africa, they include Angola, Mozambique, Guinea Bissau, Algeria, and Ethiopia, all converted into kleptocratic client regimes. In Asia, similar processes are afoot in Indo-China. Because of the disastrous consequences of imperial-centered policies administered by client regimes, the first decade of the new millennium witnessed a series of massive popular upheavals and regime changes, especially in Latin America. Popular insurrections in Argentina and Bolivia led to regime shifts from client to semi-autonomous clients. In Venezuela after thwarting a coup attempt and surviving a destabilization campaign, the Chavez government moved decisively from semi-autonomous client to an independent anti-imperialist position.

Ongoing conflicts between imperial and anti-imperialist states, between client regimes and nationalist movements, between imperial and newly emerging imperial states, will change the structure of the imperial system. The outcomes of these conflicts will produce new coalitions among the principal forces, which compose the imperial hierarchy and its adversaries.

What is clear from this account is that there is no singular omnipotent 'imperial state' that unilaterally defines the international or even the imperial system.

Even the most powerful imperial state has proved incapable of unilaterally (or in concert with clients or imperial partners) defeating or even containing the popular anti-colonial resistance in Iraq or Afghanistan. The major imperial political successes have occurred where the imperial states have been able to activate the military forces of semi-autonomous and client regimes, and secure a regional (OAS, AU and NATO) or UN cover to legitimate its conquests. Collaborator elites from the client and semi-autonomous states are essential links to the maintenance and consolidation of the imperial system and in particular the US empire. A specific case is the US intervention and overthrow of the Somali Islamic regime.

The Case of Somalia: Black Masks/White Faces

The December 2006 Ethiopian invasion of Somalia, overthrow of the de facto governing Islamic Courts Union (ICU) or Supreme Council of Islamic Courts, and imposition of a self-styled 'transitional government' of warlords is an excellent case study of the centrality of collaborator regimes in sustaining and expanding the US empire.

From the 1991 overthrow of the government of Siad Barre until the middle of 2006, Somalia was ravaged by conflicts between feuding warlords based in clan-controlled fiefdoms.[7] During the US/UN invasion and temporary occupation of Mogadishu in the mid-1990s, over 10,000 Somali civilians were massacred and a few dozen US/UN soldiers were killed or wounded.[8] During the lawless 1990s, small local groups, whose leaders later made up the ICU, began organizing community-based organizations against warlord depredations. Based on its success in building community-based movements that cut across tribal and clan allegiances, the ICU began to eject the corrupt warlords and end extortion payments they had imposed on businesses and households.[9] In June 2006 this loose coalition of Islamic clerics, jurists, workers, security forces and traders drove the most powerful warlords out of the capital, Mogadishu. The ICU gained widespread support among a multitude of market venders and trades people. In the total absence of anything resembling a government, the ICU began to provide security, the rule of law and protection of households and property against criminal predators.[10] An extensive network of social welfare centers and programs, health clinics, soup kitchens and primary schools were set up serving large numbers of refugees, displaced peasants and the urban poor. This enhanced popular support for the ICU.

After having driven the last of the warlords from Mogadishu and most of the countryside, the ICU established a de facto government, which was recognized and welcomed by the great majority of Somalis and covered over ninety percent of the population, while the so-called Transitional government, on the other hand, was restricted to Baldoa, a small town, and its survival depended on Addis Ababa.[11] All accounts, even those hostile to the ICU, pointed out that the Somali people welcomed the end of warlord rule and the establishment of law and order under the ICU.

The ICU is a broad multi-tendency movement that includes moderates and radical Islamists, civilian politicians and armed fighters, liberals and populists, electoralists and authoritarians.[12] The basis of the popular support for the Islamic Courts during its short rule (from June to December 2006) rested on several factors. The ICU was a relatively honest administration, which ended warlord corruption and extortion. Personal safety and property were protected, ending arbitrary seizures and kidnappings by warlords and their armed thugs. Most important, the Courts succeeded in unifying the country and creating some semblance of nationhood, overcoming clan fragmentation. In the process of unifying the country, the Islamic Courts government re-affirmed Somali sovereignty and opposition to US imperialist intervention in the Middle East and particularly in the Horn of Africa via its Ethiopian client regime.

US Intervention: The United Nations, Military Occupation, Warlords and Proxies

The recent history of US efforts to incorporate Somalia into its network of African client states began during the early 1990s under President Clinton.[13] While most commentators today rightly refer to Bush as an obsessive warmonger for his wars in Iraq and Afghanistan, they forget that President Clinton, in his time, engaged in several overlapping and sequential acts of war in Somalia, Iraq, Sudan and Yugoslavia. Clinton's military actions killed and maimed thousands of Somalis, caused thousands of civilian deaths and injuries in the Balkans, and the embargo he imposed on Iraq resulted in the death of 500,000 Iraqi children. In August 1998, Clinton ordered the destruction of what was purported to be a "weapons factory" in Sudan, taking out instead Sudan's main pharmaceutical plant producing vital vaccines and drugs essential for both humans and their livestock, and leading to a critical shortage of these essential vaccines and treatments.[14] President Clinton dispatched thousands of US troops to Somalia to occupy the country under the guise of a 'humanitarian mission' in 1994.[15] Washington intervened to bolster its favored pliant warlord against another, against the advice of the Italian commanders of the UN troops in Somalia. Two dozen US troops were killed in a botched assassination attempt and furious residents paraded their mutilated bodies in the streets of the Somali capital. Washington sent helicopter gunships, which shelled heavily populated areas of Mogadishu, killing and maiming thousands of civilians in retaliation.

The US was ultimately forced to withdraw its soldiers as Congressional and public opinion turned overwhelmingly against Clinton's messy little war. The United Nations, which no longed needed to provide a cover for US intervention, also withdrew. Clinton's policy turned toward securing one subset of client warlords against the others, a policy which continued under the Bush Administration. The current 'President' of the US puppet regime, dubbed the 'Transitional Federal Government' (TFG), is Abdullahi Yusuf, a veteran warlord deeply involved in all of the corrupt and lawless depredations which characterized Somalia between 1991 and 2006.[16] Yusuf had been President of the self-styled autonomous Puntland breakaway state in the 1990s.

Despite US and Ethiopian financial backing, Abdullahi Yusuf and his warlord associates were finally driven out of Mogadishu in June 2006 and out of the entire south central part of the country. Yusuf was holed up and cornered in a single provincial town on the Ethiopian border and lacked any social basis of support even from most of the remaining warlord clans in the capital.[17] Some warlords had withdrawn their support of Yusuf and accepted the ICU's offers to disarm and integrate into Somali society, further underscoring the fact that Washington's discredited and isolated puppet was no longer a real political or military factor in Somalia. Nevertheless, Washington secured a UN Security Council resolution recognizing the warlord's tiny enclave of Baldoa as the legitimate seat of government—despite the fact that the TFG's very existence depended on a contingent of several hundred Ethiopian mercenaries financed by the US. As the ICU troops moved westward to oust Yusuf from his border outpost—comprising less than five percent of the country—the US increased its funding for the dictatorial regime of Meles Zenawi in Ethiopia to invade Somalia.[18]

Despite setbacks, scores of US military advisers prepared the Ethiopian mercenaries for a large-scale air and ground invasion of Somalia in order to re-impose their puppet-warlord, Yusuf. Meles Zenawi, the Ethiopian dictator, depends heavily on US military and police weaponry, loans and advisors to retain power for his ethnic 'Tigrayan' based regime and to hold onto disputed Somali territory. The Tigrayan ethnic group itself represents less than ten percent of the Ethiopian multi-ethnic population.

Meles faced growing armed opposition from the Oromo and Ogandese liberation movements.[19] His regime was despised by the influential Amhara population in the capital for rigging the election in May 2005, for killing 200 student protesters in October 2006 and jailing tens of thousands.[20] Many military officials opposed him for engaging in a losing border war with Eritrea. Lacking popular backing, Meles has become the most loyal and subservient client of the United States in the region. Embarrassingly parroting

Washington's imperial 'anti-terrorist' rhetoric for his attack on Somalia, Meles sent over 15,000 troops, hundreds of armored vehicles, dozens of helicopters and warplanes into Somalia.[21] Claiming that he was engaged in the 'war against terrorism', Meles terrorized the people of Somalia with aerial bombardment and a scorched earth policy. In the name of 'national security,' Meles sent his troops to the rescue of the encircled warlord and US puppet, Abdullahi Yusuf.

Washington coordinated its air and naval forces with the advance of the invading Ethiopian military juggernaut. As the US advised-Ethiopian mercenaries advanced by land, the US air force bombed fleeing Somalis, killing scores, in a strike on purported Al Qaeda leaders.[22] According to reliable reports, which were confirmed later by US and Somali puppet sources, US and Somali military forces have failed to identify a single Al Qaeda leader after examining scores of dead and captured fighters and refugees.[23] Once again the pretext to invade Somalia used by Washington and its Ethiopian client—that the ICU sheltered Al Qaeda terrorists—was demonstrated to be false. US naval forces illegally interdicted all ships off the coast of Somalia in pursuit of fleeing Somali leaders. In Kenya, Washington directed its Nairobi client to capture and return Somalis crossing the border. Under Washington's direction both the United Nations and the African Union agreed to send an occupation army of 'peacekeepers' to protect the Ethiopian-imposed puppet Yusuf regime.

Given Meles precarious internal position, he cannot afford to keep his occupying army of 15,000 mercenaries in Somalia for long.[24] Somali hatred for the Ethiopian occupiers surged from the first day they entered Mogadishu. There were massive demonstrations on a daily basis and increasing incidents of armed resistance from the re-grouped ICU fighters, local militants and anti-Yusuf warlords.[25] In the wake of the US directed Ethiopian occupation, the same warlords who had pillaged the country between 1991-2005 returned.[26]

Most journalists, experts and independent observers recognized that without the presence of 'outside' support—namely the presence of at least 15,000 US and EU financed African mercenaries ('peacekeepers') the Yusuf regime would collapse in a matter of days if not hours. Washington counts on an informal coalition of African clients—what might be termed an 'Association of Sub-Saharan Stooges' (ASSS)— to repress the mass unrest of the Somali population and to prevent the return of the popular Islamic Courts. The United Nations declared it would not send an occupation army until the ASSS military contingents of the African Union had 'pacified the country'.[27]

However willing their client rulers may have been in offering mercenary troops to do the bidding of Washington, these client states found it difficult to actually send troops. Since it was so transparently a 'made-in-Washington' operation it was unpopular at home and likely to set ASSS collaborating forces against a growing Somali national resistance. Even Uganda's Yoweri Museveni, Washington's subservient client, encountered resistance among his 'loyal' rubber-stamp congress.[28] The rest of the ASSS collaborator countries refused to move their troops, until the EU and US put the money up front and the Ethiopians secured the country for them. Facing passive opposition from the great majority of Somalis and active militant resistance from the Islamic Courts, the Ethiopian dictator soon began to withdraw his mercenary troops. Washington, recognizing that its Somali puppet, 'President Yusuf', is totally isolated and discredited, sought to co-opt the most conservative among the Islamic Court leaders.[29] Yusuf, ever fearful of losing his fragile hold on power, refused to comply with Washington's tactic of splitting the ICU.

Invading Somalia: the Empire and its Networks

The invasion of Somalia—just as that nation seemed at last to have achieved peace—illustrates the importance of client rulers, warlords, clans and other collaborators as the first line of defense of strategic geopolitical positions for extending and defending the US empire. The intervention by regional and client rulers of neighboring states in defense of the empire greatly lowers the political and economic cost of maintaining the outposts of empire. This is especially helpful and necessary, given the overextension of US ground forces in Iraq and Afghanistan and its impending confrontation with the Islamic Republic of Iran.

Given such circumstances, the empire's own direct participation focuses on air and sea assaults which, combined with regional mercenary ground forces, could be used to oust an independent regime with popular backing.

Without the Ethiopian invasion, the puppet Somali warlord Abdullahi Yusuf would have been easily driven out of Somalia, the country unified and Washington would no longer control the coastal areas facing a major maritime oil transport route. The loss of a Somali puppet regime would have deprived Washington of a coastal platform for threatening Sudan and Eritrea.

From a practical perspective however, Washington's strategic plans for control over the Horn of Africa are deeply flawed. To secure maximum control over Somalia, the White House chose to back a deeply detested veteran warlord with no social base in the country, one dependent on discredited warring clans and criminal warlords. Isolated and discredited puppet rulers are a fragile thread on which to construct strategic policies of regional intervention (military bases and advisory missions). Secondly Washington chose to use a neighboring country (Ethiopia) that is already hated by the entire Somali population, to prop up its Somali puppet. Ethiopia had attacked Somali as late as 1979 over the independence of Ogadan, whose population is close to Somalia. Washington relied on the invading army of a regime in Addis Ababa, which itself was already facing increasing popular and national unrest and was clearly incapable of sustaining a prolonged occupation. Finally, Washington counted on verbal assurances from collaborator regimes to promptly send troops to protect its re-installed client. Client regimes always tell their imperial masters what they want to hear even if they are incapable of prompt and full compliance. This is especially the case when clients fear internal opposition and prolonged costly overseas entanglements, which further discredit them, and wish to bind their benefactor tightly to maintenance of their personal power.

The Somali experience demonstrates the gap between the empire's strategic projection of power and its actual capacity to realize its goals. It also exemplifies how imperialists, impressed by the *number* of their clients, their 'paper' commitments and servile behavior, fail to recognize their strategic weakness in the face of popular national liberation movements.

US empire-building efforts in the Horn of Africa, especially in Somalia, demonstrate that even with elite collaborators and client regimes, mercenary armies and regional allies, the empire encounters great difficulty in containing or defeating popular national liberation movements. The abject failure of the Clinton policy of intervention in Somalia between 1993-1994 demonstrated this.

The human and economic cost of prolonged military invasions with ground troops has repeatedly driven the US public to demand withdrawal (and even accept defeat) as was proved in Korea, Indochina and increasingly in Iraq. The effectiveness of popular movements in repelling technologically superior invaders was driven home once again in Iraq, in the recent Israeli assault on Lebanon, and in the resurgence of the Taliban in Afghanistan.

Financial and diplomatic support, including UN Security Council decisions and military advisory teams, are not sufficient to establish stable and effective client regimes. The precariousness of the mercenary-imposed Yusuf warlord dictatorship demonstrates the limits of US-sponsored UN fiats.

The Somali experience in failed empire-building reveals another even darker side of imperialism: a policy of 'rule or ruin'. The Clinton regime's failure to conquer Somalia was followed by a policy of playing off one brutal warlord against another, terrorizing the population, destroying the country and its economy until the ascent of the Islamic Courts Union. The rule or ruin policy is currently in play in Iraq and Afghanistan and will come into force with the impending Israeli-backed US air and sea attack on Iran.

Rule or ruin policies are rooted in the fact that conquests by imperial armies do not result in stable, legitimate and popular regimes. Originating as products of imperial conquest, these client regimes are unstable and depend on foreign armies to sustain them. Foreign occupation and the accompanying wars on nationalist movements provoke mass opposition. Mass resistance results in imperial repression targeting entire populations and infrastructure. The inability to establish a stable occupation and an accepted client regime leads inevitably to imperial rulers deciding to scorch the entire country with the after thought that a weak and destroyed adversary is a consolation for a lost imperial war. Who is to say whether this notion is anchored in geopolitical strategy or is simply inherent in the psychology of imperialists?

Faced with the rise of Islamic and secular anti-imperialist movements and states in Africa and possessing numerous client regimes in North Africa and the ASSS grouping, Washington is establishing a US military command for Africa. The Africa Command will serve to tighten Washington's control over African military forces and expedite their dispatch to repress independence movements or to overthrow any anti-imperialist governments which might succeed in coming into being. Given the expanded, highly competitive presence of Chinese traders, investors and aid programs which offer African states and their populations a preferable alternative, Washington is bolstering its reliable allies among the African client elites and generals and preparing them to seize the day.[30]

CHAPTER 6

IMPERIALISM: THE DRIVING FORCE OF GENOCIDE

Defining Genocides

Genocides involve large-scale, systematic state-sponsored extermination of large numbers of civilian non-combatants over an extended time period based on their national, ethnic, racial, or religious identity.[1] All the genocides of the twentieth and twenty-first centuries were preceded by state or civil society violence against the victimized peoples. Frequently, prior to the execution of the genocides, important sectors of the state and civil society opposed violence directed against the victimized population. However once the perpetrators of the genocides gained state power, they were able to neutralize, silence, repress or co-opt previous oppositionists.

Often, however, huge state-generated civilian casualties have been hidden under the general rubric of "wars": the Korean War, the Vietnam War, etc. This failure to regard empire-building wars of conquest as *policy-driven aggressions on victim states and their populations* tends to render the attendant civilian genocides largely invisible *as such*, subsuming these deaths under the age-old catch-all of "casualties of war(s)". Indeed, contemporary Western scholarship has tended to simply describe (i.e. has generated an intellectual framework for the categorization, obfuscation and disposal of) a new trend of assaults on civilian populations/civilian infrastructure as simply a disturbing possibly unavoidable trend in contemporary warfare rather than as an accelerating predisposition to genocides to accomplish political aims.

Modern genocides did not begin in the twentieth century. Nineteenth century English, US and Belgian colonial or expansionary regimes generated their own genocides: inter alia, in India, the US West, and the Congo attest to its pre-modern roots.[2] While there are important differences between nineteenth century and twentieth and twenty-first century genocides, they have one common underlying driving force—*they are all linked to empire building or a response to challenges to empire.*

Components of Modern Genocides—or Not

1. *Quantity of killings*: Six million Jews were killed in Europe under Nazi empire building.[3] During the same period the Nazis and their allies systematically slaughtered 20 million Soviet *civilians*—the majority of whom were ethnic Russians.[4] Likewise upward of 10 million Chinese *civilians* were killed by the Japanese between 1937-1942.[5] In both Indo-China[6] and Korea,[7] *civilian deaths* numbered close to 3-4 million each during massive US bombing and occupation. These were civilian and not military deaths, and they occurred as a result of policy decisions: this scale of civilian death was both planned by and acceptable to the perpetrating policymakers.

Modern imperial history is replete with other mass-scale deaths that resulted no less from policy than did direct killings. The Great Bengal Famine of 1943, which killed over five million people, has been imputed to systematic and intentional British policy, as have preceding famines, a contention which finds some resonance in the fact that none such have swept India since the British evacuation.[8] The western-guided "shock therapy" Russian privatization process[9] generated a hyperinflation that wiped out most people's life savings, which in combination with general decline of living standards and crumbling infrastructure, caused millions of premature adult deaths in Russia through the 1990s.

2. *The systematic use of the state powers pursuing a policy of genocide.* The Young Turks in the declining years of the Ottoman Empire developed a systematic extermination policy leading to the genocide of the Armenian people in 1915-1917, and over 1.5 million deaths.[10] Likewise the US employed a "counter-insurgency" policy of carpet bombings (Vietnam, Laos and Cambodia) in which over four million civilians were killed. US-directed scorched earth policies in Central America during the 1980s led to the systematic killing of over 300,000 Mayan Indians and the destruction of over 250 village communities.[11] Likewise the US planned embargo against Iraq (1991-2003) and the ongoing invasion and occupation (March 2003 to present) led to over 500,000 *infant* deaths (1991-2002) and nearly 655,000 civilian killings since the US invasion (as of October, 2006[12]—presumably this is far from the end of this mounting death toll).

3. *State promotion of a racialist-exterminationist ideology.* There was a deeply embedded racial basis in Japanese genocidal policies toward the Chinese, in the Central American puppet regimes' virulent anti-Mayan extermination campaigns, the white South African white regime's slaughter of 1-2 million Africans in frontline states, the Israeli state's ethnic cleansing of Palestinians, and the current careful yet markedly anti-Arab/ anti-Islamic campaign by the United States, to cite only a few graphic examples.

4. *Genocide occurring as a result of an historical antipathy of one culture to another—collective guilt.* This component is a matter of some

question. Is the antipathy a natural cultural aversion of one culture towards another—or is it generated by the state, as a necessary part of the process of furthering the state's imperial aims, enabling it to take policy actions which at one point in time would be repugnant to the population, and not at another point in time, as the ideologically motivated conditioning implanted under the guise of ethnic, racial or religious antipathy bears its bitter fruit?

Some historians, such as Goldhagen, argue that German genocidal policies are a result of a supposed antipathy of the entire German people towards Jews throughout German history.[13] This overlooks the fact that the Nazis only secured 37.3 percent of the German vote in July 1932 and that fell to about one-third of the electorate in November 1932 before they assumed power.[14] Goldhagen overlooks the fact that more than one-third of Germans (especially workers) voted for the Socialist-Communist candidates who were fiercely anti-Nazi and supportive of Jewish rights.[15]

Historically this argument is even weaker—the overt anti-Semitic movements, opinion leaders and politicians were marginal to German political life before the late 1920s. And, of course, it ignores the German 'high culture' based on the enlightenment, which included many Jews who contributed to a grand cultural heritage in music, sciences, literature and philosophy. Finally the notion of collective guilt of the entire civil society refuses to recognize that the Nazis' first major round-up did not target the German Jewish minority per se, but rather the victims were politically determined, and involved tens of thousands of mostly Communist, trade unionist and militant anti-fascists Germans who were exterminated in the first concentration camps including Buchenwald and Baden-Baden. The post-facto argument that there was little overt German resistance once the totalitarian terrorist regime had consolidated power had little to do with German 'acquiescence' to anti-Semitism and more to do with the effectiveness of state repression.

While popular antipathy was indeed finally aroused, the historical occurrence of this genocide factor was not confined to Jews in Nazi Germany. An even greater number (some 9-10 million) of Slavs (described by Nazi racial hygiene 'scientists' as beastlike 'Untermenschen' destined to be worked to death) met their deaths at the hands of the Nazis. In fact, Himmler had projected the elimination of some 30 million Slavs.[16] In other words, the building of the Nazi empire projected and resulted in multiple genocides, based on maximizing the exploitation of Slavic slave labor, as well as ideological efforts to create internal national cohesion via anti-Semitism

Substantial sectors of Turkish and Kurdish civil society participated in the killing and plundering of Armenians. The overwhelming majority of Israeli civil society, with the unwavering support of the powerful Zionist pro-Israel Lobby in the United States, finances and serves in the military colonization and dispossession of four million Palestinians in the Israeli-Palestinian genocide[17] —though again, this Jewish anti-Palestinian antipathy followed from the programmatic necessities of the implantation and expansion of the state of Israel on Arab lands—otherwise, Jewish and Muslim populations had historically lived together in peace. Japanese civil society by and large endorsed the Nanking massacre and its aftermath, while the anti-war concerns of Americans to date relate largely to the lives of American troops, and have not widely addressed the substantially larger Iraqi death toll of some 800,000 at this writing.

Critique of Psycho-Cultural Explanations

Explanations of genocides which focus on "irrational mass behavior" or more generally on "mass psychology" overlook the central importance of elite manipulation, anchored in the state, the economy and civil society. In none of the genocides in the 20th and 21st centuries were the "masses" in a position to initiate, organize and direct them, though, certainly, sectors of the lower class carried out the policies, and in some cases benefited directly from the spoils of the killing fields. Genocides in the first instance are state-centered activities, which exploit *one of a myriad* of contradictory attitudes among the general population (prejudice against the targeted group), and instrumentalize it to create cohesion around elite expansionist or more precisely imperialist policies.

The ruling classes which support state-sponsored genocides do so, not so much because of irrational ethnic or class hatred, but because the genocide provides the state with a legitimating ideology for their uncontested dominance, for undisputed consolidation, and economic exploitation of domestic and overseas markets. The cultural and psychological determinants of genocides are, in fact, based on the larger geo-political and economic interests of the imperial state. There is no 'single' cultural or psychological attribute embedded in any genocide-inducing society. There are many competing and parallel cultures and diverse psychologies. Under the imperatives of domestic power consolidation and imperial state expansion, aided and abetted by state-influenced religious institutions, political parties and the mass media, the largely manipulated masses of the population eventually take an active role in mass murder.

To point to cultural and psychological explanations of genocides is to distract from the central role of imperial politics and the state. To focus exclusively on ideology is to overlook the social structural framework in which 'genocidal' ideology functions, is nurtured, financed and sustained. Take away the key political and economic foundations, the imperatives of imperial conquest and the need for internal cohesion, and projected genocides fail to materialize. On the other hand, continuous imperial structures lead to the recurrence of genocides, as is witnessed by four major 20th and 21st century genocides involving US imperialism: the killing of four million Koreans

(1950-53); four million Indo-Chinese (1960-1975), 300,000 Mayans of Guatemala (1980-83), and nearing one million Iraqis (1991-2002) and (2003-present).

Genocidal elites in pursuit of imperial conquest create stakeholders among specific social classes who directly benefit. Turkish and Kurdish landholders and peasants seized Armenian property. German doctors took over their murdered Jewish colleagues' practices and university posts. Japanese business elites took over Manchurian mining companies. The US military pillaged priceless antiquities and the wealth from conquered Asia. These instances follow on what are perhaps the most evident of historical complicities: those linking governments to expansionist settler populations. Pillage and large-scale dispossession of victims creates vertical links between the imperial elite and its lowest echelons creating the transient reality of an imperial people engaged in collective genocide.

The Deployment of Collaborators

Genocides are organized through the perpetrators' recruitment of collaborators from among the targeted victims. The Germans formed "Jewish police" and "councils" to prepare for the Jewish holocaust and councils of Ukrainians and White Russian soldiers for the Russian holocaust. Japan formed "puppet Chinese regimes" while it killed tens of millions of Chinese. The US puppet rulers, Syngman Rhee in Korea and Ngo Dinh Diem in Vietnam, served as political facades while B52 bombers destroyed their countries with millions of tons of explosives, napalm and poisons like Agent Orange—killing and maiming millions. Genocides are in some cases joint ventures between imperial elites and sectors of the upper classes that feel threatened by the victimized people. Hence in Guatemala, US and Israeli counterinsurgency experts (specialists in mass murder) trained the white European-descended Guatemalan elites to massacre entire Indian populations, seizing and redistributing their lands as part of the genocide process.

In summary, genocides have deep structural roots; they are multi-layered and rooted in imperialist institutions linked to a multiplicity of collaborators, and low-level beneficiaries. They are top-down processes rather than society-wide events, in which the state plays a dominant role in order to secure the internal cohesion required in order to take on external conquest.

What is common to all 20th and 21st century genocides is their deep and intimate relation to imperialism, whether in the form of outward conquest or in terms of creating "internal cohesion" to embark on empire-building. While not all genocides are a result of or forerunner to imperialism (some result from 'internal' capital accumulations—Stalin's forced collectivization—1929-34), all imperialisms have resulted in genocides, from the 19th century to the present.

Genocides, Cohesion and Imperialism

Nazi genocide against the Jews is an example of the ruling elite victimizing a minority population to create cross-class cohesion, diverting the masses from internal labor-capital conflicts and the real or potential costs of the imperialist policies. To deflect their focus on capitalist exploitation, the ruling elite directed worker and middle class discontent to Jewish bankers and capitalists. This propaganda was especially effective in professions like medicine and the retail trade in which competition for positions and market shares between Jews and non-Jews was especially intense.

The passing from intensified exclusion and ethnic discrimination to the practice of genocide coincided with Germany's massive military, economic and political expansion and conquest of the late 1930s and early 1940s. As the costs of empire-building increased, so did the need to deflect the increasing anger and anxiety of the population by giving their ills a perpetrator's face (the Jews), and giving them lower ranking populations to despise (the Slavs). Parallel to the Jewish-Nazi Holocaust, the German imperial conquest of great swaths of Eastern Europe and especially Russia led to an even greater holocaust, the killing of some 9-10 million Slavs[18] and the enslavement of many millions more to the imperial–capital war machine.

Genocides accompanied Japanese imperialist conquests and colonial rule in China from the late 1930s to 1945.[19] The large-scale systematic murder of millions of Chinese peasants, shopkeepers, workers, teachers, in fact all but the highest elite collaborator classes, was an extreme form of colonial dispossession of property and life needed to fuel empire-building by reaping the fruits necessary to subsidize and retain the loyalty of the Japanese masses at home that was required for the perpetuation of their empire.

Genocides as Repression of Revolutionary Challenges

Genocides also occurred as a result of mass revolutionary challenges to unpopular puppet rulers that undermined the pretensions of invincible imperial dominance. The US military intervention in and occupation of Korea and Indo-China to prop up failed regimes led to the killing of eight million civilian victims. Wide areas of the local economies were destroyed through genocidal carpet-bombing and chemical warfare, leaving the industrial sectors in rubble, decimating farmland and causing long-term genetic damage to subsequent generations. The scale and scope of the imperial killing fields, however, failed to defeat the popular national liberation armies. Internal cohesion in the imperial state, especially during the US-Korean genocide, was accompanied by a deep political purge of dissidents in US civil society and public employment. It was the high human costs in terms of imperial US soldiers lost and the spiraling financial expenditures that forced the imperial rulers to sign an armistice.[20]

The greater the size, effectiveness and popularity of national liberation movements, the bigger the threat to imperial puppet rulers, and the more likely that imperial powers will resort to mass systematic killings and total warfare. As imperial policymakers develop integrated strategic views, in which the entire empire is seen as dependent on the security of each puppet ruler in each nation, the more likely they are to pursue the strategy of 'total war' in which the lines between civilians and combatants, private and public, life-sustaining economies and war industries, are obliterated.[21]

Empires are built around networks—of supply chains, raw material and labor exploitation, military outposts, puppet rulers. They are sustained by imperial armies and their domestic supporters on the basis of their being a 'superior people' to their colonial subjects. Imperial genocides result from threats to these 'global networks' and are not always directly related to any immediate economic gain in a particular site of execution. That is why genocides cannot be explained by a simple cost-benefit analysis of economic gains and losses related to a particular situation. That is why in Vietnam, say, it was not about tin and tungsten; it was about domino theory.

All imperial powers engage in what they describe as exemplary mass killings of civilians to induce surrender, submission, dispossession and obedience to imperial rule. The US massive military assault on Iraqi cities was appropriately called "shock and awe". The Nazis pursued "scorched earth" policies in Russia. The US-backed client ruler Rios Mont obliterated hundreds of Mayan Indian villages in Guatemala. Israeli exemplary killings of Palestinians succeeded in driving millions from their lands to be later occupied and exploited by Jews.[22]

When imperial powers engage in the horrors of genocides, they justify their crimes in the name of a 'sacred cause' based on the 'highest and most noble historical mission', usually of the Nation. Otherwise the repugnancy of their acts might cast some doubts on, or raise some doubts within, the imperial armies. The Jewish-Nazi Holocaust was seen as 'liberating' the German people from the tentacles of a 'Jewish conspiracy'; the conquest of Russia and its genocide was seen as 'creating living space for the German free spirit'. The US genocide in Asia was presented as 'freeing the people from the yoke of totalitarianism'. The Israeli genocide of Palestinians is described as 'delivering the Jewish people to their Promised Land'. All imperial genocides are described and justified in the name of a phony expansive 'national destiny' in which the imperial rulers assume their mantle of 'chosen people', by God, History or Genetics.

Genocides also result from the disintegration of empires. They are instruments of 'national reconstruction' intent on providing 'new blood' to sweep away decadent rulers and 'privileged' minorities. The Turkish genocide of the Armenians (1915-1917), authored by the Young Turks is a prime example of 'national revitalization' of a decaying empire via the mass murder of suspected 'separatists'. Likewise the Jewish-Nazi Holocaust was in part a result of the defeat and dismemberment of the German Empire in the aftermath of World War I and the Nazi attempt to blame internal ('Jewish') betrayals.

In summary imperialism is based on the need for domestic consensus and social cohesion in order to mobilize the entire nation for external wars and conquest, especially where there are sharp class cleavages. A war or genocide against internal ethnic minorities serves to displace discontent from class struggles to ethnic and imperial wars. Genocides are always infused with an ideology of moral regeneration and the mass slaughter of subject peoples serves to heighten the sense of moral people punishing degenerate or inferior people. Mythologies of exclusive claims based on 'folk' religions or 'historic imperative' are instrumentalized in the service of modern empire building.

Why Imperialism Leads to Genocides

By its nature imperialism involves dispossession and acquisition of economic resources and labor in order to secure political and economic dominance and/or territory.[23] Empire-building is a process which entails mass killings as well as 'diplomacy' to secure international elite acquiescence. Internal genocides such as the Jewish Nazi Holocaust can be seen as similar to the kind of 'primitive accumulation of capital' that accompanied external genocides, here seizing the economic resources of a victimized minority and transferring them to the elites that direct imperial conquests. In the case of overseas imperial genocides, the seizure of assets, territories and the pillage of agricultural, mineral and industrial goods leads to general impoverishment, refugees, a massive 'surplus labor force' and potential enemies. The genocide decisions are aimed at reducing the threat posed by the surplus population created by economic requisitions and pillage by physically annihilating real and potential guerrilla recruits among the uprooted.

In this context imperialism faces a major contradiction. On the one hand it engages in a genocide in order to dispossess millions more of their wealth and resources; on the other hand it needs the sepoys who service and sustain the imperial occupation armies. This contradiction is resolved by exploiting conquered peoples as slaves or cheap labor, and killing the non-working 'excess' population. In most cases the genocide is a parallel process of mass extermination and forced labor. In cases where genocide activity has depleted local labor or where mass resistance has emerged, it is common for the imperial-colonial power to import labor, forcibly or otherwise, from other conquered regions.

Genocides as Case Studies in Modernization and Empire-Building

From the very first genocide of the 20th century (the Turkish Armenian Genocide) the process of mass killing was seen as part of the modernization and unification of a nation based on state-centered violence. The subsequent 'ethnic cleansing' of all minorities of the former Ottoman empire followed a secular republican logic in which the military assumed the role of defender of the 'modernist' ethos against 'imagined' enemies clothed in minority guises.[24]

The foundation myth and justification for the State of Israel was the claim that Palestine was a "land without people" and the Jews were a "people without land"—a myth which became a self-fulfilling prophesy (and self-serving justification) as Israeli Jews proceeded to forcibly eject millions of Palestinian Arabs from the occupied lands.[25] The Israeli-Palestinian genocide continues to be justified by the existence of a modern democratic, albeit exclusivist, Jewish state, with exceptional links to a worldwide network of exceptionally wealthy, financially successful modern elites.[26] The interaction of genocidal behavior and modernity embedded in dense global networks has powerful resonance among imperial elites bent on reconstructing Mid-Eastern empires, especially among civilian militarists in the US.

Nazi genocide was another manifestation of dynamic industrial modernity harnessed to imperial conquest: the superior German technology and advanced scientific achievements operated on the basis of the internal cohesion fostered by anti-Semitism internally and anti-Slavism externally. The result was a 'double genocide': Jewish and Russian-Slav extermination campaigns. A basic precondition for the entire Nazi expansionist-genocide dynamic was the historic destruction of the Left and all its mass organizations.

Late imperialists like Germany, Japan and the US all exhibit the same historic tendencies toward genocidal wars and genocide-scale extermination campaigns of conquest. With the exception of Japan—an ethnically homogenous society—late imperialist states engage in large-scale genocidal extermination campaigns against diverse internal minorities (Indians and Afro-Americans in the US, Jews and Roma in Germany) creating the domestic cohesion and racialist superiority complex necessary for further imperialist conquests and genocides (Germany versus the Slavs, the US versus Asians, Arabs, and Central American Indians).

The Japanese-Chinese genocide reached its pinnacle in the infamous 'Rape of Nanking' in 1938, when over 300,000 Chinese were raped and slaughtered in a matter of days, immediately preceded and followed by the state-planned, systematic extermination of over seven million Chinese civilians of all ages and classes. Lacking a powerful genocide lobby in the West, and given the Cold War realignment of the West and Japan against the People's Republic of China, no monuments, foundations or billion-dollar compensation have commemorated the Japanese-Chinese genocide—this, despite the fact that far more Chinese civilians were murdered than Jews.

The ascendancy of the US to the position of dominant imperialist power was directly related to tri-continental genocides or multiple genocides in Asia—the US-Korean (1950-53) and the US-Indochinese (1961-1975); in Africa—the proxy genocides in Angola, Mozambique, Congo /Zaire (1961-1990s); and in Central America (1979-1990) and the Middle East (Iraq 1991-2006). For methodological reasons we have excluded the state-directed military extermination via the atomic bombing of Japanese cities (Hiroshima/Nagasaki) and the US-directed proxy extermination campaign in Indonesia in 1966 resulting in the killing of over 1.5 million unarmed trade unionists and communist party members or affiliates and family members,[27] which were politically motivated and hence excluded by the restrictions in the definition of genocide used here. The death count resulting from the extermination campaigns of 'late US imperialism' is comparable to their Japanese and German predecessors: four million each in Indo-China and Korea, uncounted millions in the genocide of Southern Africa, nearly 500,000 in the proxy genocides of Central America (300,000 Mayans in Guatemala, 75,000 in El Salvador, 50,000 in Nicaragua and 10,000 each in Honduras and Panama, the latter inflicted by a direct military invasion) and over one million in Iraq, and growing. The total war strategies employed by US imperialism lead directly to genocide-scale killing fields because the distinction between civilian and military targets are obliterated. Particularly because the resistance to US Empire is built on deeply held and widely based beliefs of the resisting masses, imperialist conquest deliberately seeks to decimate the huge reservoir of resistance supporters, recruits and suppliers of food and intelligence.

One explanation for the multiplication of genocides under 'late imperialism' is that it takes place in a historical context more resistant to a revival of colonial-imperial domination. More specifically, nations resulting from mass anti-colonial movements which earlier swept aside European and Japanese imperialism are better prepared socially, politically and militarily to resist the new US imperialist encroachments. The high levels of anti-imperialist and nationalist ideology and culture embedded in post-colonial nations from the mid 20th century onward are in sharp contrast to the feudal-mercantile societies conquered by European imperialist powers in the late 19th and early 20th century. To dispossess and disarticulate highly mobilized nationalist and/or socialist societies requires greater and wider use of genocidal methods. Murdering or exiling a few thousand leaders is no longer sufficient. Whole populations must be made 'examples', or as the Israeli genocide mongers argue in the case of the Palestinians after the latter democratically elected the Hamas government, 'they [whole populations] must assume the costs'—namely, daily military assaults and killing of civilians and a systematic blockade of food and medicine, resulting in widespread malnutrition.[28]

Technological advances in the machinery of mass extermination do not determine the frequency or occurrences of genocides, but they certainly expedite the proceedings. Labor-intensive genocides—like the Japanese Chinese genocide in Nanking—can be just as deadly as the capital-intensive high-tech gas chambers of Nazi Germany or the US carpet bombing of cities in Korea, Indochina and Iraq. Nevertheless it is certain that high technology accelerates the process of extermination and lessens the possibility that human frailty (like pity or bad conscience) will weaken the drive toward execution. Genocides provide incentives for testing, experimenting and applying, in real time situations, new extermination processes. For example, the US has now experimented with battlefield nuclear weapons in the form of depleted uranium during the two Gulf Wars and in the Balkans.

The Israeli-Palestinian genocide has all the substantive features of previously mentioned genocides: a highly militarized society given to long-term, large-scale use of state terror; dispossession of over four million Palestinians; forcing over three million Palestinians into ghettos; racial ethnic segregation and separation in all spheres of justice, property ownership, transportation and geographical movement; citizen rights based on 'blood ties' (maternal lineage); legalized and quasi-legalized torture and systematic use of collective punishment; perpetual military assaults on neighboring Palestinian communities and other Arab states; unilateral extra-territorial, extra-judicial assassinations; chronic and systematic rejection of international law; an ideology of permanent warfare and international paranoia ('anti-Semitism' is everywhere') and an ideology of ethnic superiority (the 'Chosen People').[29]

Both in the practice of mass state terror and in its legal-ideological justifications of assassinations of opponents and mass dispossession as well as its claims of the superiority of Israeli laws over international norms, the Israeli state possesses all the qualifications that exemplify a genocide perpetrator. The Palestinian ghetto, the concentration camps for thousands of suspected 'militants', the destruction of the economic base of everyday life, the forced massive evictions, systematic ethnic cleansing—all conform to the pattern of past and present genocides.

The US/Iraqi genocide, an ongoing process spanning the last seventeen years (1990-2007), provides us with a striking example of state-planned systematic extermination, torture and physical destruction designed to destroy a secular developing society and revert it into a series of warring clan-tribal-clerical-ethnic-based entities devoid of any national authority or viable economy.

The scale and scope of the US extermination policies in Iraq certainly warrant its classification as a genocide: 500,000 children died as a result of a murderous economic blockade during the Clinton Administration (1992-2000) with a further 300,000 estimated to have died up to 2003.[30] The US genocide policy was openly endorsed by the senior architect of the policy, Secretary of State Madeline Albright, who, when confronted by the scale and scope of the infant deaths during the devastating economic blockade (1991-2002), declared, "It was worth it". The indiscriminate bombing of civilian targets in both the first and especially second Gulf War—led to the total destruction of all civilian infrastructure. The widespread systematic use of depleted uranium-coated shells has deadly consequences for millions. The systematic use of torture and mass murder of hundreds of thousands of civilians has been fully documented and is justified by senior officials in the Bush regime and the majority of both parties in the Congress.[31]

In its essentials, nothing separates the US extermination campaign from earlier genocides, except that the whole world views it while it is happening. The US genocide in Iraq is a living genocide taking place before the eyes and ears of billions of spectators. While worldwide repugnance to each revelation of particulars is common, 'passive acceptance' predominates in the West where a historically-induced racism shields the citizenry from the full enormity of their governments' actions. It is hard to imagine, for instance, that Madeline Albright could glibly announce that the death of 500,000 *Belgian* babies was worth it, without creating domestic hysteria. But located in distant still exotic lands, genocidal activity can be made routine. Death squad mass murder fomented by imperial overseers is reduced to a daily death toll—immunizing the world community from the horror of a living ongoing slaughter of Holocaust proportions.

Genocides: Their Aftermaths and Dubious Legacies

With the exception of the Nazi-Slavic-Jewish genocide and possibly the Japanese-Chinese genocide, none of the rest of the perpetrators has faced international criminal proceedings. The differential treatment and general impunity of most genocide perpetrators is a direct result of military outcomes and political power. The Nazi and Japanese genocidal regimes were defeated; the US, Turkey[32] and Israel were not militarily defeated, or at least not to the point where an international court system could bring them to trial. Even in the case of the Nazis, apart from a few top leaders of the regime, almost all middle rank and below were eventually exonerated; many later pursued successful careers in business and politics. Nazi scientists and other professionals were actually recruited by the US and West German governments for a variety of strategic positions. In the case of Japan, a similar process of prosecution and then restoration of genocidal executives to positions of power took place, especially after the US and its allies launched the global counter-revolutionary policies embodied in the 'Cold War', a total misnomer given the US military attacks on Korea and Indochina within that period. In fact Japanese perpetrators of genocide played a major role in support of post-World War II US genocides in Korea and Indochina by offering military bases, supplies and logistical support.

Several highly publicized *unofficial* tribunals have taken place, specifically the Bertrand Russell Tribunal, over the US-Indochinese genocides. However their significance was symbolic as they lacked any mechanism for enforcing their guilty verdicts. None of these Tribunals received favorable treatment in the mass media or even the slightest admission of remorse or guilt from any of the perpetrating regimes, even after a change in the party in power. In other words, there is a continuing systematic consensus among the perpetrators that their actions are justified, making a shambles of any notion of the 'rule of law'.

In fact the United Nations itself is complicit: it was actively engaged in the US-Korean genocide, is incapable of intervening in the Israeli-Palestinian genocide, and provides an institutional cover to the US-Iraq genocide. If the international judicial system has failed to bring to justice all but top Nazi perpetrators, the record at the level of bi-national judicial proceedings is also appalling. The Japanese Koizumi Regime continued to pay homage to past war criminals (yearly trips by top officials to the Yoshikuni Shrine) and Japanese textbooks whitewash war crimes despite Chinese protest. This genocide nostalgia continues to poison bilateral relations with China, if only at the symbolic-diplomatic level. While Chinese-Japanese economic relations continue to flourish, there is still deep bitterness among the Chinese people against the Japanese.

Likewise, with the exception of France and Switzerland, no other Western country has officially condemned the Turkish-Armenian massacre or the Turkish denial of any responsibility for genocide. Israel, many of whose people were victims of the Nazi Holocaust, denies the Turkish-Armenian genocide and excludes any Armenian scholarly representations of their genocide at the lavishly funded Holocaust forums, conferences, publications or museums. This is especially galling since Jerusalem was once the home for many thousands of Armenian genocide survivors, but is likely due to the fact that Israel has a special strategic military pact with the Turkish genocide deniers. The same is true with regard to the United States support of Turkish deniers, where despite strong pressure from the Armenian-American community and even substantial Congressional backing, the Executive has blocked any official condemnation of the genocide.

With regard to US genocides in Asia, Washington followed up its genocidal wars by imposing murderous economic blockades particularly on North Korea and Indochina, leading to 'forced self-reliance'. In the case of Cambodia, the policy spurred the Khmer Rouge regime to engage in an irrational and deadly forced exodus from the urban centers, leading to a case of a 'joint-genocide'—Washington/Khmer Rouge. With the conversion of the Indochinese elites to capitalism and in the face of international impunity for US war crimes, US-Vietnamese reconciliation without justice became unavoidable. Ironically free-market policies have led to new imperial exploitation of cheap labor via the market instead of through military conquests.

With regard to the US-Central American genocides, there has been no effort at international criminal proceedings. At most, former President Clinton expressed a 'pro-forma' apology for US 'support' of its local murderous puppet regime in Guatemala. The incumbent regimes, themselves US clients, are direct descendants and beneficiaries of the US-Central American genocides. Having destroyed the fabric of society and undermined the local economy via war and free trade, and having demobilized the guerrilla armies, the US has turned Central America into a region of deracinated peasants, refugees turned international migrants, and criminal gangs, ruled by kleptocratic politicians and business oligarchs. Central American survivors and relatives of the US genocide victims, finding no future in their devastated homelands, dispossessed of land and employment, flee to North America where in 2007, they face highly repressive anti-immigrant legislation, massive criminalization, dispossession, imprisonment and deportation.

The Israeli-Palestinian genocide is a continuing process that is gaining momentum: daily military assaults, execution of leaders and murder of civilians, continued extension of colonies, non-recognition of elected Palestinian leaders and above all a total blockade of finances and basic food and medicine—a Nazi style 'encirclement of ghettos' and 'starvation to surrender' strategy. The powerful voice and influence of the Jewish Lobby in and out of the US government ensures Israeli impunity and US and European Union complicity.[33]

Beginning with the US Indochinese genocide and continuing to the present, the execution of genocide policies are visible to the public via the alternative media and internet, despite official propaganda campaigns transmitted by the mass media. The complicity of sectors of civil society and the mass media in non-totalitarian political systems in upholding genocide regimes, requires a reconsideration of the relationship between electoral systems and genocides, or at minimum, the notion of the peacefulness of so-called democracies.

Conclusion

From our review of 20th and 21st century genocides, it is clear that the perpetrators of great crimes against humanity for the most part are not brought to justice. On the contrary, the historical legacy is one of impunity and most likely recidivism. The record is clear: US impunity after the Korean genocide led to the genocides in Indochina, Central America and Iraq. The early Israeli ethnic cleansing of Palestinians in 1947-1950 led to new wars of conquest, land dispossession, settler occupation, ghettoization and progression toward a 'final solution' of total expulsion. Turkish-Armenian genocide denial encouraged the ethnic cleansing of Kurds throughout Anatolia. These crimes against humanity are not merely artifacts of psychopathic rulers, or derivatives from authoritarian traditions, because, as we have shown, there are competing traditions, diverse 'national psychologies' and countervailing ideologies.

What brings genocidal behavior to the foreground—the trigger and motor force—are imperialist drives for domestic cohesion and foreign conquest. It is precisely because *imperial powers* exercise the genocide imperative that they are largely unpunished, and, in most cases, their crimes remain unrecognized to this very day. Lesser powers with lesser crimes, indeed, are condemned. In contrast, the bigger the empire and the greater its power, the more likely impunity and denial will become the rule.

The failure of Western intellectuals to recognize the multiple genocides of the 20th and 21st centuries is not a result of the lack of accessible data or knowledge of the facts, because the acts of genocide are public, the bodies are strewn in public spaces, the destruction surrounds any observer, the instruments of genocide are publicly funded. What is lacking is the willingness to face the reality that *their* governments, *their* states are responsible for the genocides, that *their* elected regimes are engaged in mass terror, that *their* private mass media systematically lie and cover up the acts of genocide, that important sectors of "civil society" are either impotent critics or complicit collaborators, and that if they do not attempt to reverse this, then *they too are complicit.*

Most intellectuals embedded in imperial societies are incapable of comprehending the scope and depth of the crimes committed in their names or even of grasping the fact of naked aggression itself. Instead they describe the genocides as 'wars between states', referring to them as the 'Korean War', the 'Indochinese War', the 'Iraq War' or worse, as 'wars for democracy' or other similarly monstrous falsifications. Strange 'wars' in which all the civilians—millions by count—are on the other side, all the destruction takes place in the invaded country, all the dispossessed are the targets of the empire builders.

There is resistance: imperial soldiers are killed, puppet armies are attacked, instruments of war—helicopters and armored carriers—are destroyed. In the Warsaw Ghetto the resistance fought and killed Nazi storm troopers. Vietnamese liberation fighters inflicted 58,000 deaths and 500,000 casualties on the invaders. Fallujah (Iraq) resists, Jenin (Palestine) resists... Some genocide deniers point to these acts of heroic resistance and to survivors who crawl out of the rubble as evidence of their specious claims that the killing fields and ethnic cleansing do not amount to genocidal practices but rather to 'acts of war'... But they forget to add that *it is total war against a whole people!*

What is clear from a review of 20th-21st century genocides is that they are not single unique events committed by a particular evil people or regime, but are repeated, common practices, which recur with periodic frequency. Impunity for the commission of genocides has become the norm, incorporated in the euphemistic vocabulary of mainstream and even revisionist historians as 'wars', 'conflicts', 'crusades' and 'tragedies' instead of *recidivist criminality writ large*. There are no effective international mechanisms to bring to justice genocide elites; only tribunals organized by the imperial powers to try their defeated adversaries, as in the case of occupied Yugoslavia, Iraq and Panama. One might well expect the new International Criminal Court to act with alacrity against lesser perpetrators from underdeveloped countries who do not enjoy imperial protection.

New capitalist elites among the victimized people (as in Indochina) are more than willing to forgive and forget genocide crimes in exchange for hard currency and a privileged place in the world market.

As long as international judicial processes are inoperative, only a series of sustained popular revolutions can bring to justice at least the puppets and collaborators of the genocide perpetrators. Only the final defeat of the imperial state will open the possibility of a truly international court of justice, which can make the genocide perpetrators answer for their crimes.

CHAPTER 7

THE GLOBAL RULING CLASS: BILLIONAIRES AND HOW THEY "MADE IT"

While the number of the world's billionaires grew from 793 in 2006 to 946 as at March, 2007,[1] major mass uprisings became commonplace occurrences in China and India. In India, which has the highest number of billionaires (36) in Asia with total wealth of $191 billion USD, Prime Minister Singh declared that the greatest single threats to 'India's security' were the Maoist-led guerrilla armies and mass movements in the poorest parts of the country. In China, with twenty billionaires with $29.4 billion USD net worth, the new rulers, confronting nearly a hundred thousand reported riots and protests, have increased the number of armed special anti-riot militia a hundredfold, and increased spending for the rural poor by $10 billion USD in the hopes of lessening the monstrous class inequalities and heading off a mass upheaval.

The total wealth of this global ruling class grew 35 percent year to year topping $3.5 trillion USD, while income levels for the lower 55 percent of the world's six-billion-strong population declined or stagnated. Put another way, one hundred millionth of the world's population (1/100,000,000) owns more than over three billion people. Over half of the current billionaires (523) came from just three countries: the US (415), Germany (55) and Russia (53). The 35 percent increase in wealth mostly came from speculation on equity markets, real estate and commodity trading, rather than from technical innovations, investments in job-creating industries or social services.

The Russian oligarchy, among the newest, youngest and fastest-growing group of billionaires, stands out for its most rapacious beginnings. Over two-thirds (67 percent) of the current Russian billionaire oligarchs began their concentration of wealth in their mid to early twenties. During the infamous decade of the 1990s under the quasi-dictatorial rule of Boris Yeltsin and his US-directed economic advisers, Anatoly Chubais and Yegor Gaidar, the entire Russian economy was put up for sale for a 'political price', which was far below its real value. Without exception, the transfers of property were achieved through gangster tactics—assassinations, massive theft, and seizure of state resources, illicit stock manipulation and buyouts. The future billionaires stripped the Russian state of over a trillion dollars worth of factories, transport, oil, gas, iron, coal and other formerly state-owned resources.

Contrary to European and US publicists on the Right and Left, very few of the top former Communist leaders are now to be found among the current Russian billionaire oligarchy. Wealth was not transferred to high Communist Party Commissars (lateral transfers) but was seized by armed private mafias run by recent university graduates who quickly capitalized on *corrupting*, intimidating or assassinating senior state officials and benefiting from Boris Yeltsin's mindless contracting of 'free market' Western consultants.

Further, contrary to the spin-masters' claims of 'communist inefficiencies', the former Soviet Union-developed mines, factories, and energy enterprises were profitable and competitive before they were taken over by the new oligarchs. This is evident in the massive private wealth that has been accumulated in less than a decade by these gangster-businessmen. Virtually all the billionaires' initial sources of wealth had nothing to do with building, innovating or developing efficient new enterprises.

Forbes magazine puts out a yearly list of the richest individuals and families in the world. What is most amusing about the famous *Forbes* magazine's background biographical notes on the Russian oligarchs is the constant reference to their source of wealth as 'self-made' as if *stealing* state property created and defended for over seventy years by the sweat and blood of the Russian people demonstrated the entrepreneurial skills of thugs in their twenties. Of the top eight Russian billionaire oligarchs, all got their start from strong-arming their rivals, setting up 'paper banks' and taking over aluminum, oil, gas, nickel and steel production and the export of bauxite, iron and other minerals. Every sector of the former Communist economy was pillaged by the new billionaires: construction, telecommunications, chemicals, real estate, agriculture, vodka, foods, land, media, automobiles, airlines, etc.

With rare exceptions, following the Yeltsin privatizations all of the oligarchs quickly rose to the top or near the top, literally murdering or intimidating any opponents within the former Soviet apparatus and competitors from rival predator gangs.

The key 'policy' measures that facilitated the initial pillage and takeovers by the future billionaires were the massive and immediate privatizations of almost all public enterprises by the Gaidar/Chubais team. This 'shock treatment' was encouraged by a Harvard team of economic advisers and especially by US President Clinton in order to attempt to make the capitalist transformation irreversible. Massive privatization led to capitalist gang wars and the disarticulation of the Russian economy. As a result there was an eighty percent decline in living standards, a massive devaluation of the ruble and the sell-off of invaluable oil, gas and other strategic resources at bargain prices to the rising class of predator billionaires and US-European oil and gas multinational corporations. Over a hundred billion dollars a year was laundered by the mafia oligarchs in the principal banks of New York, London, Switzerland, Israel and elsewhere—funds which would later be recycled into the purchase of expensive real estate in the US, England, Spain and France, and as investments into British football teams, Israeli banks and joint ventures in minerals.

The winners of the gang wars during the Yeltsin reign followed up by expanding operations to a variety of new economic sectors as well as making investments in the expansion of existing facilities (especially in real estate, extractive and consumer industries) and overseas. Under President Putin, the gangster-oligarchs consolidated and expanded—from multi-millionaires to billionaires to multi-billionaires, and growing. From young swaggering thugs and local swindlers, they became the 'respectable' partners of American and European multinational corporations, according to their Western PR agents. The new Russian oligarchs had 'arrived' on the world financial scene, according to the financial press.

Yet as President Putin recently pointed out, the new billionaires have failed to invest, innovate and create competitive enterprises, despite optimal conditions. Outside of raw material exports benefiting from high international prices, few of the oligarch-owned manufacturers are earning foreign exchange because few can compete in international markets. For that reason the oligarchs have 'diversified' into stock speculation (Suleiman Kerimov $14.4 billion USD), prostitution (Mikhail Prokhorov $13.5 billion USD), banking (Fridman $12.6 billion USD) and buyouts of mines and mineral processing plants, activities better suited to their "entrepreneurial talents".

The Western media has focused on the falling out between a handful of Yeltsin-era oligarchs and President Vladimir Putin related to the increase in wealth of a number of Putin-era billionaires. However, the biographical evidence demonstrates that there is no rupture between the rise of the billionaires under Yeltsin and their consolidation and expansion under Putin. The decline in mutual murder and the shift to state-regulated competition is as much a product of the consolidation of the great fortunes as it is the 'new rules of the game' imposed by President Putin. In the mid 19th century, Honoré de Balzac, surveying the rise of the respectable bourgeois in France, pointed out their dubious origins: "Behind every great fortune is a great crime." The swindles begetting the decades-long ascent of the 19th century French bourgeoisie pale in comparison to the massive pillage and bloodletting that created Russia's 21st century billionaires.

Latin America

If blood and guns were the instruments for the rise of the Russian billionaire oligarchs, the Market, or better still, the US-IMF-World Bank-orchestrated Washington Consensus was the driving force behind the rise of the Latin American billionaires. The two countries with the greatest concentration of wealth and the greatest number of billionaires in Latin America are Mexico and Brazil (77 percent)—the two countries that privatized the most lucrative, efficient and largest public monopolies. Of the total $157.2 billion USD owned by the 38 Latin American billionaires, thirty are Brazilians or Mexicans with total holdings of $120.3 billion USD. The wealth of 38 families and individuals exceeds that of 250 million Latin Americans; the holdings of 0.000001 percent of the population exceeds that of the lowest fifty percent. In Mexico, the income of 0.000001 percent of the population exceeds the combined income of 40 million Mexicans. The rise of Latin American billionaires coincides with the real fall in minimum wages, public expenditures in social services and protective labor legislation, and with a rise in state repression, weakening labor and peasant organization and collective bargaining. The implementation of regressive taxes burdening the workers and peasants and tax exemptions and subsidies favoring the agro-mineral exporters contributed to the making of the billionaires. The result has been downward mobility for public employees and workers, the displacement of urban labor into the informal sector, the massive bankruptcy of small farmers, peasants and rural labor, the out-migration from the country-side to the urban slums and emigration abroad.

The principal cause of poverty in Latin American is the very conditions that facilitate the growth of billionaires. In the case of Mexico, the privatization of the telecommunication sector at rock bottom prices resulted in the quadrupling of wealth for Carlos Slim Helu, the third richest man in the world (just behind Bill Gates and Warren Buffet) with a net worth of $49 billion USD. Two fellow Mexican billionaires, Alfredo Harp Helu and Roberto Hernandez Ramirez, benefited from the privatization of banks and their subsequent de-nationalization with the sale of Banamex to Citicorp.

Privatization, financial de-regulation and de-nationalization were the key operating principles of US foreign economic policies implemented in Latin America by the IMF and the World Bank, and dictated the fundamental conditions shaping any loans or debt re-negotiations there.

The billionaires-in-the-making came from old and new money. Some began to raise their fortunes by securing government contracts during the earlier state-led development model (1930s to 1970s) and others inherited wealth. Half of Mexican billionaires inherited their original multi-million dollar fortunes which provided their boost to the top. The other half benefited from political ties to reap big payola from buying public enterprises cheap and then selling them off to US multinationals at great profit. The great bulk of the 12 million Mexican immigrants who crossed the border into the US have fled from the onerous conditions that allowed Mexico's traditional and nouveaux riche millionaires to join the global billionaires' club.

Brazil has the largest number of billionaires (20) of any country in Latin America with a net worth of $46.2 billion USD, which is greater than the net worth of eighty million urban and rural impoverished Brazilians. Approximately forty percent of Brazilian billionaires started with great fortunes—and simply added on—through acquisitions and mergers. The so-called 'self-made' billionaires benefited from the privatization of the lucrative financial sector (the Safra family with $8.9 billion USD) and the iron and steel complexes.

How to Become a Billionaire

While some knowledge, technical and 'entrepreneurial skills' and market savvy played a small role in the making of the billionaires in Russia and Latin America, far more important was the interface of politics and economics at every stage of wealth accumulation.

In most cases there were three stages:

1. During the early 'statist' model of development, the current billionaires successfully 'lobbied' and bribed officials for government contracts, tax exemptions, subsidies and protection from foreign competitors. State handouts were the beachhead or takeoff point to billionaire status during the subsequent neo-liberal phase.

2. The neo-liberal period provided the greatest opportunity for seizing lucrative public assets far below their market value and earning capacity. The privatizations, although described as 'market transactions', were in reality *political* sales in four senses: in price, in selection of buyers, in kickbacks to the sellers and in furthering an ideological agenda. Wealth accumulation resulted from the sell-off of banks, minerals, energy resources, telecommunications, power plants and transport, and the assumption by the state of private debt. This was the takeoff phase from millionaire toward billionaire status. This was

consummated in Latin America via corruption and in Russia via assassination and gang warfare.

3. During the third phase (the present) the billionaires have consolidated and expanded their empires through mergers, acquisitions, further privatizations and overseas expansion. Private monopolies of mobile phones, telecoms and other 'public' utilities plus high commodity prices have added billions to the initial concentrations. Some millionaires became billionaires by selling their recently acquired lucrative privatized enterprises to foreign capital.

In both Latin America and Russia, the billionaires grabbed lucrative state assets under the aegis of orthodox neo-liberal regimes (Salinas-Zedillo regimes in Mexico, Collor-Cardoso in Brazil, Yeltsin in Russia) and consolidated and expanded under the rule of supposedly 'reformist' regimes (Putin in Russia, Lula in Brazil and Fox in Mexico). In the rest of Latin America (Chile, Colombia and Argentina) the making of the billionaires resulted from bloody military coups and regimes that destroyed the socio-political movements and started the privatization process. This process was then even more energetically promoted by the subsequent electoral regimes of the right and 'center-left'.

What is repeatedly demonstrated in both Russia and Latin America is that the key factor leading to the quantum leap in wealth—from millionaires to billionaires—was the vast privatization and subsequent de-nationalization of lucrative public enterprises.

If we add to the concentration of $157 billion in the hands of an infinitesimal fraction of the Latin American elite, the $990 billion USD taken out by the foreign banks in debt payments and the $1 trillion USD (one thousand billion) taken out by way of profits, royalties, rents and laundered money over the past decade and a half, we have an adequate framework for understanding why Latin America continues to have stagnant economies with over two-thirds of its population with inadequate living standards.

The responsibility of the US for the growth of Latin American billionaires and mass poverty is several-fold and involves a wide gamut of political institutions, business elites, and academic and media moguls. First and foremost the US *backed* the military dictators and neo-liberal politicians who set up the billionaire-oriented economic models. It was ex-President Clinton, the CIA and his economic advisers,[2] in alliance with the Russian oligarchs, who provided the political intelligence and material support to put Yeltsin in power, and backed his destruction of the Russian Parliament (Duma) in 1993 and the rigged elections of 1996. And it was Washington, which allowed hundreds of billions of dollars to be laundered in US banks throughout the 1990s as the US Congressional Sub-Committee on Banking (1998) revealed.

It was Nixon/Kissinger and later Carter/Brzezinski, Reagan/Bush, and Clinton /Albright who backed the privatizations pushed by Latin American military dictators and civilian reactionaries in the 1970s, 1980s and 1990s. Their instructions to the US representatives in the IMF and the World Bank were writ large: privatize, deregulate and denationalize before negotiating any loans.

It was US academics and ideologues working hand in glove with the so-called multilateral agencies, as contracted economic consultants, who trained, designed and pushed the privatize-deregulate-denationalize agenda among their former Ivy League students-turned-economic and finance ministers and Central Bankers in Latin America and Russia.

It was US and EU multinational corporations and banks which bought out or went into joint ventures with the emerging Latin American billionaires and who reaped the trillion dollar payouts on the debts incurred by the corrupt military and civilian regimes. The billionaires are as much a product and/or by-product of US anti-nationalist, anti-communist policies as they are a product of their own grandiose theft of public enterprises.

Conclusion

Given the enormous class and income disparities in Russia, Latin America and China (twenty Chinese billionaires have acquired a net worth of $29.4 billion USD in less than ten years), it is more accurate to describe these countries as 'surging billionaires' rather than 'emerging markets' because it is not the 'free market' but the political power of the billionaires that dictates policy.

Countries of 'surging billionaires' produce burgeoning poverty, submerging living standards. The making of billionaires means the unmaking of civil society—the weakening of social solidarity, protective social legislation, pensions, vacations, public health programs and education. While politics is central, past political labels mean nothing. Ex-Marxist former Brazilian president Cardoso and ex-trade union leader President Lula da Silva privatized public enterprises and promoted policies that spawn billionaires. Ex-Communist Putin cultivates certain billionaire oligarchs and offers incentives to others to shape up and invest.

The period of greatest decline in living standards in Latin America and Russia coincides with the dismantling of the nationalist, populist and communist economies. Between 1980-2004, Latin America—more precisely Brazil, Argentina and Mexico—stagnated at 0 to 1 percent per capita growth. Russia saw a fifty percent decline in GNP between 1990-1996 and living standards dropped eighty percent for everyone except the predators and their gangster entourage.

Recent growth (2003-2007), where it occurs, has more to do with the extraordinary rise in international prices (of energy resources, metals and agro-exports) than with any positive developments derived from the billionaire-dominated economies. The growth of billionaires is hardly a sign of 'general prosperity' resulting from the 'free market' as the editors of *Forbes Magazine* claim. In fact it is the product of the illicit seizure of lucrative *public resources*, built up by the work and struggle of millions of workers, in Russia and China under Communism and in Latin America during populist-nationalist and democratic-socialist governments. Many billionaires have *inherited wealth* and used their *political ties* to expand and extend their empires—it has little to do with entrepreneurial skills.

The billionaires' and the White House's anger and hostility toward President Hugo Chavez of Venezuela is precisely because he is reversing the policies which create billionaires and mass poverty. He is re-nationalizing energy resources and public utilities, and expropriating some large landed estates. Chavez is not only challenging US hegemony in Latin America but also the entire privatize-deregulate-denationalize edifice that built the economic empires of the billionaires in Latin America, Russia, China and elsewhere.

PART II

ZIONIST POWER
IN THE UNITED STATES

CHAPTER 8

NO EXIT: THE JEWISH LOBBY SINKS THE IRAQ STUDY GROUP

Introduction

Late in 2006, a blue ribbon panel comprising the Iraq Study Group convened under the leadership of former Secretary of State, James Baker and former Senator, Lee H. Hamilton, to present a report for President Bush after several months of study and interviews. The official report, entitled **The Iraq Study Group Report: The Way Forward—A New Approach**, *was released on December 6, 2006. The recommendations in the report were attacked even before they were made public.*

Chances for a change in the direction of US Middle East policy have been extremely unlikely. The reason has been the growing power of the Jewish Lobby in Congress, the massive Zionist propaganda campaign in all the mass media, Israeli Prime Minister Ehud Olmert's 'nose leading' of Bush, and a host of related activities. The end result has been that Congress has failed to withdraw or reduce US troops and funding for the Iraq War. Bush, with the support of McCain and Clinton, Lieberman, Reid and Hoyer, pushed for more troops in pursuit of an all-out bloodbath in Baghdad. The Baker Iraq Study Group, under siege from the Zioncons and Zionlibs, was unable to deal with Israeli violence against Palestinians or enter into a dialogue with Syria and Iran on any but the most narrow and unpromising terms.

The Baker Camp

There was no doubt that Baker's Iraq Study Group's proposals to the White House and Congress took place in a generally favorable setting. Domestically, anti-war sentiment in the run-up to the Congressional election in 2006 was at an all-time high; the forty percent of the electorate that voted repudiated numerous Republican candidates identified with Bush's policies (and even others who were not). Top advisers to the Bush regime publicly supported opening a discussion with Iran—a major recommendation of the Baker Group. David Satterfield, a senior adviser to Secretary of State Condoleeza Rice, told the Senate Armed Services Committee, "We are prepared to discuss Iranian activities in Iraq. The timing of such a dialogue is one we still have under review."[1] Satterfield's comments followed the Congressional testimony of General John Abizaid (the top US general to Iraq) who had categorically rejected sending more troops to Iraq. Interviews with top military officials, retired and active, called for a phased withdrawal. Equally important, in an unprecedented turn of events, the weekly publications of the three military sectors (Army, Navy and Marine Corps) had editorialized in favor of the firing of Secretary of Defense Rumsfeld just two days before the midterm elections—and succeeded in precipitating his ouster.

A feature article in *Newsweek* favorably referred to the Baker Group as the "Rescue Squad."[2] Other sectors of the media followed suit. The *Financial Times* editorialized:

> The last five years have seen Israel extend and consolidate its hold on the West Bank and Arab East Jerusalem despite western rhetoric. That, every bit as much as the unprovoked invasion of Iraq, is what constantly threatens to set the region alight.
>
> The bipartisan Iraq Survey Group, led by James Baker, a former Secretary of State, and Lee Hamilton, an influential former congressman, is likely to focus on these issues and the need to re-launch the peace process. That, in turn, will require engagement with Iran and Syria, and should lead to the reconsideration of the Arab peace plan of 2002—full Arab recognition of Israel in return for Israeli withdrawal from all occupied Arab land. Ignoring the roots of Middle East volatility, as the accelerating cycle of conflict in the region should remind us, is a dangerous abdication of responsibility.

By including former leading Republican and Democratic Congress people (Hamilton and Simpson) and cabinet members, Baker had secured at least the support of some sectors of the two parties and Congress. By ensuring that one member of the Iraq Study Group, Robert Gates, would be named to replace Rumsfeld in the crucial position of Secretary of Defense, Baker potentially had some direct leverage in the executive branch. With the exception of Edwin Meese, a leader in the far-right Heritage Foundation,

Clifford May of the Zioncon Foundation for the Defense of Democracy and Michael Rubin (who has since resigned)—all members of the Israel First crowd—Baker had limited the influence of the Zioncons who designed Middle East war policy in the Bush Administration.

Equally important, Baker had the backing of the major petroleum and gas companies of Houston-Dallas, who had been sidelined from Middle East policymaking during the Zioncon-militarist ascendancy in the White House. They were eager for an "even-handed" Middle East policy to better serve their economic and personal relations with Middle East oil producers which unbalanced US support for Israel continued to fray, and to facilitate commercial negotiations with Iran and the Gulf States. Major US investment houses, including those whose CEOs had been prominent donors to the pro-Israel lobbies, were eager for a peace settlement that included Iran, in order to move into the new multi-billion dollar Islamic investments funds, which emerged among the Arab Gulf States.

On the domestic front, it *seemed* that Baker and his Group were in a strong position to reorient US Middle East policy by engaging Syria and Iran, Sunnis and Shia, and even Israel and Palestine in a "Grand Settlement". Most US big business interests favored an approach which would have limited Israeli-Zioncon influence over the use and abuse of US military power in the Middle East, facilitated US multinational corporations' and banks' dealings with conservative Arab/Iranian rulers, widened and secured US access to oil, and expanded US influence in the oil and gas rich former Soviet Republics in South and Central Asia.

Conditions and circumstances on the international front were even more favorable to the Baker Group. Iran had accepted a place at the negotiating table with the US, to discuss stabilizing Iraq. This was central to any settlement as Iran had ties and influence with sectors of the Shia leadership in Iraq.

Of course the *quid pro quo* for any agreement between the US and Iran would have involved the US agreeing to end its confrontational policies and military threats directed at Teheran. As we will discuss shortly this was a point of intense contention within Washington, meeting intense resistance from the entire 'Israel First' power structure (Lobby-Congress-Mass Media-Democratic Party Donors). To facilitate the opening of a dialogue with the US, Iran had offered the United Nations access to all its major nuclear installations in order to neutralize the hysterical warmongers among the formidable army of Israel First ideologues. According to the BBC:

> Iran will give inspectors access to records and equipment from two of its nuclear sites, the head of the UN's atomic agency, the IAEA has said. Mohamed El Baradei said he hoped Iran's move would begin a series of measures that

would clear suspicions over its nuclear program... According to Mr. El Baradei, Iran has agreed to let...the IAEA inspectors take environmental samples from the equipment at a former military site at Lavizan. Iran has also said it will give the UN access to records from a uranium enrichment plant in Natanz.[3]

These reports by the IAEA provided the Baker Group with ample justification for opening a dialogue with Iran and assuring the US public and members of Congress—at least those not under the thumb of the Lobby—that they were not "appeasing" a nuclear menace. Contrary to the claims of the Israeli warlords and their Lobby propagandists that Iran was an "*existential nuclear threat to the survival of Israel*", a report by the IAEA issued on November 14, 2006 sent to the governor of the nuclear watchdog, confirmed that Iran was now principally using two 'cascades' of 164 centrifuges apiece to enrich uranium.[4] This meant that Iran "still falls well short of the 3,000 or so centrifuges that would be needed to enrich uranium on an industrial scale".[5] Baker, if he so wished, could have neutralized the entire Israel chorus by pointing out that Iran had grossly insufficient weapons-grade enriched uranium for bomb making. He could have pointed out that, in any case, enriching uranium was in total compliance with the Nuclear Non-Proliferation Treaty and that the IAEA had extensive access to oversee Iran's nuclear projects.

Moreover, Baker could have pointed to the ongoing tacit working agreements between the US and Iran in opposing the Taliban, reconstructing Afghanistan and in pursuing Al Qaeda everywhere. In addition, Iran had intelligence-sharing agreements with the US puppet regime in Iraq. Even more important, Baker could have pointed out that Iran had supported the US overthrow of Saddam Hussein and had recognized the US puppet regime.

Syrian diplomatic moves, especially the restoration of relations with the US client regime in Iraq, certainly provided a positive setting for Baker to propose opening a dialogue with Damascus. Simultaneously, Iran had met with Iraqi President Jalal Talabani. At a time when the US client regime in Iraq was losing control and the US military was increasingly incapable of sustaining it, the Iranian desire to stabilize Iraq was a signal to Washington that it was willing to cooperate on a joint policy on Iraq. Syria's clear overture to the US was evident in its statement restoring ties: "Syria accepted the Iraqi and UN formula about the presence of US troops in Iraq. Instead of demanding their immediate departure, Syria agreed that they should withdraw gradually when not needed."[6]

Baker had the backing of the White House's major European ally, British Prime Minister Blair, who supported the idea of including Syria and Iran in a deal to stabilize Iraq. Blair argued for a 'general plan', which would have included an international agreement to resolve the Palestine/Israel conflict. Given the mood of compromise, that left only Israel pitted against the entire European continent and Middle East in refusing to negotiate with Iran, Hamas and Syria. With regard to the Palestinian conflict, Hamas had implicitly endorsed a two state solution based on the 1967 borders, for all intents and purposes recognizing Israel. Hamas' offer forcefully put the lie to Israel's claims that Hamas was a terrorist organization, which refused to negotiate a two state solution or recognize Israel.

Most important of all, the Bush strategy of "staying the course" in Iraq had been (with the sole exception of Israel Prime Minister Olmert—the war's only beneficiary) universally rejected—by his own generals, "coalition" partners, the American people and the majority of the US combat soldiers in Iraq. The White House disaster in Iraq had even led some Zioncon propagandists and architects of the war to abandon and opportunistically attack Bush. In other words, Baker's proposals would have been directed at an isolated President with a totally discredited policy, whose only clutch of supporters were economically and diplomatically insignificant but who possessed a powerful, wealthy and well-placed configuration of disciplined 'influentials' in the US known as the Jewish Lobby.

With formidable domestic allies and an extremely favorable international environment, one would have thought that Baker's proposals for moving forward in a new direction in the Middle East would be a 'cakewalk.' Clearly, the ball seemed to be in Baker's corner.

Unfortunately, that was not the case at all. What most of the critics, commentators, self-styled investigative reporters, politicians and media pundits favorable to Baker forgot to mention was the great elephant in the parlor—the Israeli/Jewish Lobby and its extended reach in Congress, the Democratic Party, the media and other vehicles for shaping US Middle East policy.

The Jewish Lobby Rolls Back the Baker Initiative

The American Jewish Lobby, at the behest of the Israeli state, had been leading a large-scale, intensive and partially successful campaign to demonize Iran and Syria, successfully pushing the US to pressure the United Nations in favor of economic sanctions. Through their blustering political clone, US Ambassador to the UN John Bolton, they pulled Washington closer to launching a military attack on Iran. An examination of AIPAC's agenda shows a new war against Iran on behalf of Israel at the top of its list of priorities. For the last three years, the publications, conferences and press releases of the Conference of Presidents of the Major American Jewish Organizations (CPMAJO) had urged their members to go all-out to fund and back candidates (mostly Democrats) who supported Israel's 'military solution' to Iran's nuclear enrichment program.

Never a day went by when the CPMAJO publication—the *Daily Alert*—did not reproduce articles endorsing Israel's war crimes and civilian killings and fabricating tissue thin 'explanations' justifying each and every brutality. Whether it involved murdering a family of ten at a beach outing in June 2006 or an extended family of nineteen in their beds in Beit Hanoun or dropping one million anti-civilian cluster bomblets in Lebanon two days before the ceasefire, or the cold-blooded murder of American activist, Rachel Corrie, the *Daily Alert* was ready to cover up for the Israeli State.

An army of 'Israel First, Last and Always' ideologues ('Resident Scholars' from some Washington institute or 'Middle East Experts' from a prestigious university) had been churning out articles every day calling for the US to spill more of its soldiers' blood for 'Greater Israel' by going to war with Iran. The brazen arrogance of these intellectual trollops defies the imagination. The US was still bogged down in a losing war, which their Zionist cohorts in the Pentagon had designed and executed, and which the 'Lobby' celebrated, and here they were, arguing, pushing and shoving for the US to engage in a bigger, bloodier and costlier war with Iran.

Numerous articles and opinion pieces appeared in the *Los Angeles Times*, *Washington Post*, *Wall Street Journal* and *New York Times* written by 'Israel First' writers, which attacked any attempt by Baker to change the US's confrontational policy towards Iran, not to mention a proposal calling for an international conference to resolve the Palestine-Israel conflict. Led by arch-Zionist Michael Ledeen of the American Enterprise Institute, some in the Jewish Lobby dismissed the Baker Iraq Study Group as 'the realists and anti-Semites'. Kagan and Kristol explicitly mocked them as 'defeatist' and traitors.[7]

The Jewish Lobby has had formidable allies—not only in Congress and the majority Democratic Party but also powerful representatives in the executive branch, including key operators like Vice President Cheney, National Security Coordinator of the Middle East, Elliot Abrams, Presidential Spokesperson Joshua Bolten, Vice Presidential Adviser David Wurmser and a pack of other long-serving 'Israel Firsters'. The Zionist-influenced Congress could have dredged up Gates' previous involvement in the Iran-Contra scandal too, if he had decided to ally with Baker, just as they sabotaged Murtha by digging up a 30-year old caper to undercut his quest for House Majority Leader.

Along with White House support, Israel successfully mobilized its political apparatus (the Jewish Lobby) in the US to direct political campaign funding toward the election of unconditional supporters of Israel. Democratic campaign finance directors, Israeli-US Congressman Rahm Emanuel and 'Israel Firster' Senator Charles Schumer, were backed by a multi-million dollar Wall Street slush fund (as reported by *Time*, *Newsweek*, and the *Wall Street Journal*). They ensured that over thirty Jewish Congressmen and women and 13 Senators were elected, including all of the Jewish incumbents, a number of senatorial and Congressional leaders married to Zionists as well as Lobby-certified 100 percent Israel supporters like Congressional Speaker of the House, Nancy Pelosi, and Senate majority leader, Harry Reid (praised by the Jewish Lobby for his life long unconditional support for Israel).[8] In the first test of Congressional Zionpower, Nancy Pelosi was defeated by a large majority in her effort to nominate the Iraq war critic Congressman John Murtha as Majority Leader in the House, which instead installed Steny Hoyer, a Congressman much more sympathetic to Israeli Prime Minister Olmert's pro-war views.

The Jewish Lobby was working hard to erect a 'firewall' to any US rapprochement with Iran, and in particular any initiative in that direction from the Baker Iraq Study Group. This was especially necessary because of the dire crisis of the US in Iraq and public perception of the possibility of a new, bloodier and costlier war against Iran. Moreover the Lobby was desperate to counter the positive confidence building measures adopted by Israel's Middle East adversaries, Syria and Iran, with regard to Iraq.

The Israeli countermeasures were not long in coming.

Olmert Swoops In

Shortly after the November 2006 US midterm Congressional elections, Ehud Olmert, Israel's Prime Minister, swooped in to impose the party line for the Conference of Presidents of Major American Jewish Organizations (CPMAJO) and related pro-Israel groups, and forestall any potential damage to Israel that might have gained momentum through the American elections, where what was widely-regarded as an anti-war vote had swept the Republicans from power in Congress. During his November 13th visit to Washington, he stated his categorical support for Bush's Iraq War policy and confrontational strategy with Iran. In fact, on November 10th, just prior to Olmert's visit, the Israeli deputy defense minister had suggested that Israel might be forced to launch a military strike against Iran's disputed nuclear program.[9] This statement from a high-ranking Israeli official just prior to the visit to the US of its prime minister set the stage in which what Olmert termed his "support for the US administration's strategy" against Iran occurred. According to the Israeli daily *Haaretz*:

> Olmert said Israel and other countries in the area should be thankful to the United States and Bush. He said the Iraq war had a dramatic positive effect on security and stability in the Middle East as well as strategic importance *from Israel's perspective* [my emphasis] and of moderate Arab states. Olmert said he was satisfied with the position Bush

took on Iran which *went further* [my emphasis] than in their
previous meeting in May. "Iran's role in the conversation
was quite clear, very serious and very significant and I left
the meeting with an outstanding feeling," said Olmert.[10]

Nothing expressed the power of the Jewish Lobby over US politics as clearly
as the cowardly silence of the leading Democrats before this gross intervention
by a foreign ruler into the internal politics of the US: Democratic Congressional
leader Pelosi swallowed the frog in silence. The few congressional critics
who complained about Olmert's 'partisanship' (taking sides with Bush) still
tacitly accepted that Olmert's impinging on US sovereignty was a principle
widely accepted by the fifty-odd Jewish Senators and Congress people, and
their numerous Gentile pro-Zionist camp followers.

Clearly Olmert had succeeded in pre-empting any new, more flexible
proposal that might have emanated from Baker's Iraq Study Group,
successfully leading President Bush 'by the nose'—as former Prime Minister
Sharon had once so colorfully boasted. Following the meeting with Olmert,
Bush duly called for the world to unite in isolating Iran until it "*gives up its
nuclear ambitions...If they continue to move forward with the program, there
has to be consequences. And a good place to start is working together to
isolate the country...Iran's nuclear ambitions are not in the world's interest.
If Iran had nuclear weapons, it would be terribly destabilizing.*"[11]

Prime Minister Olmert had succeeded in committing President Bush
to a position incompatible with Baker's proposals for meeting with Iran: a
strategy of isolation, sanctions and military threats was clearly incompatible
with any opening or meaningful dialogue let alone the achievement of Iran-
Syria co-operation in stabilizing Iraq—a matter most clearly in the best
interest of the increasingly discredited Bush administration (to say nothing
of that of the US). Yet as Olmert explicitly stated, the strategy Bush actually
committed to was that which was in line with *Israel's* 'strategic interest' of
extending its power and domination in the Middle East by weakening or
destroying its adversaries. Moreover Olmert had shown little concern at
how his statements publicly praising the US invasion and occupation of Iraq
might have embarrassed Jewish Zionists, when 85 percent of Democratic
voters and sixty percent of the US electorate were fed up with the deaths
(2890 plus by the November elections) and maiming (25,000 plus) of US
soldiers. For the 'Israel First' Democratic Congressmen and women (the
vast majority) who had known all along Israel's pro-war position, their faint
outcry was over the fact that Olmert had been so public, overt and aggressively
pro-war, just after the same Zionlibs had won the election by 'criticizing' the
war (mainly over the 'management' of the occupation).

The fact that Olmert had intervened in US politics so openly and
Bush followed so docilely should have been no surprise to observers of US-

Israeli relations. Further, it was the height of hypocrisy for the Democrats to express 'surprise' or chagrin, as they knew from direct experience that the Israeli state intervened on a daily basis through its proxy lobby on every policy having to do with the Middle East. AIPAC has even boasted of writing legislation, of securing massive Congressional majorities and of close Congressional 'co-ordination' (read subordination) with the Israeli regime in synchronizing its political operations. What made the Democrats angry was that Olmert had exposed their servility to Israel. While they stomped and belched over Bush's pro-war policy, they did not even dare convene a press conference to criticize Olmert, for fear of alienating the pro-Israel millionaires who had been providing an estimated 65 percent of the funds for the Democratic Party.

Olmert's pro-war position on Iraq, Iran and Syria had been preceded by an unprecedented propaganda campaign in all the major media by all the principle Zioncon/Zionlib ideologues: articles, opinion pieces and editorials had flooded the pages of the *Wall Street Journal, Foreign Policy, Washington Post, New York Times, New Yorker,* and *Christian Science Monitor.* The usual crowd of unconditional Israel apologists dubbed Middle East experts were pushing Tel Aviv's line of continual bloodletting in Iraq and military aggression in Iran. Michael Rubin, Charles Krauthamer, Clawson, Eisenstadt, Ledeen, Wolfenson ("American Jews should work hard for Israel and maximize gains for it"), Wurmser, Chertoff ("the US is threatened by international law"), Abraham Foxman ("Iran is worse than Nazi Germany") and an unprecedented one hour long uncontested tirade against Iran ("Iran is Germany, and it's 1938, except that this Nazi regime is in Iran") by Benjamin Netanyahu on Glenn Beck's prime time CNN television program preceded and followed Olmert's political intervention in Washington. The *Wall Street Journal* editorialized a full-scale attack on the Baker group even before it had issued any report, backing Israel's position on war with Iran, and reiterating its support for continuing war in Iraq and the massive ethnic cleansing of Palestinians (40,000 Palestinians had fled Gaza in the period between June and November 2006 in the face of Israeli missiles and tank shelling which killed 400 and maimed thousands). US Ambassador to the United Nations, "Blowhard" John Bolton let out a maniacal screed against the United Nations General Assembly and all its agencies for having voted to condemn Israel's deliberate, cold blooded massacre of an extended family of 19 mostly women and children in their beds in the Gaza village of Beit Hanoun on November 8, 2006. Bush expressed 'pride' in the use of the US's 31st veto to stop UN resolutions condemning Israel's savaging of Palestinians.

If Bolton represented the furthest right of an already highly skewed conservative spectrum (the 'loony right'), he was not without support, especially among the most respectable and representative organizations of the Jewish Lobby. "The Jewish community remains supportive and would want to see (Bolton) stay", said Malcolm Hoenlein, Vice-Chairman of the Conference of Presidents of Major American Jewish Organizations. The Jewish weekly, *Forward*, claimed, "He has been an effective advocate and he is appreciated by the diplomatic corp."[12] It should be remembered that most major Jewish groups had publicly endorsed Bolton when his appointment became a political battle in Washington in early 2005. There is no doubt that Bolton has indeed been an "effective advocate" *for Israeli* Middle East interests over and above the lives of Americans, Iraqis, Lebanese and Palestinians. Hoenlein however mistook the appreciation of the Israeli diplomatic corps for that of the rest of the world's diplomats who have been amused or appalled by Bolton's frothing rants against Europe, Asia, Africa, Latin America, the UN, International Lawyers or anyone that disagreed with him or dared to criticize Israel.

Israel's certainty of its stranglehold on the White House's Middle East policy was explicitly revealed by Israel's outgoing US Ambassador Danny Ayalon, who asserted in an interview: "US President George W. Bush will not hesitate to use force against Iran in order to halt its nuclear program, I have been privileged to know him well, he will not hesitate to go all the way if there is no choice."[13] According to Ambassador Ayalon's timetable:

> First the President will try to exhaust the diplomatic process, I estimate there is a 50 percent chance that the diplomatic effort will succeed. If not he will advance another step and consider imposing isolation and a blockade on Iran, like the US imposed on Cuba in the past. If this too does not succeed, he will not hesitate to employ force. If sanctions succeed, all the better. Otherwise, he will act by all means possible, including military action. (The Iraq War) is not the model. This (attack on Iran) is more a case employing air power combined with limited ground force…He (Bush) told me personally, in one of these difficult moments, that if you continue and persevere in your path, the people will ultimately follow you.[14]

Ayalon's interview revealed several important aspects of what the future course of White House policy toward Iran would be, underlining the fact that it was an Israeli (not Congress, not the American people), who felt some certainty that he knew what that would be.

First and foremost, the Israelis had inside knowledge of and access to the While House, and they were able to successfully impose their confrontational policies on the Presidency. Even as the majority of the US electorate, numerous high-ranking voices within the US military, the people and nations of the world and even some of Bush's advisers were against 'his path', the Israelis had the chutzpah to stand nearly alone in encouraging the President "to continue and persevere" in his war policies. That their isolation in so doing was unlikely to remain unnoticed did not deter them; such disregard of the risk of exposure indicated both the extent of Israeli confidence in their control of US policy, and the depth of their determination to undo all regional rivals. As *Forward* pointed out, the disregard of Zionist elites even included disregard of the opinion of American Jews:

> Even as a new study found that American Jews are significantly more opposed to the Iraq War than are Christians, Jewish organizations decided not to take up the issue at their annual policy conference. Drawing from the results of 13 polls conducted since 2005, the Gallup Organization found that 77% of American Jews think the Iraq War was a mistake, compared with 52% of the general American. [15]

The Israelis pandered to Bush's fundamentalist Christian belief that 'the people would ultimately follow' him in his Messianic delusions, even when all the evidence was to the contrary. Bush's belief was not distant from the Israeli belief—that he was exercising a superior moral compass than that of the world, on behalf of a superior nation whose interests superceded and could righteously ignore and annul international norms and principles. But while Israel had the backing of US vetoes in the United Nations and the military of a support of a superpower, Bush lacked a superior power (unless we include the mighty Jewish Lobby) to counteract his political isolation—though it may be the case that numerous contenders for the US presidency in 2008 will soon compete to join him in this lonely spot.

Bush has the dubious distinction of being the President-most-servile-to-a-foreign-power in US history (exceeding his predecessor, ex-President Clinton, Zionist Emeritus), a point emphasized by ex-President Jimmy Carter in his latest book, *Palestine: Peace Not Apartheid*. No American President had ever confided his war plans to a foreign emissary even before meeting with his top advisory commission, thus precluding the possibility of influential domestic leaders like the members of the Baker group from any substantial role shaping policy. Moreover Bush's servility to the Israel/Jewish Lobby extended to blocking his European allies from formulating an alternative Iran policy to Israel's military 'pre-emptive strike' proposal. According to the Israeli daily *Haaretz*:

> Bush told his French counterpart (President Jacques Chirac) that the possibility that Israel would carry out a strike against

Iran's nuclear installations should not be ruled out. Bush also said that if such an attack were to take place he would understand it.[16]

The single-minded stranglehold of the Jewish Lobby expressed in White House support for an Israeli sneak attack on Iran was such that Bush not only ignored the advice of Secretary of State Rice, but dismissed the fateful consequences: a massive Iranian military response against US occupation forces in Iraq resulting in thousands of deaths, massive oil and political dislocations throughout the entire Middle East, destabilization of the Gulf States and rising oil prices. The unprecedented Zionist control over the White House was summed up by Zioncon executive director of the Jewish Institute for (Israeli) National Security Affairs (JINSA), Thomas Neumann: "The administration today was stronger on Israel than any administration in my lifetime".[17]

While proponents of a 'turn' in US policy in the Middle East had hailed the resignation of Donald Rumsfeld on November 8, 2006, just two days after the midterm elections, and the appointment of Robert Gates, a member of the Baker Iraq Study Group, to be the new Secretary of Defense––as auguring a more 'realist', less bellicose policy—Zionist leaders were confident that their dominant influence over Bush would keep Gates in line with Israeli policy. Mara Rudman, a Zionlib former member of Clinton's National Security Council, speaking at the Zioncon "Israel Policy Forum" in Washington accurately put the Gates appointment into its proper perspective: "It's not really where he (Gates) goes, its where the president goes". Thomas Neumann, JINSA's propaganda master, dismissed the possibility that Gates would front for the Baker Iraq Study Group: "Gates was appointed more because he has a record of doing what he's told (by Bush). There's nothing good or bad about Gates, they (the White House) wanted someone who doesn't make waves."[18]

And as the evidence indicates, *the President appears to be going where the Israelis and their US transmission belts told him to go.*

The Defeat of Peace Initiatives from Syria

In November 2006, after a visit to the Middle East, British Prime Minister Blair issued a policy statement calling for a dialogue and negotiations for an overall peace settlement in the Middle East including all interested parties, especially Syria and Iran. The Israeli regime immediately rejected the proposal. The Lobby echoed their patrons' policy and subsequently the White House and Congress followed suit. Syria proceeded to establish diplomatic relations and intelligence and economic cooperation with the US-backed Iraqi regime, demonstrating a major gesture toward 'stabilizing' the Mesopotamian region. The Israeli regime branded the policy a means of influencing Iraqi 'terrorists'. Predictably, the Jewish Lobby, its scribes and media outlets downplayed its significance or put a negative spin to the Syrian initiative, demanding that "Syria follow words by action", namely stop the flow of militants into Iraq. Syria responded by pointing to its far more extensive frontier patrol posts on the border than those maintained by either the US occupation forces or its Iraqi client government. The Israeli regime and its Lobby, the White House and Congressional clients' rejection of Syrian (and Iranian) peace initiatives was as much directed at neutralizing these overtures as it was in pre-empting similar initiatives emanating from the Baker Iraq Study Group. The Lobby's vehement dismissal of Syria's role as a stabilizing force set the stage for linking it with Baker and undercutting his recommendations. A similar Lobby propaganda effort was directed at Iran and indirectly at Baker's proposals for negotiating with them.

The efforts by the White House, Brussels and Tel Aviv to isolate Syria, undermine its conciliatory steps and block any overture from the Baker group were centered on the unsubstantiated accusations that Damascus had assassinated two 'anti-Syrian' Lebanese leaders, Rafik Hariri and Pierre Gemayel. In the case of the February 15, 2005 assassination of former Prime Minister Hariri, the main witness against Syria later recanted and perjured himself even as the European Union lent its weight to the accusation against Syria. The principal Turkish investigator later resigned after having unsuccessfully pursued only one line of investigation—to demonstrate the complicity of Syria—discounting the equally plausible hypothesis of Israeli involvement. The two major beneficiaries of the Hariri assassination were the US and Israel, whose interests in fomenting chaos in Lebanon far exceeded those of Syria. Despite the contest of pro and anti-Syrian demonstrations in Beirut which took place in the wake of the Hariri assassination, a barrage of anti-Syrian publicity led to the resignation of Lebanon's pro-Syrian prime minister, Omar Karami, and Syrian withdrawal of its forces from Lebanon, rather than to a consolidation of Syrian influence.

The historical benefits from the anti-Syrian Hariri campaign were likely not lost on the subsequent political manipulators of the November 21, 2006 Pierre Gemayel assassination. As a result of it, the US and its Israeli ally had already succeeded in forcing Syria to withdraw its forces from Lebanon, making Southern Lebanon and, in particular, Hezbollah, vulnerable to Israeli military attack. Shortly thereafter, Israel had used a routine border incident as a pretext to invade and attempt to destroy Hezbollah and decimate its social base among the millions of residents in Beirut and Southern Lebanon. But rather than strengthen Israel's position in Lebanon and increase the power of its longstanding Phalangist clients, the invasion had strengthened Hezbollah, raising its support to over sixty percent of the Lebanese population.[19] The subsequent campaign to pin the Gemayel death on Syria and Hezbollah was designed to promote Israeli interests in Lebanon by provoking internal civil conflict, orchestrating and mobilizing a mass smear campaign against Hezbollah to pre-empt the latter's effort to secure a more equitable representation of its electoral support in the Lebanese Cabinet.

But more tactically important, targeting Syria with the accusation of dual assassinations served to weaken Syria as a possible interlocutor for the Baker Group, undermining Baker's proposal to open a dialogue with Syria.[20] More specifically it neutralized the positive fallout in Washington of Syria's establishment of relations with the US client-regime in Iraq. For this reason the rabidly pro-Israel *Wall Street Journal* screeched: "Another Murder in Beirut for Jim Baker to Contemplate".[21]

The fact was that Israel and its Zionist representatives in the US were the main beneficiaries of the dual assassinations. There was both hard and circumstantial data pointing to Israeli complicity in the killings. There had been several earlier cases of notorious Phalangists being murdered just prior to their scheduled testimony in Brussels related to a case brought by Palestinian survivors against top Israelis involved in the notorious massacres in Lebanon, especially at the Palestinian camps of Sabra and Shatila in September 1982. On January 24, 2002, Elie Hobeika, a Phalangist warlord directly involved in the massacre, was blown up in his Beirut neighborhood along with three bodyguards just two days after agreeing to testify against the Israelis on behalf of the Palestinian survivors. Hobeika, who was the notorious Phalangist chief liaison with the IDF during the Israeli occupation of Beirut, claimed to have worked with the Israeli Mossad in orchestrating the massacre. A mysterious group, 'Lebanese for a Free and Independent Lebanon', claimed responsibility from Cyprus and then just disappeared. Weeks earlier, another witness for the Belgian case and close Hobeika associate, Jean Ghanem, had been killed in an auto accident. A few months later, a third close Hobeika associate and potential witness in the Belgian case, Michael Nassar, was assassinated along with his wife in Brazil.

In these assassinations and unexpected deaths, most experts and Lebanese politicians, including Phalangists, pointed to Mossad operations. Pointedly, the fact that Phalangists were Israeli clients did not preclude selective assassinations when it was in Israeli state interest: they treated the Phalangists, their former allies, like used condoms. Pierre Gemayel, the grandson of the founder of the Lebanese fascist Phalange Party, had been a marginal figure in the Lebanese political equation; in death he became a pivotal figure in Israel's Middle East power grab.

In June 2006 Lebanese military authorities had announced the arrest of Hussein al-Khatib, a Lebanese prisoner who had been held in Israel during the 1980s. He confessed to having worked in Lebanon as part of a Mossad-led assassination team killing Lebanese and Palestinian leaders using car bombs. Throughout Lebanese history, Mossad operatives have been imputed with political assassinations of Palestinian and Lebanese adversaries, car bombings and commando operations in Beirut as well as throughout the country. As early as the foundation of Israel, its leaders, including Ben Gurion, had advocated promoting civil war in Lebanon in order to establish a Christian Maronite government allied to Israel.

In summary, Israel had a motive for killing Hariri and Gemayel, had a history of killing 'clients' to further their state interests, and certainly had exercised the practice of executing Lebanese political figures before. Given the high stakes involved in a possible re-direction in US policy toward engaging Syria, as had been proposed by the Baker Iraq Study Group, and given Damascus efforts to facilitate such a dialogue by giving legitimacy to the bloody US client in Baghdad, the Israeli ploy of political murder and the Zionist media blitz condemning Syria for the deaths made political sense from the point of view of furthering Israel's quest for Middle East dominance.

Fending Off the Iranian Peace Overtures

Iran stands out as a potentially key interlocutor for a general Middle East settlement, offering a means whereby the US might retain its strategic Arab allies in the Middle East through dialogue, negotiations and power sharing with Teheran. Contrary to the propaganda spewed by the Israeli regime and the Jewish Lobby in the US, Iran had repeatedly demonstrated that far from fomenting 'terrorism' it had co-operated with the US on a whole series of important measures compatible with US imperial policies in Iraq and Afghanistan.

In the run-up to the US invasion and subsequent occupation of Iraq, it was a publicly known and officially acknowledged fact that Iran had supported the US overthrow of Saddam Hussein, provided intelligence to the US, advised and supported Shia co-operation in the formation of a US client regime, and recognized, established and maintained formal relations with the puppet regime despite its collaboration with the killers of hundreds of thousands of Iraqi civilians.

Iran had been a major bulwark against Al Qaeda, arresting and in some cases offering to extradite its members to the West, thus showing a decided partisanship to some aspects of the US 'War on Terrorism'. Equally important, Iran played a major stabilizing role in Western Afghanistan, especially in Herat, severely limiting Taliban influence (though at the time, and indeed given its early US-supported provenance, Iran might well have regarded the Taliban as an American instrument threatening its eastern border). Iran worked closely with Italian and ISAF reconstruction teams in rebuilding the region. The *Financial Times* reported: "The main factor holding the west of Afghanistan together is the positive influence of neighboring Iran which is 'pumping a lot of money into the reconstruction of the west', says a senior US administration official in Washington".[22]

The army of Israel-First publicists in the US and Europe continued to lump Iran with Al Qaeda, the Taliban, and Iraqi terrorists despite all the evidence to the contrary. The 'Big Lie' campaign was directed toward isolating Iran and securing United Nations sanctions against it as a prelude to a US/Israeli sneak attack on Iranian cities, infrastructure, military and scientific research installations and nuclear research facilities. To proceed toward the destruction of Iran and the consolidation of Israeli dominance in the Middle East, the immediate goal was to pre-empt the Baker Group from proposing a dialogue with Iran or at a minimum, setting parameters, which would have virtually undercut that possibility.

The most vicious, effective and duplicitous Israel-centered propaganda campaign against Iran focused on its nuclear research programs. The Zionist-led campaign against Iran had not provided any basis to contradict the IAEA inspection team's findings that no evidence for a nuclear weapons program existed. Iran's forthright offers to the US and the EU for detailed inspection tours by all inspectors were dismissed outright by the White House as a 'propaganda ploy', a ploy which Israel refused to match with regard to its own illegal nuclear and chemical-biological arms facilities. No expert or political leader in the world, now or in the recent past, had argued that Iran was violating the Nuclear Non-proliferation Treaty. Israeli-US opposition toward uranium enrichment was applied selectively to Iran. Otherwise all one hundred nations with nuclear energy programs should likewise have been threatened with preventive war.

Shooting Down Palestinian Peaceful Overtures

Despite sustained bloody attacks from the Israeli military machine (the Orwellian Israeli 'Defense' Forces) the Palestinian Hamas government had made two peace proposals. Between January 2005 and June 24, 2006, the Hamas government refrained from responding to Israeli military attacks on Gaza and the West Bank (despite numerous assassinations, house demolitions and illegal arrests of activists) in hope of inducing Tel Aviv to begin peace negotiations. The Israeli state, backed by the US, categorically rejected peace and imposed a total blockade on the Gaza Strip. It was only when the IDF shelled a Palestinian beach filled with families, murdering 18 picnicking children and their parents, that Hamas responded with sporadic shell firing and the capture of an Israeli tank soldier engaged in shelling into the Gaza neighborhoods.

The subsequent Israeli massacre of 400 Palestinians (over 200 of whom were non-combatant civilians, mainly women and children) between

July and November 24, 2006 failed to dampen Palestinian resistance. Palestinian and international proposals to end the blood bath were consistently rejected by the Israeli regime. On November 24, 2006 the BBC News reported:

> Israel has dismissed an offer by Palestinian militant groups to stop firing rockets into Israel if Israel ends attacks on Palestinians. An Israeli government spokeswoman, Miri Eisen, said...the offer of an end to firing rockets from Gaza showed the lack of real commitment to peace [*sic!*]

By that twisted logic, Israel's continued artillery barrages of Palestinian towns demonstrated a 'real' commitment to peace! The BBC pointed to what most experts acknowledge has been Israel's long-term bellicose posture: "Israel has in the past consistently rejected ceasefire offers by Palestinian militants, saying it *refuses to do deals of any kind* [my emphasis] with what it describes as terrorist organizations."[23]

The Olmert regime rejected outright a new peace initiative proposed by Italy, France and Spain, which would have allowed United Nations peace forces to safeguard the frontier between Gaza and Israel.[24] In the face of Israel's systematic daily killing of Palestinians and ethnic cleansing of over 8,000 Palestinians each month (40,000 since June), the United Nations General Assembly voted 150 to 7 on November 13, 2006 to condemn Israel for mass murder in Beit Hanoun, and called for an investigation. The Israeli Ambassador walked out. The Israeli regime rejected the UN resolution and, as a sign of its contempt for the United Nations, continued in its slaughter, killing a dozen Palestinians in the immediate aftermath.

Israel's disdain for world public opinion had the unequivocal support of the Conference of Presidents of the Major American Jewish Organizations and their counterparts in Canada, England, France, Argentina and elsewhere throughout the world. But it was in the United States where the Jewish Lobby's power really counted: the US exercised its 31st veto protecting Israel from a censorious UN Security Council resolution. The White House's dismissal of the UK Prime Minister Tony Blair's proposal for an all inclusive Middle East conference, including Syria, Palestine, Iraq, the Jewish State and Iran, allowed Israel to ignore the entire European Union, the Middle East, and, for that matter, the rest of the world. The *Financial Times* reported:

> Tony Blair's call this week for a 'whole Middle East strategy' sent a message that the road to peace in Iraq passes through Jerusalem and Beirut. In his foreign policy speech to the City of London, the UK Prime Minister recognized

the region's crises were interlinked and required a comprehensive approach.[25]

It was clearer than ever that the Israeli ethnic cleansing of Palestine, rather than being a *catalyst* for Israeli extremism, was a *reflection* of the pervasiveness of racist attitudes which had characterized Zionist extremism since its inception[26] and that this threatened everyone in the Middle East, Europe and the United States. Zionists' distrust of the non-Jewish world, their unwillingness to compromise, their belief that the future is theirs alone, the denial of the legitimacy of the Other's narrative, and their determination to pursue their ideology even at the expense of their own people, have been defining characteristics of the movement that have made resolution of the Israeli-Palestinian conflict impossible. These characteristics have been at the heart of the extremist Zionist assault on Western nations and people who propose constraints on Israeli militarism. In 2003 the West failed to act in time to protect its own interests in the Middle East from a Zionist-backed war in Iraq, and ended up paying a price. But the Iraqis and Palestinians have paid infinitely more. With the US occupation forces in a quagmire in Iraq and with the same White House/Israeli forces pushing for a new pre-emptive war against the much stronger Iran, the consequences have become much more threatening.

The Israeli rejection of Palestinian, European and United Nations proposals for peace negotiations targeted the Baker Iraq Study Group as well, since it also saw that the road to peace in Baghdad passes through Jerusalem.

Conclusion

Despite the advantageous international situation and broad domestic support, the Baker Group faced the enormous power and opposition of the Jewish Lobby in its quest to break new ground in US Middle East Policy. Each and every proposal had to pass the scrutiny of an army of 'Israel First' Lobbyists, their compliant Congress members and staff, and had to withstand the hostility of members of the Executive, including George W. Bush, aligned with the Jewish state. If Baker's proposal made any headway, the Jewish power bloc in Congress and the Executive was expected to impose a political straightjacket that precluded any effective and meaningful exchange. This meant that they would have proposed the White House follow a 'two track' approach: vigorously continuing to pursue economic sanctions and military threats on one track while, on the other, approaching Iran to intervene and stabilize the US client regime in Iraq. The Zionists and their followers already knew that a two-track approach would be a non-starter. Iran would not lend its political leverage to stabilize Iraq in order to free up US military power to blow up Iranian cities as well as its nuclear facilities, ports, refineries and other vital infrastructure. Not even Baker's much vaunted diplomatic skills could have convinced Iran to make one-sided strategic concessions to the White House in exchange for nothing—not even an elementary security or non-aggression agreement.

When Great Britain's Defense Minister, Des Browne, announced a sharp reduction of troops in Iraq at least by half for 2007,[27] Baker was then under even greater pressure to propose a timetable for the reduction of US troops—a position however, which apparently had divided his group.[28]

A proposal to gradually reduce US troops in Iraq and reposition them to military bases was not likely to meet stiff opposition from the Jewish state or its representatives in the US—unless the White Office offered stiff resistance. For Israel and its Lobby, the US invasion and occupation had already accomplished its primary mission of destroying the Iraqi state, thereby fragmenting Iraqi society into warring ethno-religious-tribal divisions and eliminating a strong secular republic opposed to the Jewish state's ethnic cleansing of Palestine. For Israel and its US Lobby, it was now time to move on to eliminating other adversaries to Israeli Middle East dominance—namely Iran and Syria. That was why the Lobby spent more resources and exerted greater pressure on the White House and Congress to escalate the confrontation with those two countries. And that was why the Lobby had already launched a full-scale propaganda campaign to block any openings to Iran, which might have led to some sort of security accommodation.

Could Baker have 'conned' the Iranian and Syrian leaders into believing that their political support of the US in Iraq would be rewarded later? That aiding the US in Iraq would create 'confidence' in their good will in Washington and enhance Iran's image as a "responsible" Middle East power? Baker might have argued that their co-operation strengthened the 'good guy realists' in Washington, weakened the 'bad guy Zioncons' and would lead to an end to the confrontational military blackmail. No doubt there were Iranian politicians and diplomats among the competing forces who were eager to cooperate with the US at *almost* any price, but even they could not publicly embrace the restrictive terms that the Lobby/White House proposed. A dialogue was impossible if the White House and Israel continued to threaten a pre-emptive attack. It was highly unlikely that Baker's Group would dare confront the powerful Jewish lobby by proposing a restriction on Israel's militarist posture or even diplomatically asking the Jewish State to refrain from setting 'deadlines' for an air assault against Iran.

Despite the otherwise universal consensus (Israel and the Jewish Lobby excluded) that the Palestine-Israel conflict was at the center of Middle East discord and the public and private acknowledgment that Israeli land grabbing and ethnic cleansing was the major factor in the conflict, despite the fact that James Baker had publicly acknowledged as much when he served as Secretary of State in Bush Sr.'s government, it was highly unlikely that the Baker group would advance a proposal convoking an international conference to deal with the Palestinian issue. He knew in advance that it would provoke a firewall of opposition in a Lobby-controlled Congress and denunciations of 'anti-Semitism' from the fanatic Zionist Middle East 'experts', pundits and Ivy League 'academics in uniform'.

What the Baker Iraq Study Group intended and proposed was an alternative way of defending and enhancing the US Empire. More specifically the Group sought to 'stabilize' Iraq in order to open the Middle East for US financial investors and petroleum companies. This strategy was severely constrained by a formidable bloc led by the Jewish Lobby with far reaching influence in the mass media, the Congress and Senate and their committee chairpersons especially in the Democratic Party, which preferred military devastation as a prelude to domination.

While neither the Baker Group nor the 'Israel Firsters' represented a pro-democracy alternative to empire building, it was important to note one significant difference. The Jewish Lobby was acting directly and consistently to promote the agenda of a foreign colonial power that was beyond the reach of American voters, the constraints of the US Constitution, and international law. Equally important, Israel and its US Lobby were and are largely unmoved by the death and injury of US soldiers in Iraq and the squandering of the US taxpayers' money. This has been reinforced by the fact that less than 2/10 of one percent (0.2 percent) of the US soldiers in Iraq were Jewish (predominantly immigrants from Eastern Europe) and probably very few of those were on the front lines. More young American Jews volunteer to serve in the Israeli Defense Forces.

The Baker Group, in contrast, had a very heterogeneous group of supporters — including a few anti-war democrats, military officials offended by Zionist-Pentagon manipulation, sectors of the media, several petrol and financial moguls, and sectors of the electorate. While the Bush Administration may have shredded the Constitution and corrupted the electoral system, there still was space and voice to articulate popular opposition to the White House and the Jewish Lobby, unlike the public's incapacity to influence the Israeli state. As the Baker proposals advanced toward a rapprochement with Iran and Syria, this weakened the capacity of Israel and its Lobby to plunge the US into another Middle East war, at least temporarily. Insofar as the Baker proposals moved toward a timetable for withdrawing US troops, it opened space for accelerating and deepening the troop reduction. The almost total absence of the Left and "progressives" from this impending power struggle, given its world-historic significance and consequence, has been in large part attributable to the influence which Jewish progressives exercise on the anti-war movement. The anti-war movement's refusal to recognize the Jewish Lobby as the prime obstacle and major opponent of a new US Mid East policy crippled any effective public protest.

A prime example has been the writing of investigative journalist Seymour Hersh, who was a constant reference for the progressives. In his November 2006 article on the likelihood of the Bush Administration attacking Iran,[29] Hersh excluded any mention of the Jewish Lobby and its powerful role as the only major national interest group promoting and supporting a war with Iran. In his earlier texts on the Iraq war planning and execution, he had pointedly omitted identifying the longstanding and deep ties of top Pentagon policymakers (Wolfowitz, Feith, Rubin, Perle, Shulsky, et al.) with the Israeli state. By once again systematically omitting mention of the Zionist power configuration in any analysis of what was pushing US policy toward a war with Iran, he helped to render this influence invisible, thereby undermining efforts by his readers in the peace movement to act against the principal architects of a pre-emptive war on Iran.

Even worse, in his article Hersh repeated Israeli (and Lobby) fabricated propaganda about Iran's imminent nuclear bomb threat albeit while mentioning a CIA detailed study discounting those very claims. In a word, Hersh's reportage gave legitimacy and credibility to Israeli-Lobby war propaganda, providing yet another means to embed it in public consciousness while sowing doubts about serious studies by the UN-sponsored International Atomic Energy Agency, which refuted Israeli claims. What has been pervasive and suspect in Hersh's investigative reporting were his references to anonymous highly placed sources who provided highly confidential information, *which already had been public knowledge for weeks and sometimes months* and reported on websites, in public documents and even by news services. Whatever inside dope Hersh cited that had not been public was based on anonymous sources which could never be double checked or verified, whose analysis incidentally coincided with Hersh's peculiar penchant for blaming the Gentiles (WASPS) and exonerating the brethren.

The peace movement's refusal to take a stand and confront the Zionist Lobby condemned it to playing a passive 'spectator role' in the 'Baker versus-Lobby' battle for control over US Middle East policy. No doubt some leftists adopted a 'pox on both your houses' posture, while others welcomed some of Baker's initiatives for an open dialogue even as they refused to recognize that those proposals would go nowhere unless the influence of the Zionist power configuration in Congress and the White House was defeated, hoping perhaps that as the 'heavyweights' at the top jousted and clamored, space would open for a real debate from below. This might then supersede the debate on the 'best way to manage the war and the empire' and enable activists to propose the immediate withdrawal of troops as part of 'a grand settlement' among democratic people. However, real peace in the Middle East can only come about with the closing of foreign military bases, the ending of Israel's colonial occupation, and public control or nationalization of energy resources.

In the end the Baker Iraq Study Group recommended a long-term, large-scale US military presence in Iraq, in the Gulf States and in adjoining Arab states. The redeployment strategy the Baker proposed still meant keeping seventy to eighty thousand US armed advisers, trainers and special operation forces embedded with the Iraqi puppet army for the foreseeable future. The open-ended nature of the Baker proposals, without specific time, date and place for withdrawal and/or deployment—even had it been unopposed—would have allowed the White House a free hand over the next two years to stay the course, continue the war and occupation, escalate the number of troops, deceive the public, incur more deaths of US troops and perpetuate the slaughter of the Iraqi people.

With those proposals, Baker's call for a broader dialogue involving Iran and Syria was already dead in the water. Understandably Iran has conditioned negotiations on a timetable for US withdrawal and a less bellicose policy to itself. Syria, under severe pressure from the White House, was unlikely to embrace an agenda based on an extended US military presence, especially one that increased US firepower in neighboring countries and ignored Israel's control over the Golan Heights and its bloody overt and covert operations in Lebanon to destroy Hezbollah.

In the end, the Baker Iraq Study Group raised false expectations about new directions by proving unwilling or impotent to resist Bush's pre-emptive cries to carry on with war as usual. Baker's one contribution to modifying the bellicose thrust of the Bush regime—Robert Gates as Secretary of Defense—gave every indication that he would be following Rumsfeld's policies, a blue-blooded Yes Man, as the leading lights of the Jewish Lobby had predicted.

CHAPTER 9

FACING DOWN THE FACTS: THE LOBBY AND THE MEDIA ON LEBANON

Introduction

It is not possible to discuss the US imperial system without drawing attention to the anomalous position that Israel holds within it. While Israel has long been dismissed — including by the Left — as a client state subordinate to the dictates of Washington, that classification has become increasingly untenable — not simply because of its academic inaccuracy, but because recent and ongoing events in the Middle East indicate that this is an arena in which nothing less than the future of world peace is at stake.

My 2006 book, *The Power of Israel in the United States*,[1] documented not just the power of Israel to influence US Middle East policy, but also the fact that this power derived from the existence within the US of an extensive pro-Zionist lobby advocating Israel First policies, echoing the objectives and defending the actions of the state of Israel, whatever these might be. The Zionist power configuration far exceeds the organizational reach and financial resources of AIPAC or 'the Lobby'. It includes seven major propaganda [*sic*] 'think tanks' which crank out thousands of position papers, editorials and op-ed pieces appearing on a daily basis in dozens of national and local newspapers, as well as providing ideological experts to appear on innumerable TV and radio 'news' programs. The line is uniform — Israel is always right; the Arabs and Muslims are a threat to peace and the US should provide unconditional support for Israel.

The propaganda 'think' tanks that follow the Israel-First line include: the American Enterprise Institute, the New Citizenship Project, the Project for the New American Century, the Center for Security Policy, the National Institute for Public Policy, the Jewish Institute for National Security Affairs, the Washington

Institute for Near Eastern Policy and the Institute for Advanced Strategic and Political Studies.

The Zionist power configuration includes: The Conference of Presidents of the Major American Jewish Organizations (51 national organizations, including AIPAC, the Anti-Defamation League and American Jewish Committee), several hundred local and regional Jewish Federations, whose prime agenda is defending Israel, right or wrong; scores of political action committees (PACs) with non-descript names (i.e. not indicative of ties to Israel) but who are fundraisers for Israel nonetheless; several dozen regional and Washington-based propaganda 'think tanks'; millionaire Jewish donors and philanthropists or cultural activists who act to censure any activity critical of Israel; billionaire political contributors; media moguls; and so on.

The Israeli influence on American Middle East policy has led to the devastation long into the future of one of Israel's most significant enemy states. In fact, the elimination of an external Israeli adversary has been the primary reason for the illegal pre-emptive US assault on Iraq, and more visibly so—for the clear absence of any other credible reasons than the urging of Israel—for ongoing US bellicosity towards Iran.

These objectives, however, have not served the best interests of US imperialism either in the Middle East or globally. As a result, a growing fissure is opening between the interests of the pro-Zionist sector of the American ruling elite and those of the traditional American elites whose larger imperial interests are threatened by the ongoing Middle East debacle.

The intent of the present chapter is to demonstrate pro-Israel influence by illustrating how an Israeli interpretation of events dominated English-speaking media even during the Israeli assault on Lebanon. As the whole world watched, TV cameras continued to roll as Israeli munitions blew huge sectors of Beirut and most of the infrastructure of southern Lebanon to smithereens. Then the Lobby and the media commentators set about their Herculean task of making viewers re-conceive what their eyes had seen until it could fit once again into America's traditional image of Israel as a victim whose purely retaliatory actions were appropriate and reasonable.

The Lobby Rallies to the Destruction of Lebanon

As adjuncts of the Israeli Foreign Office, not a single one of the 51 organizations which make up the Conference of Presidents of the Major Jewish Organizations in the US voiced a single public criticism of Israel's massive destruction of civilian homes, hospitals, offices, supermarkets, refugee convoys, churches and mosques in Lebanon, and its deliberate killing of civilians, UN peacekeepers[2] and rescue workers with precision bombing. On the contrary, the entire Jewish lobby echoed in precise detail the Israeli lies that Lebanese deaths were caused by the Lebanese resistance's "use of human shields", despite the overwhelming visual evidence carried by the major media of the devastation of the heavily populated southern suburbs of Beirut by Israeli air bombardment, which were completely out of range of any Hezbollah rockets and posed no threat to Israel's northern border.

The magnitude of Israel's military assault can be measured in great detail. From July 12 to August 14, 2006 the Israeli Armed Forces (IDF) launched 5,000 missiles, 5-ton bunker-buster bombs and cluster bombs as well as anti-personnel phosphorus bombs each day into Lebanon for 27 day—totaling over 135,000 missiles, bombs and artillery shells. During the last seven days of the war Israel launched 6,000 bombs and shells per day—over 42,000, for a grand total of 177,000 over a heavily populated territory the size of the smallest state in the US. In contrast, the Lebanese national resistance launched 4,000 rockets during the entire 34-day period, an average of 118 per day. The ratio was 44 to 1—without mentioning the size differentials, the long-term killing effects of the hundreds of thousands of unexploded cluster bombs (nearly 50 killed or maimed in the first 4 months since the end of hostilities) and Israel's scorched earth military incursion. [3]

Under the rubric of the United Jewish Communities, the national, state and local Jewish organizations launched a $300 million fundraising and propaganda campaign[4] in support of the 26 Jewish civilians and 119 soldiers killed[5] during the Israeli invasion of Lebanon—not for the 18 Israeli Arabs who were excluded from Jews-only bomb shelters?[6]

The Jewish Lobbyists published the number of Israel's civilian dead as 44[7] without mentioning that 26 were Jews and the remaining 18 were members of Israel's Arab Muslim and Christian minority[8] who constitute around twenty percent of the population, thereby enhancing the image of Israeli (Jewish) suffering. The disproportionate number of Israeli Arabs killed might well be viewed as a result not just of the Israeli government policy of providing shelters and siren warning systems to Jews while ignoring the security needs of its Arab citizens in their villages where state services are deliberately minimal, but also of its practice of housing armaments in these Arab communities.[9] The proportion of civilian deaths to soldiers was 44 to 119 or nearly 37 percent of the total Israeli dead (but if we only consider Jewish Israelis and IDF members the proportion is 26 to 119 or nearly 22 percent of the Jewish dead were civilian.) Contrary to the Lobby's allegation of Hezbollah's war crimes, the Lebanese resistance was clearly aiming most of its fire at the invading IDF. In contrast, in Lebanon, of the 1,181 known to have been killed, 1088 were civilians and only 93 were fighters. In other words 92 percent of the Lebanese dead were civilians—over twice the rate of Israeli civilians killed by the Lebanese resistance and more than four times the rate of Jewish civilians killed by the Lebanese resistance. To put it more bluntly: over 41 Lebanese civilians were slaughtered for each Jewish Israeli civilian death.

The Jewish Lobby's claims of Israeli moral and military superiority in the Middle East—the latter was paradoxically evoked combined with warnings that Israel's survival was at stake—was shredded to tatters as a result of its failure to annihilate Hezbollah even as worldwide broadcasts made clear the relative inequalities in firepower and destruction for all who had eyes to see.

The Lobby echoed Israeli military claims of the invincibility of the Israeli armed forces—a claim that for years had rested on their 'fighting' against rock-throwing Palestinian school kids. Their vulnerability became clear when they were faced with well-armed veteran Lebanese guerrilla fighters.

Over much of the period that the carnage in Lebanon was going on, and almost unnoticed because of it, Israel killed 202 Palestinians from June 26 to August 26, 2006, 44 of whom were small children, while losing only one soldier.[10] In Lebanon, Israel lost 119 soldiers compared to the loss of 93 Lebanese fighters in 34 days (almost half the time). In other words, 160 times more Israelis were killed as a result of the Israel's invasion of Lebanon in one month—than died in Palestine in two months. The Jewish Lobby's propaganda campaign in the US Congress, throughout the mass media and even in our small US communities, in defense of Israel's "Summer Rain" (of bombs on civilians) against the Palestinians was thoroughly exposed as a murderous scorched earth policy by the United Nations Report and indeed, to its credit, summarized in the Israeli daily *Haaretz*:

> The (campaign)…is still taking a severe toll on 1.4 million Palestinians…thousands of Palestinians have been forced to flee their homes following continuing IDF incursions into the Strip (Gaza) and heavy shelling…the Israeli Air Force has conducted 247 aerial assaults in Gaza…more than a million people have been left with no regular supply of water and electricity.[11]

The Lobby, with Orwellian duplicity, reversed the roles by calling the Palestinian victims (all 202 of them at the time of the invasion of Lebanon) "terrorists" while calling the executioners (the Israeli Defense Force) victims (1 dead soldier who was more likely to have been killed by 'friendly fire'). Calling those who resist an *occupying* army " terrorists" could only make sense if the intention was to willfully redefine the legitimate ownership of the territory on which the events occurred, and to seek to enforce and embed that conceptualization on others.

The Lobby and Media Re-interpret Lebanon for the Credulous

A survey of the *Daily Alert*, the propaganda sheet prepared by the

Jerusalem Center for Public Affairs (a semi-official propaganda arm of the Israeli regime) for the Conference of Presidents of Major American Jewish Organizations (CPMAJO) did not reveal a single mention of the fact that the Jewish state was killing almost ten Lebanese civilians for each Lebanese fighter it killed, while the Hezbollah resistance, to the contrary, was killing four times as many Israeli *soldiers* as Israeli civilians (Jews and Gentiles combined). Not a single opinion article, editorial or commentary reproduced by the *Daily Alert*, from the *Wall Street Journal, Washington Post, The National Telegraph,* the *New York Sun, USA Today, Boston Globe, New York Times, Haaretz, The Jerusalem Post* or *The Times* (UK) addressed what had nonetheless become obvious: that Israel's much ballyhooed 'precision' bombing succeeded in targeting mainly civilians, while the Lebanese defenders' far less sophisticated weaponry hit mostly IDF invaders.

These omissions by the Jewish Lobby and its members and supporters in the Anglo-American-Israeli respectable and yellow press and electronic media were absolutely necessary to perpetuate the myth of Israel waging a 'defensive', 'existential' [*sic*] war for 'survival' against Islamic 'terrorists' embodied in Hezbollah and the Lebanese National Resistance, which fought alongside it.

Could Israel's destruction of 15,000 homes up to Beirut and beyond to Northern Lebanon possibly have been *defensive* actions as the CPMAJO claims? Did these very articulate, very wealthy, highly educated Princeton, Yale, Harvard, Johns Hopkins and Chicago-educated Jewish apologists for the Israeli invasion really believe that bombing hospitals, supermarkets, water treatment plants, churches and mosques in Southern Lebanon, oil refineries and milk, food and pharmaceutical factories in Beirut, transport, highways and bridges in Northern Lebanon were 'existential' acts essential for the survival of the 'Jewish State'? Why did they ignore the obvious scale of destruction presented above—with its implications of genocide? Did the investment bankers, professors, dentists and armies of rabbis of all Talmudic readings truly believe, in the face of such overwhelming visual evidence to the contrary—that Israel had been the innocent victim of any aggression that could justify the slaughter of 1088 Lebanese civilians, who numbered over 90 percent of those it killed, and the displacement of nearly one million?

Well-informed and educated professionals would have known that from January 1996 to August 2006, there had been weekly incidents all along the Israeli-Lebanese border, involving Israeli raids, killings and kidnapping of Lebanese civilians, as well as rocket firing in both directions. Wouldn't the Hollywood moguls, who have given so generously to the Israeli war machine, have known that Elliott Abrams, President Bush's chief adviser on the Middle East (stern defender of Jewish purity and intimate collaborator with the Israeli high command) gave full support in early summer to an Israeli plan to destroy Hezbollah, at least one month before the border incident?[12]

Of course the educated elites *knew*. Unlike the 'good' Germans in the 1940s, who conceivably might legitimately have claimed they didn't see the smoking chimneys or the grim trains, in the 2006 assault, images of devastated apartments and slaughtered children were visible, easily accessible and followed by well-publicized reports by all the human rights groups on Israel's crimes against humanity. They knew and supported Israel's crimes before and after the ceasefire—and they *chose* nonetheless to endorse the war, the policies and the state as true accomplices after the fact.

While the Jewish Lobby focused on Hezbollah's capturing of two soldiers across the Israeli border as the detonator for a full-scale invasion, numerous sources around the world disputed the Israeli account of a Hezbollah cross-border attack. According to the big business US magazine *Forbes*,[13] the French news service AFP,[14] the respectable *Asia Times*[15] and the Lebanese police, the Israeli soldiers were captured *within Lebanon* in the area of Ai'tu Al-Chaarb, a Lebanese village a few kilometers from the Israeli border—a contention given further credibility by the remarkable March, 2007 admission of Israeli Prime Minister Ehud Olmert that the attack on Lebanon had been planned months in advance,[16] and presumably only awaited a pretext.

While the Jewish lobby was raising funds exclusively for Israeli-Jewish soldier and civilian victims of the conflict, Hezbollah engaged in a non-sectarian reconstruction program that embraced all Lebanese communities and households, regardless of religious or ethnic preferences. This underlined the broader national (rather than sectarian) character of the Lebanese resistance movement. Contrary to the Lobby's propaganda, the Lebanese resistance was not exclusively Shia or even Muslim in make-up. Israel's invasion had managed to unite Lebanon's factions in defense of their homeland. Of the 93 Lebanese fighters killed, *twenty percent* were from organizations other than Hezbollah, a point ignored by the Lobby's ideologues.

Consequences of the Israeli War of Aggression

The Israeli military's failure to achieve its goal of defeating and eliminating the Lebanese resistance, particularly Hezbollah, had a major impact in both Israel and throughout the pro-Israel Jewish support networks. In Israel, the major criticism of the Olmert-Perez regime and General Halutz from both soldiers and civilians was that the government was too *timid*—there was insufficient bombing, too few ground troops and too much 'concern' for Lebanese civilians. The ceasefire was premature, they complained; the territory occupied was too limited. The big Israeli demonstration in early May 2007 against Olmert was not against the Israeli invasion of Lebanon, but rather against its failure to win the war.

While many US and Israeli progressives cited the 'turmoil', 'dissent' and harsh polemics in the aftermath of the war as typical of the 'rough and tumble' of Israel's democracy, they ignored the savage militarist substance and ultra-rightwing direction of Israeli public opinion. The 'who lost the war' polemic in Israel was basically anchored not in the need for peace or negotiation, but in preparation for a new, more violent attack on Lebanon and other adversaries of Israeli regional ambitions. Likud and other parties in the Knesset have called for the Israeli bombing of Syria and Iran.

This militaristic rage found outlet in the brutal daily assaults on the Palestinians in Gaza and the West Bank where Israeli warplanes bombed homes and ground forces assassinated and injure dozens of civilians — 'existential' murders of stone-throwing schoolboys. Israel's rage affected Jewish religious notables. The Rabbinical Council of America called for the Israeli military to re-evaluate its military rules of war in light of Hezbollah's "unconscionable use of civilians, hospitals, ambulances, mosques and the like as human shields", according to the *Jerusalem Post* of August 21, 2006. The RCA and the modern Orthodox women's organization, Eminah, which represent over one million US Jews, called for maximizing Lebanese civilian deaths in order to lessen the 'risk' to 'our' (Israeli Jewish) soldiers — in the finest spirit of Nazi chaplains egging on the Wehrmacht's scorched earth policy during World War Two. Their Israeli counterparts, Chief Rabbis Eliyahu and Drori, echoed the RCA's 'delicate criticisms' in more colorful and uninhibited terms. "Our corrupt military, which tells us that our soldiers must endanger their lives to protect enemy civilians, is the reason we lost the war", complained the gentle Rabbi Eliyahu, who regarded all non-Jewish civilians opposing Israeli policy as enemies worthy of incineration. Not to be outdone, the good Rabbi Drori accused the rest of Western humanity as 'anti-Semites' for being horrified at Israel's savage destruction. *"Anti-Semites demand that we use Christian morality while our enemies act like barbarians."*[18] Apparently the killing and maiming of over a thousand Lebanese civilians, mostly women and children, did not satisfy him.

Lest one think that these US and Israeli Rabbis were simply loose cannons or isolated psychopaths, three weeks earlier, Rabbi Dov Lior, *in the name of the Yesh Council of Rabbis* (with hundreds of thousands of Israeli followers), announced that

> when our enemies hold a baby in one hand and shoot us with the other, or when missiles are purposely aimed at civilian populations in the Land of Israel in blatant disregard for moral criteria, we are obligated to act according to Jewish morality, which dictates that 'he who gets up to kill you, get up yourself and kill him first'.[19]

The holy men of the Holy Land provided a post-factum religious blessing for the more than three hundred Lebanese children killed and urged the future killing of even more. The readers were assured that all this was 'according to Jewish morality'. Many US Jews, especially liberals and even conservatives, might have objected privately to rabbinical fiats for the slaughter of children, but their polite silence on the matter was deafening. The Lobby conveniently ignored the Jewish morality spiel, even as it defended the 'moderate' secular line of Israeli civilian deaths resulting from Hezbollah fighters using Lebanese babies and old grannies as shields to commit their crimes. Did a raging debate ensue among US and Israeli rabbis, and secular and religious apologists over whether killing Lebanese civilians and children should be based on tactical military or religious-ethical considerations—or did each just respond according to their sphere of expertise?

The Executive Director of the American Jewish Committee, David A. Harris, put to the lie the nasty bit of propaganda by the US 'Left' Zionists of downplaying the role of the Jewish Lobby in securing wholehearted US White House and Congressional support for Israel's destruction of Lebanon. In discussing US subservience to Israel, Harris declared,

> No other nation has been prepared to define such an intimate relationship with Israel in all bilateral spheres—from arms sales, foreign aid and intelligence-sharing to a free-trade zone, scientific co-operation and diplomatic support. No other nation has the capacity, by dint of its size and stature, to help ensure Israel's quest for a secure and lasting peace [*sic*]…In the recent conflict with Hezbollah, once again the United States demonstrated its willingness to stand by Israel, provide vital support and withstand the pressure of many US allies who would have wished for an earlier end to the fighting even if it meant keeping Hezbollah largely intact and in place…Whatever the primary factor, *there can be no doubt that American Jewry is an essential element of the equation* [yoking the US to Israel] [italics added]. This is all the more reason why American Jewry need to work day in and day out to ensure that the mutually beneficial link [*sic*] goes from strength to strength.[19]

In plain English, the Jewish networks and lobbies secured 98 percent support *from Congress* for a resolution supporting Israel's invasion of Lebanon, even as 54 percent Democrat and 39 percent Republican *voters* favored a policy of neutrality as opposed to alignment with Israel.[20] The Lobby did indeed convince, pressure and threaten the White House to prolong the Israeli terror bombing as Harris so proudly announced. The Jewish Lobby worked 'day in and day out' to make sure that Israel could ethnically cleanse Palestine, drop 5-ton bombs on Lebanese apartment buildings, bulldoze villages and isolate the US from even its closest allies at the expense of the US taxpayers, their democratic ideals and their national sovereignty. And, as the height of political dishonesty, the American Jewish Committee labeled these war crimes as 'our mutually beneficial link'. Now that's chutzpah!

CHAPTER 10

US EMPIRE AND THE MIDDLE EAST: ZIONISM, PUPPET REGIMES AND POLITICAL ALLIES

An understanding of US imperial policy in the Middle East requires an analysis that centers on four points:

1) The power and influence of Israel and the Zionist power configuration over US *political institutions* (Congress, the Executive branch, the mass media, the two major political parties and electoral processes), their *economic leverage* on investment and financial institutions (state and trade union pension funds, investment banks), and their *cultural domination* of journals, the performing arts, magazines, films and newspapers. Zionist political, economic and cultural power is directed exclusively toward maximizing Israel's military, economic and political expansion and superiority in the Middle East even when it conflicts with *other* US imperialist interests.

2) The capacity of the US empire to construct and instrumentalize Middle East client states and mercenary forces to implement US policies. The most prominent and important current instruments of US policy in the Middle East include the puppet regime in Iraq, the Abbas-Dahlan group in Palestine, the Kurds in Iraq, the Sinoria-Hariri-Jumblat regime in Lebanon, the Mujahideen-e Khalq organization targeting Iran, Kurds and Sunni

tribalists in Iran and the puppet Somali 'regime' backed by Ethiopian-Ugandan mercenaries.

3) The US alliance with right-wing regimes and rulers in Jordan, Egypt, Turkey, Saudi Arabia, the Gulf States and Israel to provide military bases, intelligence and political backing for the colonial occupation in Iraq, the division of Iraq, and economic sanctions and war against Iran, Hezbollah, Hamas and any other clerical-nationalist and leftist movements in the Middle East.

4) The capacity to contain, repress and limit the opposition of the majority of the US public and a minority of Congress members to the current war in Iraq and a future war against Iran. The key problem for traditional US imperialism is the discrediting of the Zioncon civilian-militarists in the White House and their increasing tendency to resort to new political adventures and provocations to recover support and to concentrate dictatorial powers in the President's office to ensure future impunity for their various crimes after the present administration passes into history.

These vectors of US Middle East policy are increasingly *challenged* from within and without, are subject to sharp *contradictions* and face the probability of failing. Nevertheless the machinery of imperial power is still operating and defining the nature of US Middle East policy.

The Vectors of US-Middle East Power

The Israel-Zionist Power Configuration

For the first time in the history of world empires, a tiny ethnic-religious minority representing less than two percent of the population is able to shape US policy in the Middle East to serve the colonial interests of a foreign country (Israel), which represents less than one percent of the population of the Middle East. And indeed, within Israel itself, given occasional polls indicating Jewish Israeli preference for peace over maintenance of settler colonies, that number shrinks even further. The Zionist power configuration in the US, with several hundred thousand fanatical activists throughout the country, can mobilize close to 98 percent of the US Congress on any legislation favoring Israel, even when their approval prejudices the interests of major US oil multinationals. AIPAC (the America-Israel Political Affairs Committee), with one hundred thousand members and 100 full time agents *writes* over 100 pieces of Congressional legislation affecting US trade, military aid, and sanctions policies favoring Israel every year. In March 2007, the leaders of both political parties, Congress and the Senate, and over fifty percent of all members of the Congress attended and pledged allegiance to the state of Israel at the most recent AIPAC convention in Washington. This was despite the fact that two leaders of AIPAC are currently on trial for spying for Israel and face twenty years in prison![1]

The Zionist power configuration (ZPC) includes far more than the AIPAC 'lobby'. In the run-up to the invasion of Iraq, Zionists controlled the Vice President's office including convicted felon Irving 'Scooter' Libby, the Pentagon and its 'intelligence' operations (Wolfowitz, Dov Zakheim, Feith and Shulsky) and held strategic positions in the White House and National Security Council (Frum—author of Bush's 'Axis of Evil' speech, Abrams—pardoned felon from Iran Contra scandal, now in charge of Middle East policy, and Ari Fleischer—President Bush's spokesman). Zionists dominate the editorial and opinion pages of the major newspapers (*Wall Street Journal*, *Washington Post* and *New York Times*), major television networks and Hollywood. Hundreds of regional state and local Jewish federations intervene to prevent any criticism of Israel, attacking any critics, meetings, theatrical or cinema productions and successfully forcing cancellations.

The Zionist power structure has been the leading force pushing US war plans and sanctions against Iran. They backed Bush's invasion of Iraq. The ZPC secured US backing for Israel's bloody attack on Lebanon, no matter that it weakened the successfully installed US puppet ruler, Prime Minister Fouad Siniora. The ZPC authored and secured Congressional legislation blocking any contact with the Palestinian unity government. They successfully lined up US congressional support for Israel's starvation blockade of Palestine put in place to try to roll back the democratic election of Hamas, and to punish the Palestinians for it. The scope and depth of Zionist power over US Middle East policy goes far beyond influencing 'public opinion' (the major media expression of which it largely has locked up)—it penetrates key institutions, designs and enforces policy implementation and promotes wars which benefit Israel.

In a word, the Zionist power configuration's primary loyalty is to the state of Israel and its policy is designed to colonize the US Congress on behalf and to the benefit of the 'mother country', Israel.

The Zionists have thirty Jewish Congress people and thirteen senators and lead some of the key committees in Congress. The head of the key Democratic Party Caucus is Rahm Emmanuel, a former member of the Israeli Defense Forces. Emmanuel was instrumental in having the Democratic Party majority in Congress eliminate a key clause in a war appropriations bill which would have prevented Bush from going to war with Iran without consulting Congress. The ZPC has secured the absolute, unconditional support of all presidential candidates for Israel and its promotion of a 'war option' against Iran. The Zionist power configuration succeeded in driving the US to war with Iraq but it has not been able to prevent the great majority of Americans (including about 77 percent of American Jews[2]) from turning against the war. The Zionist power configuration, following the line from Israel, has now made US sanctions and war with Iran its top priority. Having accomplished their goal of destroying Iraq, the ZPC are downplaying their support for the Bush regime's policies in Iraq, in order to focus all their efforts on pushing the US to secure UN Security Council approval for harsh economic sanctions on Iran. The Israeli-Zionists' policy of escalating sanctions has succeeded—as they openly declare in their publications. Their overwhelming effectiveness in deciding US-Iran policy has even led their Israeli mentors to urge words of caution against overplaying their power. Assuredly, the ZPC's own various assertions of the extent of their influence are a prima facie source for demonstrating it.

The ZPC's blatant and open dominance of US Middle East policy has for the first time provoked widespread opposition among patriotic nationalists among US military officials and conservatives, as well as a growing number of academics, and even among a tiny group of Jewish millionaires (Soros) and intellectuals. For the first time major debate has opened up regarding whether Israel is a 'strategic asset' or 'strategic liability' to US imperial interests. The opposition to the ZPC includes both pro-empire and anti-imperialist individuals. The pro-empire critics of Israel argue that Israel has taken over $110 billion dollars in outright grants and loans and they have privileged access to US weapons technology and compete with the US arms industry. They argue that Israeli colonial oppression in Palestine creates tensions and conflicts prejudicial to the US oil industry. They argue that the Zionist-backed Israeli war policies in the Middle East undermine the economic expansion of US financial and oil interests allied with conservative Arab 'oil states'.

The anti-empire opponents to Zionist control of US Middle East policy argue that the invasion of Iraq led to the killing and wounding of millions of Iraqis and tens of thousands of US soldiers, has cost over $500 billion USD, and has led to the destruction of US constitutional protections of civil rights. They call for the immediate withdrawal of US troops and demand the denuclearization of the Middle East, starting with Israel.

As the Zionists lead Congress by the nose toward another major war with Iran (the 'military option'), they have to face growing resistance worldwide. Iranian allies in Lebanon, Palestine and Iraq and throughout the Middle East can attack and destroy the most important oil installations in the world—in Saudi Arabia and the Gulf States—and the world's most important oil tanker routes (Hormuz Straits). The ZPC's fanatical extremism in support of Israel is evident in their willingness to risk a world war and world depression in furtherance of Tel Aviv's ambitions to rule the Middle East and destroy its key adversary, Iran, a country of eighty million people.

The struggle against the ZPC in the US is the key to peace in the Middle East, the key to stopping the US from pressuring the Security Council and NATO, and to keeping the Middle Eastern countries from committing collective suicide. Unfortunately, the US Left, especially the Zionist-influenced peace movement, refuses to face this reality. If this were to fail, then only one road to changing US war policy in the Middle East would remain—outside resistance. Then, only mass resistance in the Middle East and elsewhere could impose the heavy costs on the US economy and military that would force the American people to counter the ZPC. Only when the costs of the Zionist-influenced Middle East wars have devastated the US could we expect a major popular backlash against the Zionist power structure's stranglehold over Congress. Only then could we hope for the beginning of a US military withdrawal from the Middle East. Needless to say, by then, Israel's goals of leveling the region would have been accomplished. Whether that would ultimately serve Israel's own interests in the region, however, is far from certain.

Instrumental Clients

Given the high political and economic costs of prolonged, large-scale and extensive involvement of US armed forces in colonial wars, Washington has increased its reliance on client regimes and terrorist organizations with its own role reduced to supplying mercenary military and intelligence forces.

The massive US financing of the 'Iraqi' security forces to eventually replace US ground soldiers as the prime defenders of the puppet regime and US military bases is one example. Washington and Israel's training, advising and financing of the Kurds in northern Iraq, Iran and Syria is another. By 'instrumentalizing' local mercenaries, Washington achieves several political and propaganda goals. The use of local mercenaries creates the illusion that Washington is gradually handing over power to the local puppet regime. It gives the impression that the puppet regime is capable of ruling, and propagandizes the myth that a stable and reliable locally-based army exists. The presence of these local mercenaries creates the myth that the internal conflict is a civil war instead of a national liberation struggle against a colonial power.

The imperialist use of the Kurds of Northern Iraq serves strategic US imperial goals in several ways. First the Kurds are utilized to repress opposition from Iraqi Arab and Turkmen anti-colonial forces throughout Iraq but especially in the North. Secondly the imperialist project to break up the Iraqi republic into three or more fragments is aided by Kurdish separatism and seizures of the oil fields in ethnically mixed regions and the contracting out of exploration rights to foreign multinationals.[3] The US has pressured the Iraqi puppet government to allow the Kurds to engage in massive ethnic cleansing of Arabs and Turkmen in Kirkuk and other ethnically mixed cities in Northern Iraq.[4] The US client Kurdish regime also serves as a base of operation for Kurdish separatists and commandos into Iran, Syria and Turkey (despite US denials).

US client regimes in the Middle East and the Horn of Africa have specific functions in building the US Middle East empire and serving Israeli interests. In Lebanon, the Christian Maronites and the puppet Fouad Sinoria regime are financed and armed to undermine the independent mass-based anti-imperial Hezbollah-led political-military coalition. The client Gulf States and Saudi Arabia provide oil, intelligence and military bases as launching pads for policing the Middle East. Egypt and Jordan provide intelligence via torture interrogation of US captured and kidnapped political and military prisoners, especially from the Afghan and Iraqi resistance. Afghanistan is headed by a US puppet 'president', Hamid Karzai, in alliance with Afghan narco-warlords who produce and supply eighty percent of the heroin sold in Europe and the rest of the world. US-backed and directed Ethiopian dictator, Meles Zenawi, intervened in Somalia to overthrow the independent Union of Islamic Courts government and install the US puppet Mohammed Yousuf. Subsequently a new contingent of African mercenaries was sent by Ugandan dictator-client, Yoweri Museveni, to prop up the Ethiopian imposed Yousuf regime in the face of massive armed resistance from the Somali anti-imperialist insurgency.

A rigorous analysis of the performance of US client regimes and mercenary forces reveals numerous failures and declining support. The Iraqi mercenary army has high levels of desertion and plays a continued double role—ostensibly serving the US but in actuality providing the resistance with intelligence, arms and off-duty fighters. More important, the failure of the US policy of using Iraqi mercenaries to defeat the resistance is evident in the escalation of US combat military forces in Iraq in the spring of 2007, after five years of colonial warfare—from 140,000 to 170,000 troops, not counting the presence of some 100,000 mercenaries from American firms such as Blackwater.[5]

In Lebanon Hezbollah defeated the Israeli invasion and has increasingly isolated the Sinoria puppet regime in Beirut, even though the US secured a UN military presence in a *failed* attempt to isolate Hezbollah. Washington's massive arms shipments to the Maronite rightwing, rightist Sunnis and the Jumblatt sector of the Druze in 2007 portend a new effort to provoke a so-called civil war in Lebanon to weaken Hezbollah and its anti-imperialist Palestinian allies.

The US-Israeli blockade and massacres in Palestine (Gaza and the West Bank) since the election of the Hamas government and their use of the US clients Abbas and Dahlan have failed to weaken the Palestinian national liberation struggle. Nevertheless they succeeded in provoking a mini civil conflict.

In Somalia the resistance has regrouped and advanced throughout the country, especially in Mogadishu where fighting has intensified around the Presidential Palace. The US-Ethiopian conquest has failed to defeat the anti-imperialist movement and to stabilize the puppet regime. With the forced withdrawal of Ethiopian colonial mercenaries it is highly likely at this writing that the puppet Yousuf regime will collapse despite the presence of Ugandan mercenaries.

The US backing of the 'autonomous' client Kurdish regime in Northern

Iraq and its expansionist pretension toward 'Greater Kurdistan' including wide swaths of Turkey, Iran, Iraq and Syria has created intense contradictions with its Turkish 'allies'. A new Kurdish state carved out of Northern Iraq serves as a jumping off point for cross border attacks into Anatolia, especially by the PKK but also backed by the governing Iraqi Kurdish elite. This may lead to a Turkish invasion of Northern Iraq to destroy the PKK bases. This, in turn, could lead to a general Turkish-Kurdish war and severely weaken the US mercenary strategy in Iraq and the fragile structure of its alliance sustaining US-Middle East dominance.

The US-Israeli strategy of dividing and destroying the Palestinian resistance through an economic boycott is collapsing. Since the Mecca agreements between Hamas and the Palestinian Authority, numerous European and Arab countries have opened negotiations, renewed economic aid and trade and recognized the Hamas-led coalition as legitimate.

In Lebanon, the Sinoria regime holed up in Beirut has failed to weaken Hezbollah and only exists because of US, European and Saudi financial (and military) support. The Lebanese army is divided. The UN forces refuse to attempt to disarm Hezbollah. Israel has no appetite for another invasion. Clearly the US has lost influence in Lebanon while increasing the power of the Hezbollah-Hamas-Iranian bloc.

The US effort (despite US struggle to prop up a Shia government in Iraq) to coalesce a purported "Sunni" alliance stretching from Saudi Arabia through the Gulf States, Jordan, Israel and Egypt has failed mainly because of Israel's colonial ambitions in Palestine and its military threats to all 'Muslim' countries. Israel's disastrous invasion of Lebanon forced the US client regimes into opposition to the US-Israeli policies. Israel's rejection of the Mecca-Palestinian pact and AIPAC's power to force Washington to follow Israel's lead has alienated Saudi Arabia and several European allies. In fact as a result of US rejection of the Saudi-authored, Arab League-approved peace proposal, the Monarchy has criticized the US occupation of Iraq and its threats to Iran. Even the Gulf mini-states, like the Emirates, have declared their opposition to a US military attack on Iran. The opposition of the US Gulf clients indicates the decline of US dominance and the failure of its pro-Israel policies. There can be no stable relation between US imperialism and its Middle East Arab clients that includes an expansionist, colonial Jewish regime in power in Israel. The Zionist power configuration has successfully ensured the instability of US-Arab client relations throughout this key region by means of its capacity to subordinate US policy to Israeli interests.

The US strategy of 'instrumentalized' local clients and mercenary armies to police the Middle East in the interest of the US empire is failing and finds little basis for restoration under present circumstances.

Regional Alliances: Middle East Power Sharing?

The major obstacle preventing Washington from advancing its 'Arab agenda'— consolidating its influence over its Arab clients, organizing Arab state support for the war in Iraq, isolating Iran and expanding US oil interests— is the pervasive veto power of the Israeli fifth column, the Zionist power configuration with control over the US Congress and power in the Executive branch. As a result, Washington has rejected the Saudis' proposal to Israel of 'land for peace and recognition' by the entire Arab world; it has rejected the Saudis' Mecca agreement creating a unified Palestinian government; it has rejected Arab Gulf state, Syrian, Iraqi, Saudi, Russian and Chinese proposals for diplomatic negotiations with Iran and Syria.

The US has completely failed to construct a power-sharing NATO-style alliance in the Middle East (except with Turkey and Israel) for several reasons. The overwhelming majority (ranging from 80-95 percent) of the Arab population reject such an agreement which would undermine the little authority which the client regimes still retain. The US offers nothing in political concessions in exchange for Arab support for US imperial supremacy—not even pressure on Israel to concede semi-arid territory in the West Bank to the Palestinians. The power structure of a US-Middle East alliance is so asymmetrical—the balance of power so skewed in Washington's favor—that there is little basis for negotiations and sharing of costs and benefits. Because of the inequality of power, some governments (like that of Saudi Arabia) with a wealth of economic power are fearful of being absorbed by the US.

As a result, rather than a formal Middle East US-Arab alliance, there are bilateral agreements and specific concessions, such as military bases (Iraq, Oman, Saudi Arabia and Turkey), intelligence and torture/interrogation agreements (Syria, Egypt and Jordan) and petroleum distribution agreements (Gulf States-Saudi Arabia). These bilateral agreements provide Washington with significant leverage and influence but not the *formal* control of wealth (because of Arab state ownership of oil) nor the use of local military forces for promoting US and Israeli regional supremacy.[6]

The US 'alliance' with Israel is based on a different kind of asymmetrical influence and benefits. Because of Israeli-Zionist power over US political institutions, the US can only pursue policies that further Israeli strategic interests in the Middle East. The asymmetry of power in Israel-US relations is evident in the costs and benefits of economic, military, political and diplomatic relations. The US pays tribute of over $3 billion USD a year (mostly in outright grants) to Israel, a country with a per capita annual income of $25,000 (as of 2006), higher than 25 percent of the US population! Israel receives free entry to US markets, unhindered and unlimited immigration to the US, tax exemptions on the purchase of Israel bonds, and the most advanced US military technology which allows Israel to successfully 'out compete' the US military industrial complex in major arms markets such as billion dollar sales to India, Africa and in the US! Israel runs a massive 100,000-member Zionist lobby influencing US policy: Washington does not have a single pro-US lobbyist in Israel.

During the Reagan years, to cover up Zionist influence in shaping US policy to serve Israeli interests, key lobbyist and indicted spy suspect, Steve Rosen promoted the idea that Israel was a 'strategic asset' of the US in the Middle East[7]—the line now parroted by 'Left' Zionists who downplay the role of the Lobby.

In other words, the so-called US-Israel alliance subordinates Washington's foreign and diplomatic policy and military resources in the Middle East to the needs of 'Greater Israel' because the Zionist power configuration has greater political leverage in the Congress than the petroleum and arms industries, the military and even the President.

The US-Turkish alliance too is asymmetrical: Turkey supplies the US with military bases, allies itself with Israel (despite majority popular opposition), and supports the US war against Iraq at an enormous loss of trade and tax revenues. In exchange, Turkey faces a US-sponsored separatist Kurdish state on its border with Iraq that permits cross border attacks by Kurdish armed insurgents. US policymakers have given the highest priority to satisfying Kurdish territorial demands as a mechanism to secure Peshmerga military support in repressing Iraqi national resistance. Turkish demands for US control over Kurdish expansionist claims over Anatolia are ignored. Washington believes that the Turkish government will submit to the US alliance with the Kurds. The White House dismissed Turkey's threats to invade de facto 'Kurdistan' as inconsequential. Given the Turkish government's pursuit of European Union membership (which the US supports), Washington believes that Ankara will refrain from any military intervention into Northern Iraq.

On the other hand, there is reason to believe that the Kurdish guerrilla strongholds in Northern Iraq are receiving arms, money, recruits and a green light from the 'autonomous' Kurdish government. It is likely that the conflict in Anatolia will intensify now that the Kurds have the financial backing from the US military in Iraq and oil revenue from recently seized well sites. There are few doubts that US arms to the Kurds in Iraq are passed on to the Kurds in Anatolia. The question is whether and for how long the Turkish military will continue to submit to the US-Kurdish strategy in Northern Iraq and its spillover effects in Anatolia, or whether Ankara will launch a full-scale military incursion against the Kurdish 'revolutionary' supporters of 'democratic colonialism' as the PKK has referred to the US imperial army occupying Iraq.

The 21st Century Experience of US Empire-Building in the Middle East

A serious analysis of US empire building strategy must take account of the *changing* tactics and unchanging *rigid* strategic goals. Washington launched the invasion of Iraq unilaterally; confronted with intensified resistance Washington turned multilateral, seeking support and mercenary forces from European allies and Third World clients. As the national liberation forces gained the upper hand, Washington recruited a large contingent of over 100,000 overseas professional mercenaries and 200,000 Iraqi collaborators. At first Washington brought over 'exiled' Iraqi politicians to form a puppet regime; then it backed the conservative Shia clan leaders; then it recruited heavily among the Kurds. As each imperial 'tactic' failed to defeat the resistance, Washington increased its occupation army and its Iraqi colonial army. But each escalation increased domestic opposition. Each tactical alliance created new antagonisms with Sunnis, Baathists and Turkmen. Major military allies and client regimes began to retire their forces from the US dominated 'coalition' in the face of an inevitable defeat.

Facing increasing military isolation in Iraq and declining public support in the US, Washington's response is to increase the militarization of the Middle East and prepare a new war against Iran. Washington believes that an attack on Iran will mobilize the entire Zionist power configuration (from hundreds of local Jewish federations to Washington lobbies), which will exercise control over Congressional behavior, the two parties (especially the Democrats) and the mass media. Further, the White House believes that an attack on Iran will serve to rally the American people behind the President, arousing chauvinist fervor and increasing Bush's popularity. The White House believes it can engage in an air and sea war in which the US air force can destroy Iran's defenses without suffering serious US casualties—on the US mainland, that is, since US military personnel based in Iraq and its naval fleets in surrounding waters would serve as Iran's primary targets. Washington believes it can isolate the conflict to Iran and subsequently attack Syria, Hezbollah and facilitate the Israeli's genocidal 'final solution' of the Palestinian question.

Washington's policy of permanent warfare is a wild irrational gamble comparable to Hitler's attack on Russia following its conquest of Poland and parts of Western Europe. New wars in the face of failed wars can only lead to greater defeats, greater domestic rebellion and wider wars.

Launching an attack on Iran means facing a country three times larger than Iraq with a highly motivated army easily capable of crossing the frontier and attacking US ground troops in Iraq, in alliance with pro-Iranian militias in Baghdad and elsewhere. The regional configuration of Arab countries is already highly polarized against the US, unlike the period prior to the US invasion of Iraq. Iran has powerful allies in Lebanon, Iraq and throughout the Muslim world who will retaliate against US strategic assets and clients. Iran can easily target the Hormuz Straits and major oil installations in the Gulf States, Saudi Arabia, and Iraq as well as Iran—leading to massive shortages of petroleum and quadrupling of oil prices.

However a US attack against Iran goes in the short run, ultimately the US loses: the military losses will be felt throughout Iraq, the oil catastrophe will reverberate throughout the world, and the political consequences will be greater polarization against the US-Israel axis throughout Europe, Asia and of course, the Middle East. The result will be the final demise of the Bush regime and the total discrediting of the Zionist-controlled Democratic Party. A major economic recession will incite open class and national conflicts. Once again, an imperialist war may be the midwife of revolutions: the Russian Revolution followed World War I; the Chinese Revolution followed World War II. Will World War III lead to a new revolutionary cycle?

PART III

THE POSSIBILITY
OF RESISTANCE

CHAPTER 11

PAST, PRESENT AND FUTURE OF CHINA: FROM SEMI-COLONY TO WORLD POWER?

Introduction

The general consensus is that China is emerging as the next great economic superpower. Despite growing awareness of severe ecological problems and occasional recognition of the growing social inequalities,[1] many writers foresee China (and lately India) as the next world powers, challenging and surpassing Japan, Europe and the United States.

This chapter raises serious methodological, conceptual, historical and empirical questions concerning the notion that China is the next world superpower. Without denying its tremendous increase in exports, investments and growth, this paper focuses on a more basic question: what is the character of the principal economic enterprises responsible for this expansion, and how do they project into the future? This is not a semantic issue but one of methodological and conceptual clarity, without which we cannot comprehend exactly who are the 'agents' of growth and transformation. This requires that we go beyond simplistic national labels to identifying the socio-political character of the economic units acting within China and in particular the most dynamic of these units in terms of their future power.

The second section will provide a schematic historical analysis of the stages of Chinese development, focusing on the continuities, ruptures, transitions and projections over the past half-century. The purpose is to identify the rise, fall and revival of social classes and the politico-economic project in which they are embedded.

The third section will focus on the performance of the Chinese political economy, both its growth and its explicit and inherent contradictions.

The fourth section will focus on the impact of deepening liberalization on China's economic and class structure, and particularly on the role of foreign capital. Specifically this section will discuss the long-term implications of the takeovers of Chinese enterprises by foreign multinational corporations and banks.

The fifth section will discuss the external political, economic and military threats and challenges which China faces, as well as the internal conflicts that are the cause and consequence of China's insertion into the world capitalist system.

The final section provides an overview of the future trajectory of China's development. This section will be directed at the political and economic consequences of the cumulative purchases by foreign capital of the most dynamic sectors of the economy. It will examine whether a self-interested and directed Chinese state is harnessing foreign capital to the Chinese growth engine or whether the Chinese state will become increasingly carved up into sectoral and regional fiefdoms by competing imperial capitals. This in turn will lead us to address the question of whether China's national and international capitalist classes will become protagonists of an emerging competing Chinese empire, partners of and competitors to existing imperial powers or whether they will succumb and become satraps of older imperialist states.

The viability of Chinese capitalism ultimately rests not only on its growth rates and job generating capacity, but also on the social relations of production, circulation and reproduction. The ferocious exploitation of labor, the massive displacement of peasants, the firing of millions of skilled/semi-skilled industrial workers from state and bankrupt firms and their increasing propensity to engage in direct action foretells the emergence of large-scale class warfare pitting the new billionaire class of foreign and domestic capitalists and their 'protector state' against the hundreds of millions of dispossessed and alienated workers and peasants. The class struggle, its extent, intensity and political course will test the sustainability of the Chinese growth model of 'maximum exploitation' under autocratic control.

We will conclude by looking at the twin forces of growing foreign capital takeovers and intensifying class struggle as they intersect, to modify or transform Chinese society and economy.

Methodological and Conceptual Clarification

In any attempt to evaluate and analyze the Chinese economy, it is essential to determine what it means to write of "China". The most obvious discussion focuses on the geographical border, which demarcates the country from other countries, and on the nature of the political regime. But a discussion of "China" requires us to go beyond this elemental designation, to a discussion of the principle economic activities and the ownership of the dynamic sectors of the economy. "Made in China" does not necessarily mean owned by Chinese. Insofar as the political-legal-territorial framework contains non-Chinese economic units engaged in large-scale, long-term trade, production, distribution, finance, research and development, it is incumbent on the analyst to draw a distinction between the performance of "Chinese" and "non-Chinese" economic units and actors. To lump them altogether as simply "China" obscures differential performances and divergent middle and long-term consequences. Moreover it is important to delineate, the dynamic tendencies between Chinese and non-Chinese economic units to determine which will ultimately predominate.

Beyond the important quantitative differences in ownership between Chinese and non-Chinese capitalists, is the question of whether non-Chinese investors are 'harnessed' to a Chinese-directed growth strategy or vice versa? Almost all academics, journalists, consultants and officials from the international financial institutions (IFI) lump together the Chinese and non-Chinese economic institutions and actors in calculating exports, investments, production, financing, imports and so on. Moreover they generally overlook the fact that non-Chinese firms are growing faster, increasing their share of exports (and imports), profits, royalty payments and control over new growth sectors of the Chinese economy.

This is particularly true since China joined the World Trade Organization, and deepened and extended its liberalization strategy. The growth of foreign owned enterprises means that investments, trade, exports, financing, location, and decisions are made according to the *global needs* of the MNCs and backed by their imperial states—outside of the framework of the legal entity called "China". As the presence of non-Chinese MNCs increases, so does their influence over the dynamic growth sectors of the economy; conversely the range of influence over the economy by the Chinese state declines. Even more important, given the close relation between strategic growth sectors and the state, the increasing presence of the MNCs is likely to change the nature of the state, making it less "Chinese" and more attuned and responsive to the policies of the foreign-owned MNCs.

Needless to say this is a middle to long-term *process* which depends on several factors beyond the dynamics of capital expansion. For example, intensified internal class and national conflict or external military-economic threats and confrontations could weaken or even undermine the dynamic expansion and control of foreign MNCs.[2]

In any case the method of measuring China's growth performance requires that the politically sensitive factor of Chinese versus non-Chinese owners be taken into account. The result is likely to downgrade or diminish the performance of China per se. On the other hand if we conceive of the MNCs as extensions of the major imperial powers (US, EU and Japan), as dynamic outposts or enclaves of empire embedded in the Chinese economy, we should consider their expansion as part of the growth of imperial empires.

In other words, does "China" grow as the imperial powers expand or does China expand through Chinese owned and controlled economic enterprises? Over the past quarter of a century—as it probably will for the next several decades—foreign capital penetration has expanded rapidly, especially with the decline of the public sector and via buyouts or joint ventures with local Chinese capital. This suggests that the arguments about Chinese power challenging the US, EU and Japan is based on a questionable premise, namely that what is called "Chinese" includes the growing number of foreign-owned multinational corporations and banks which operate in China. The growth of foreign capital in China is occurring at the same time that the Chinese state and private capital compete for raw materials, especially energy resources, and especially in less developed countries in Africa and Latin America while exporting finished manufactured goods. In other words, China is beginning to take on features of both a neo-colony and an emerging imperial power.

The assumption of growing Chinese power is based on the idea that Chinese-owned and controlled enterprises in strategic sectors of finance, manufacturing and export are growing faster than the sectors of the Chinese economy dominated by imperial-based MNCs and international investment houses. As we will demonstrate below, the data do not support such an assumption.

Another questionable presumption is the notion that foreign investment and MNCs are being subordinated or harnessed by the Chinese state to serve Chinese strategic goals just as the US used British investment in the railroads to expand US capitalism. There are several problems with this argument.

1) The Chinese state, its policies and leadership are not fixed in time: initial foreign investment has led to accelerated entry in a wide range of sectors, both cause and consequence of increasing liberalization. However, Chinese governing elites have mutated over time from dominant partners to co-owners to minority shareholders in the latest investment ventures. The notion of 'harnessing' foreign investors to serve Chinese development strategy is losing relevance as MNCs capture the commanding heights of several firms or at least management positions in key enterprises. As the Chinese state invests in infrastructure (railroads, ports, air transport and so on) the MNCs increase their role in the dynamic sectors of the market. China's 21st century strategy reverses the US' 19th century strategy with regard to foreign investment—the lucrative growth sectors pass on to foreign capital, while the Chinese treasury funds the high cost, long-term, large-scale, low-return infrastructure.

2) The spectacular Chinese growth performance occurs within an extremely limited geographical area and the working population that it encompasses. One could almost write of "Two Chinas"—the coastal region and the interior. The fact of the matter is that China's productive grid is extremely limited to its port regions, with links to mining enclaves in the interior. Given the lack of national economic integration and the high level of integration (trade and investment) with external imperial powers (Japan, USA and EU) it is problematic to refer to China as having a *national* economy. This is particularly the case when the coastal economic zones concentrate almost all of the foreign-owned or managed enterprises. In analytical terms what is termed Chinese growth is rather zones of expansion within which foreign-owned enclaves operate. Geographically speaking, Chinese growth is profoundly circumscribed; within these circumscribed zones, the most dynamic enterprises are both foreign and Chinese.

State revenues and expenditures reinforce the "zonal" and enclave nature of what is effectively "China". At best the interior of China provides a source of cheap labor, and a declining share of food and raw materials.

3) The issue of the class-specific process of accumulation and distribution. The entire process of accumulation, reproduction and distribution is directed, owned and benefits an extremely limited class of foreign and domestic capitalists and Chinese state directors and their extended family networks.

The extreme and growing class inequities in power, wealth, ownership, access to state credit, contracts, licenses, incentives and land concessions is totally mystified by references to "China" invests, grows... etc. While the foreign and domestic ruling classes compete for government subsidies, concessions and market shares, they share at least two essential characteristics: a common support for increasing capital's share of national income; and a common opposition to any efforts by labor to organize, protest or improve working and living conditions. Conceptually this requires us to discard the undifferentiated notion of "China" and to focus on the class actors who act in the *name* of China, but who design or demand development policies compatible with their class interests. Otherwise the presumption is that the collective population embodied in the notion of 'China' is somehow implicated in the essential economic decisions or that those who make the decisions in some way "represent" the interests of the Chinese workers, unemployed and peasants rather than the class-controlled institutions in which they are embedded.

An equally important methodological issue arises from measuring the standard of living in China. Most analysts equate standard of living with monetary income and conclude that there has been a vast increase in living standards, an "historic" massive reduction in poverty and improved opportunity.

But measuring the standard of living involves far more than a discussion of monetary income, especially in economies in transition from socialism to free-market capitalism. These are very questionable inferences for several crucial reasons:

1) The elimination of free education and health care, paid vacations and pensions in the transition signals a decline in living standards; the costs of privatization should result in a major deduction from monetary earnings.

2) Capitalist displacement of millions of farmers, artisans and others with sideline earnings in kind (food, utensils and so on) means another deduction from monetary income.

3) The increase of living costs (rents, energy, electricity, water and so on) must be deducted from monetary income.

4) The stress and physical abuse from the intensified exploitation of labor in export factories increases the likelihood of physical disabilities, workplace injuries and deaths. Worsening conditions at the workplace means a further decline in living standards.

5) The added multiple tax burdens on peasants by exploitative local officials, the delays and avoidance of paychecks by private factory owners, the eradication of workers' neighborhoods and housing to benefit real estate speculators all have worsened living standards. While personal consumption has increased— very unequally over time and place—employment, land tenure, price and retirement insecurity are negative determinants of living standards.

If the estimates of mass living standards are distorted upwardly by reference to monetary income, they are understated for the new class of billionaire and millionaire capitalists and their progeny. Monetary income is an important but partial measure of their living standards. The new wealthy classes have access to the best private foreign and domestic health services, elite private foreign and domestic educational institutions, and they have easy direct access to government policy makers. They control a conglomerate of physical assets (productive and financial). Their extended families inherit their wealth, partake of their luxurious vacations, mansions, automobiles…to name only a few of their non-monetary assets. In sum, this means that monetary measures of income underestimate the living standards of the capitalist class.

By any measure, the relative standard of living of the Chinese masses, as a share of the total goods and services and quality of life has declined precipitously. This is especially the case if we examine the 'ecology' of habitation and work and its unequal impact on classes. Scientists and all observers have written and spoken to the vast increase in air, water and ground pollution generated by unregulated capitalist expansion by private and state enterprises. What most observers fail to note however is that the sickness and deaths accrue overwhelmingly among the workers, peasants and low-paid salaried classes who are most exposed to pollution at their workplace, in their movements through the cities, their dependence on public water facilities and the location of their dwellings.

The ruling and upper classes live in less polluted locations, drink bottled water, have country and seashore villas to escape the contaminated air, have air-conditioned cars, homes and country clubs, and are located far from the highly contaminated mines, factories, sewers, waste dumps and incinerators. The advent of capitalism has certainly increased respiratory illnesses and childhood diseases especially in "high growth" industrial zones. Ecological impoverishment is a major factor in reducing living standards because it adversely affects the quality and length of life.

Given the vast and growing inequalities, the worst measures of living standards are those that rely on 'per capita income' (income divided by population). Per capita income obscures the elephantine inequalities between the top five percent and the bottom 75 percent of the population. The 'average' is a deceptive statistical artifact which obscures the real income levels of the vast majority. It would be more appropriate to average the monetary income by decimals, minus the costs of social services (health, education and pensions, rents, energy, travel and taxes). In addition, to convert the remainder of monetary income into a measure of living standards, we would have to counterpoise gains in purchases of consumer goods to losses in fresh air, leisure time, job security, near rent-free housing, paid vacations, benign working conditions and family separations.

The measure of monetary income and living standards is much more complex than what is argued by most orthodox economists. If we expand our discussion of living standards to what needs to be called the social pathologies, the argument in favor of rising living standards becomes even more dubious. The decline of public morality in the transition to capitalism is universally recognized. China ranks among the worst countries in the world in terms of corruption by public officials, usually but not exclusively in terms of transactions with the private sector. In terms of the monetary costs of corruption and white-collar crime, China surely ranks at the highest level of the big US enterprises like World Com, Enron and the US savings and loan corporations. Tens of billions of dollars are illegally transferred (laundered) by Chinese elites overseas, purchasing real estate in the US, Canada and

England, stocks, bonds and Treasure notes, as well as financing expensive education and health care for progeny and family.

Corruption permeates Chinese economic and public life down to local village officials—reinforcing class privileges and creating new ones. While corruption existed during the Communist period, it was on a far lower scale and scope than the present, as most Chinese attest. Corruption has enormous class consequences: enhancing the power, property and privileges of the wealth while increasing the taxes for the peasants eroding public services and lowering public investments in social welfare for the vast majority. Equally important has been the massive increase in crime, including drugs, prostitution, sex slavery, fraud and public assaults on protestors deprived of land, jobs, pensions and homes. The geometric growth of street, office and state crime and the ensuing insecurity, loss of property, income and life, is a product of the new regime ethos of "get rich". This doctrine undermines the civic virtues of the collective good which reigned in the previous period, even as it was frequently breached in practice. Living with pervasive corruption, crime and arbitrary authority guided by motives of private gain at public expense is certainly an indication of declining *living* standards.

These methodological considerations will guide our discussion of the transition of the Chinese economy to 21st century capitalism.

Stages of Chinese Development: From Semi-Colony to Revolution

Historical changes occur in unequal time frames: relatively slow processes involving small-scale changes and gradually emerging contradictions are followed by rapid and abrupt transformations. China is illustrative of this proposition. Over the past half century China has passed through two major transformations and two "transitional regimes" which have changed property relations, the class structure and the nature of state power. Each political transformation, guided by a new configuration of socio-political power, has set in motion a re-organization of the economy and changed the nature of the class struggle.

Each new stage grows out of the previous period, carrying forth to the new political-economic regime some of the practices, values and classes from the old. Moreover the transition from socialism to capitalism, in particular, the high growth rates and many of the attractions for private foreign and domestic investors were products of the basic human and capital investments undertaken under the socialist regime. Each political-economic regime contains the seeds of its own destruction and the social agencies for the emergence of the new regime.

Stage I: From Colony and Neo-Colony to a Revolutionary Socialist Regime
The Chinese socialist revolution (CSR) (1949) created the most basic

political and economic conditions for any sustained and consequential economic development. The revolutionary movement played a major role in the military defeat of Japanese colonialism, ended the European enclaves and the coastal concessions and defeated provincial and local warlords and their allies in the Kuomintang, thus creating a unitary state. It ended skyrocketing inflation, monumental corruption and pillage of the public treasury and financial system, laying the groundwork for a stable currency, fiscal discipline and a functioning economy capable of reconstructing the war-devastated economy. It repulsed US threats to its frontiers during Washington's invasion of North Korea. Within the framework of a sovereign national state, free of intrusive imperial tutelage, the CSR organized vast infrastructure projects (roads, ports, airfields, railroads, irrigation dikes, flood control facilities, water and electrical linkages) that stimulated high rates of economic growth in industry, trade and agriculture. The CSR ended decades of mass starvation under Western and Eastern imperial domination.

The CSR brought about several strategic reforms which provided the basis for long-term growth. It inaugurated a mass public literacy and health campaign at all levels of society—created an educated, healthy labor force, and produced millions of engineers, scientists and highly skilled machine/tool operators. Equally important the CSR converted a mass of rural peasants into a disciplined, skilled and productive urban industrial labor force, raising living standards in the course of creating a complex division of labor. Upstream industries in steel and coal and the capital goods sector created the basis for downstream light industries and inexpensive consumer items. In the countryside, fragmented and unproductive mini-agricultural holdings were consolidated leading to greater mechanization and facilitating the provision of social services to cooperatives and, later, to larger collectivist units.

Without these profound structural changes, the emergence of a high growth productive economy would never have been possible. The development process was not altogether a linear, stable process. Over-ambitious goals that over-estimated the regime's organizational and technical capacity, such as the Great Leap Forward (1957-58), led to temporary setbacks which had substantial negative consequences, especially in the countryside. Equally important, the new system and regime, despite the radical changes in property relations, class structure and the new egalitarian norms, contained many of seeds of the past 'commercial-landlord-hierarchal-colonial' society, which preceded it. Party cadres acting on behalf of the state transferred the rural surplus extracted from the peasant coops to the central government engaged in rapid urban industrialization. They used the same mixture of coercion and persuasion as had the "tax collectors" in the semi-feudal past, even as the ends pursued were totally different. The vertical-centralized organizational structure of the regime in pursuit of egalitarian goals reflected the ruptures and continuities with the past, the combination of "feudalism" and socialism.

For nearly a decade after the revolution, a substantial number of pre-existing capitalist enterprises continued to operate under the tutelage of the Communist regime. Subsequent to nationalization, many of the business leaders either fled the country or were incorporated into the economic planning and industrial ministries. Some of these capitalist holdovers or their kin later made a comeback with the reversion to capitalism and the revival of private enterprise. In addition to the incorporation of capitalists into the public sector, the new enterprise directors adopted what they considered the "modern forms of production"—namely, mass production line, Taylorist production methods, unbalanced growth emphasizing heavy industry and production goals over agriculture and mass consumption.

The influence of the Soviet model of economic development played a major role in defining growth and accumulation strategies, and the priorities and methods of economic development. Social consumption—investment allocations to public health, transport and education—took far greater precedence over individual consumption based on quality goods, including clothing, housing, recreation, food and household appliances.

The feudal-capitalist-Soviet methods and organization emphasizing vertical control and public-defined priorities increasingly came into conflict with mass demands for greater popular participation, horizontal solidarity and personal consumption. The latent and overt conflicts between the Party elite and the masses over participation took place within a general consensus on the iron rice bowl (guaranteed employment), universal free public education and health, 'affirmative action' (promoting individuals from worker or peasant background) and public ownership of the means of production. The major exceptions among the masses to this consensus existed in the countryside among peasants who cultivated small private lots for self-consumption, barter or occasional sale, and among a limited stratum of urban vendors. The most influential exception to the socialist consensus in the elite was an important stratum of party leaders, ideologues and followers who argued for a greater role for "the market", greater enterprise autonomy and the introduction of market reforms. The open conflict between these forces eventually led to the "Cultural Revolution" (1966-1974), which sought to set the revolution on a course toward deepening the socialist perspective. Paradoxically the outcome of the Cultural Revolution severely weakened the mass movements and led to the ascendance of what later became the "capitalist roaders" under the leadership of Deng Tsiao Peng.

The Cultural Revolution, at the onset, challenged the "feudal" extraction of the rural surplus, the Soviet-style hierarchy, the abuse of authority and the "Taylorist" organization of work. The struggle reaffirmed the primacy of the workers' role in society precluding any openings toward the market for at least for 15 years. The urban mobilizations, especially of the young generation, were aimed at ending the abuse of power by public authorities and professionals who monopolized the public institutions of education, health, science and culture. It sought to bring them into line with egalitarian norms. The mass excesses, the conversion of the ideological/class struggle into an elite-bureaucratic conflict controlled from above, and the lack of any concrete participatory institutions led to the exhaustion and disillusion of the mass movements.

The eventual ascendancy of the 'capitalist roaders' in the late 1970s was not so much a result of any decisive political-military victory as it was a byproduct of the demise and dissolution of the mass movements under the leadership of an aging Mao Tse Tung and what came to be called the 'Gang of Four'.

Stage II: From Communism to State Capitalism 1970-1989

The eclectic communism of the 1949-78 period and the demise of the renovating forces in the Cultural Revolution (1966-73) strengthened the bureaucratic elite favorable to opening the economy to the market. These policies in turn reinforced the capitalist remnants still embedded in the regime. More important it opened room for advancement for economists, scientists, engineers and other party cadre educated or influenced by Soviet experiments with profit-based enterprises and calculus. Mao's foreign policy right turn embracing Washington (Nixon and Kissinger) and a host of right-wing, anti-communist dictators and leaders from Pinochet in Chile, Marcos in the Philippines and Savimbi in Angola, opened the entire party to a reassessment of its international politics and the centrality of the world capitalist market. This reassessment, in turn, strengthened the emerging new generation of professionals and cadres who came to maturity in the post-revolutionary period. Their thinking was shaped in sharp reaction to the plebian-egalitarian thrust of the Cultural Revolution and particularly by its excesses and its attempts to circumvent objective problems by 'creating facts' and by its frontal attack on scientists, experts and academics.

The new pro-capitalist power configuration was made up of technocrats, market-oriented Communist leaders, aspiring private entrepreneurs, ideologues for the new capitalist class and sectors of the old bourgeoisie restored to respectability. They developed a strategy of liberalization in stages. This new power elite sought to avoid a frontal attack on the social welfare system and collective property. Instead they adopted a series of liberalizing measures throughout the 1980s. They substituted a land lease policy—a de facto privatization of land—via the dismantling of the collective farms. Even those farms which were successful were forced into the 'family leasehold' system. Party cadres encouraged private trade, individual accumulation and gradual land concentration. High party and state officials and cadres acted as agents of the state transfers of property to the private sector. They allocated contracts and import licenses, signed off on land use permits, credits, loans and incentives, and enriched themselves in the process. Many soon became capitalists in their own right. These perquisites were distributed by state officials to the new class of capitalists at a price. Corruption was the link between the state apparatus and the new capitalists, often blurring the line between public and private ownership especially as a high percentage of the new capitalist class were progeny or kin of state officials.

"State Capitalism" became the transitional regime between socialism and neo-liberal capitalism.[3] This transitional regime's most important role was to create the optimal framework for the rapid accumulation of private capital and wealth. This involved the imposition of a harsh regimen of labor control and repression of workers' demands while deregulating the exploitation of labor by capital. Total labor control allowed the regime to privatize and close numerous state enterprises, engage in a massive pillage of resources and create a new class of millionaires within a decade. Economic liberalization encouraged the growth of two sets of opponents both seeking democracy, but with differing goals: on the one hand, a pro-Western liberal student opposition directed against state capitalism's continued control of the economy and on the other a worker-based opposition which demanded democracy in the name of defending the heritage of full employment, trade union rights, the 'iron pot' and other welfare measures being undermined by the state capitalists with liberal leanings. The Tiananmen Square (1989) uprising was dominated by the student-liberals, while in Shanghai and elsewhere the worker opposition predominated.

Both oppositions were defeated, strengthening the state apparatus and the advance of liberalization in the 1990s and beyond. The 'state capitalist' regime attempted to ride two horses: a continued strong state sector, nourishing a privileged and corrupt official elite and a market opening for commercial, agricultural and private business and investors to 'complement' the state sector. The statist sector, initially the dominant group, insisted that public banks continue to favor loans to state enterprises, while the liberal factions pushed for greater public loans for private firms and wider areas for private investment.

By the end of 1990s, the internal relation of forces shifted inexorably toward the 'liberalizing' sectors of the state ruling elite, as the private sector gained momentum and secured greater concessions from the state. In other words, state capitalism became the breeding ground for private capitalism.

State capitalism as a "transitional regime" to liberal capitalism combines the *outer forms* of socialism (the predominance of state enterprises and state planning) while the *inner* dynamics moved toward capitalist relations (land leasing, export strategy, openings to foreign investments, and privatizations). A new "ideology" encouraging individual enrichment served as a justification and stimulus for the emerging new class of capitalists. Accelerated and unequal growth during the 1980s was underwritten by the basic foundations for development constructed during the preceding Communist period. The newly emerging capitalist regime benefited from a healthy, trained and skilled urban industrial working class. It expanded on the foundation of basic industries (steel, coal, heavy machines) and light industries (textiles, shoes and related activities) which served as the take-off points for the export strategy. Basic infrastructure (railroads, ports, airports and shipping) and an orderly, stable and unified state capable of defending national sovereignty built under the Communist regime were essential conditions for the capitalist take-off.

The key element within the state capitalist formation that facilitated the movement away from communism and toward the transformation of China into a liberal capitalist state was the ideological makeover of the entire policymaking and advisory elite. This involved the unquestioning adoption of capitalist criteria, methods, motivations and organizational structures. During the 1980s, a whole generation of children of the state capitalist elite was educated by Western liberal economists both in China and abroad. They were taught market economic models, the equation of 'modernization' with capitalist liberalization, the positive role of the multinational corporations and foreign investment. They were indoctrinated to believe that efficiency was identical with profitability and privatization, that inequality was a result of 'merit' (or lack of it). The entire litany of capitalist virtues was almost universally and unquestionably accepted by the educated elite—and put into practice—because it provided a justification and incentive for their own class ambitions.

The progeny of the state capitalist elite became the political and economic agency for the transformation of state capitalism to its liberal variant. The emerging new class of liberalizing capitalists benefited educationally and in terms of economic opportunities from the privileged position of their families in the state apparatus. They also benefited from their political links to state sector officials in terms of the rigged privatization of state property, largely based on corruption, illegal transfers, swindles, under-pricing and other political mechanisms.

The transition from state to liberal capitalism was based on a kind of 'primitive accumulation' or pillage of public resources, as the motor force of expanded capitalist reproduction in the subsequent liberal capitalist phase. The state capitalist elite still justified the opening to liberalization as a means of "developing the forces of production as a prelude to socialism" but the emergence of a powerful, influential billionaire capitalist class diminished the credibility of this slogan.

The principal groundwork for the liberal transition performed by the state capitalist regime was the abolition of all restraints on the most savage forms of capitalist exploitation of labor. The regime cheapened labor costs by displacing a mass of 400 to 500 million rural and urban workers. They became available for employment in low-paid factories, construction industries controlled by real estate plutocrats and domestic services. By 2005 China had the worst inequalities of any Asian country—a far cry from the early 1970s when it was one of the most egalitarian countries.

Transition from State Capitalism to Liberal Capitalism

The growing presence of Chinese capitalists throughout all sectors of the economy and their high concentration in the dynamic growth sectors was cause and consequence of their greater political presence directly and indirectly in the top spheres of the political system. The result was the deepening of liberalization: the accelerated dismantling of trade barriers and protective labor laws, the savaging of the countryside, the massification of the reserve army of unemployed and the orientation toward the export market strategy. This led to the emergence of a class of billionaires— 'super-rich'—comparable to the richest of the rich in the imperial countries and generating the world's greatest inequalities between the top one percent and the bottom fifty percent of the class structure.

The 'victims of the Cultural Revolution' became the executioners of one of the harshest capitalist restorations in modern history (perhaps only exceeded by the Russian and some of the Eastern European ex-Soviet Republics) if we measure the social losses and the extraordinary concentration of profit, rents and land seizures which took place under the ascendant liberal elite.

The predominant group, at least in the early to middle years of the liberal regime, were Chinese national capitalists, though early on a substantial stake was taken on by overseas Chinese from Hong Kong, Taiwan and elsewhere. The advance of national private capitalism took two routes: either through the takeover of privatized state factories or via investments in new enterprises or services. In nearly all cases corruption of state officials played a major role in "lubricating" the process over and above the "entrepreneurial talents", market savvy and innovative behavior of the new class. Privatization beneficiaries—the new owners—were in part former Party-State officials who simply turned elite control into capitalist ownership and in part aspiring private business people with close ties to the local, provincial or state authorities. Likewise the new private enterprise bourgeoisie benefited enormously from state contracts, land grants, tax exonerations, state-controlled cheap labor and (especially at the beginning) nearly oligopolic markets. In both cases liberalization was as much state-driven as it was market-oriented. The interventionist state remained a key factor but its role changed dramatically from a direct investor to a promoter of private investment. But still, at this point, the state and business managers of the Chinese economy were largely Chinese, whether domestic or foreign, and might be presumed to be also safeguarding Chinese control over the economy. The new foreign investment fund that China proposes to create using a small fraction of its foreign currency reserves will probably benefit overseas money fund managers, and if the investments yield expected returns, allow the state to increase social programs to lessen some of the world's worst class inequalities.

Rules limiting market activities were superseded by new regulations (or at least practices), which gave capitalists land sites, investment incentives and protection of property rights. Throughout the 1990s and into the new millennium, the one constant was the growing proportion of production, exports, investments and profits controlled by private capitalists. What began in the early 1980s as a 'market opening' turned into market domination in the following two decades. By the middle of the first decade of the 21st century, private capital accounted for 75 percent of non-agricultural production. In large part, the growth of private capitalism was the result of the closing of state factories or their sell-offs and the vast infusion of private capital both local and foreign.

The rapid reproduction of private capital at the national level resulted from the expansion of consumer goods production, both durables and non-durables, based on the pent-up demand and initially scarce competition. The property, real estate and construction boom turned well-connected "entrepreneurs" into multi-millionaires. The buyouts of state enterprises also led to the rise of a new industrial bourgeoisie. By hook or crook, through captive markets and, above all else, the freedom to plunder cheap labor, the emerging capitalists catapulted in less than a decade from small-scale businessmen into tycoons with multiple mansions, million-dollar condos, Mercedes, mistresses and overseas bank accounts.

Given the initial high levels of exploitation of labor, the hundreds of millions of poverty-stricken unemployed workers and peasants, and the high concentration of wealth in the upper tenth percentile, domestic demand was relatively constricted. The regime and the new capitalist ruling class looked toward the export market as a mechanism to retain class privileges and find a profitable outlet for growing production.

Given that the locus of markets was overseas, it was logical and profitable to develop the coastal regions of China, closest to the ports and force labor to move from the interior to the production sites. The export markets determined production sites and the latter determined the direction of mass internal migration. The coastal production sites, ports, and commercial and banking center became the hotbed for neo-liberal ideology spawned by the academic and research centers. The coastal cities also were the centers for the biggest economic transactions between state officials and the new big bourgeoisie, and between the latter and foreign investors seeking "strategic partners" and entry into the Chinese market. All the major urban coastal centers became centers for the most rancid forms of real estate speculation and corrupt land deals. These transactions led to the construction of luxury apartments, upscale shopping malls, boutiques, five-star hotels and high rent skyscraper office buildings—to provide work space and cater to the whims and conspicuous consumption of the new bourgeois multi-millionaires and the first billionaires.

Millions of construction workers, miners, domestic servants and assembly-line workers labored under the most abominable conditions. The longest hours, the worst safety conditions, lowest pay and least sanitary and regulated work conditions in Asia produced huge profit margins. The licit and illicit gains financed the private domestic services and the physical facilities within which the new rich got richer and conspicuous consumption became a daily ritual. Never in Chinese history or for that matter in the history of capitalism had so much private wealth been accumulated, in such a short time, exploiting so much labor which enjoyed so few rights and benefits. Superimposed on the geographical concentration of production and distribution was the class concentration of wealth, consumption and political power. The notion of "Two Chinas" took on an altogether new meaning (no longer referring to the US distinction between China and Taiwan): it referred to the China of the coastal regions dominated by the new big bourgeoisie and the China of the interior made up of hundreds of millions of unemployed former peasants supplying cheap labor, foodstuffs, raw materials and finished goods to the coastal areas for processing, finishing, exporting and…profit.

Foreign Capital: The First Beachheads

Parallel to the growth of an elite Chinese bourgeoisie, big foreign investors established manufacturing beachheads and enclaves in key sectors, such as transport, banks, hotels, computer chips, and scores of other growth sectors. Major MNCs subcontracted with local Chinese manufacturers in all the major export sectors (clothes, shoes and toys) or directly invested in these sectors.[4] In most cases foreign corporations were required to form joint ventures with majority Chinese ownership. In the special economic zones foreign-owned MNCs were given free land, tariff free import privileges, tax holidays followed by rates of taxation half the rates paid by Chinese firms. The latter privileges are scheduled to be leveled in 2008.

The turning point came with China's entry into the World Trade Organization (2001). Large-scale, long-term policies involving state factory closings followed and were accompanied by privatizations and the transfer of ownership to private national or foreign capitalists. Entry into the WTO decisively shifted the balance between private and state capital, and facilitated the ideological predominance of the former.

Private capital surpassed state capital in the value of output, exports and employment offerings. Big private firms began to receive an increasing percentage of loans from state banks where in the past they had been excluded or restricted. Under the cover and protection of equal treatment for foreign and national capital, Japanese, US, Hong Kong, Taiwanese and European Union MNCs accelerated their entry, spreading to most sectors of manufacturing, as well as financial services, banking, etc. From face creams to golf courses, from factories to high tech enterprises, practically no manufacturing areas were 'off limits'.

Table 1

Share of Gross Industrial Output Value by Registration Status[5]

	State Owned Industry	Collective Owned Industry (private and local)	Limited Liability Corporations and Shareholding Enterprises (private)	Private Enterprise	Foreign Investment
1985	64.9	32.1	n.a.	1.8	1.2
2002	15.6	8.7	30.9	11.7	29.3

The "bureaucratic statists" engaged in rear-guard actions meant to slow the pace of privatization via regulatory delays and non-implementation of political decisions. Some of these objections were based on political beliefs, others as a means of extracting pay-offs. In the end, however, the statists were clearly in retreat.

High growth meant the expansion of conglomerates under the ownership of billionaires and family-based capitalists intertwined with overseas Chinese and Western investment houses.

The state capitalist model based on a triple alliance of state capital/ national private capital/foreign investment was gradually replaced by a new dual coalition of national and foreign capital. By the middle of the first decade of the 21st century, the Chinese national bourgeoisie had reached the apex of its power—surpassing state capital and not yet challenged for dominance by the ascending foreign multinationals. Labor unrest was spreading at a geometrical rate, but so were the systems of repressions and special police and paramilitary forces. Cheap labor pools were declining but the inflow from the countryside compensated for high labor turnover. Competition was intensifying but overseas financing was increasing and opportunities for strategic alliances were growing. Opposition to foreign capital penetration was as yet limited to bureaucratic sectors. Most Chinese capitalists preferred to subcontract from and form partnerships with foreign capital. Most university graduates were looking to careers in the private national monopolies and foreign MNCs. A state-anchored career was a lesser preference. Bankruptcies among small and middle size firms proliferated as competition intensified and profit margins declined; new and bigger monopolies took their place.

China was not only a capitalist's 'paradise'—it was a magnet for capitalists and investors worldwide. Everyone wanted to get into the act of unrestricted exploitation of labor and access the market of 200 million middle class consumers, thousands of millionaires and dozens of super-rich billionaires.

The Future: Will the Transition from Liberalism to Neo-Liberalism Lead to the Eclipse of the National Bourgeoisie?

The present tendencies, now in the latter part of the first decade of the 21st century, mark out a clear trajectory toward a deepening of capitalist, especially foreign capitalist, expansion. This process could be adversely affected by a major crisis in the global trading system, a social revolution in China, a serious recession in the US or a Sino-US military confrontation. Foreign investment and overseas MNCs are growing at a rapid rate, moving beyond their initial beachheads as minority shareholders in select firms. From the present to the next decade, MNCs and foreign investment banks will buy into and extend their reach into production, distribution, transport, telecommunications, real estate and the service sectors throughout the lucrative coastal economies. This process proceeds via three routes: via direct investments in new enterprises; through joint ventures with a strategic partner; buying shares in existing enterprises. Laws regulating majority control to Chinese nationals have been liberalized in the 21st century. In all cases there is an unmistakable tendency for the MNCs to extend their influence and investments over time, eventually taking control over the strategic management positions. This process is not uniform, particularly where there are conflicts with Chinese management, political interference and sustained economic losses, in which case the MNCs withdraw.

As labor, rent and start-up costs rise in the principle cities and as a relatively prosperous bourgeoisie and petit bourgeoisie emerge in the hinterland, the MNCs extend their operations toward the Chinese heartland.

Despite the lower living standards among the great mass of workers, peasants and unemployed, there is an internal market of 100-200 million active consumers in the heartland. The historic shift of FI and MNCs is toward capturing a substantial and eventually majority share of the domestic market even as China continues to serve as an assembly and export platform for foreign-owned firms.

The MNCs have now launched a multi-pronged economic offensive to:

1) capture control of the banking and financial system
2) dominate the high and middle sectors of the domestic consumer goods market
3) penetrate into the telecommunications sector, and
4) gain shares in the cultural, entertainment, publicity and commercial markets.

Through the banking system, foreign capital will gain access to huge sums of internal savings, control credit to large, medium and small firms and more important, will be able to finance MNC investments with Chinese savings. China's leading banks are already selling shares to foreign investors and several major multinational banks have purchased local banks. By the end of 2007, when restrictions on foreign ownership are lifted, the foreign takeover of the banking sector should accelerate. By the beginning of the second decade of this century, foreign banks will likely be a major force in the financial sectors of the Chinese economy. From control over the strategic levers of loans, credit, refinancing and investment, foreign capital will be in a position to penetrate the peak industries of the country.

Foreign investors are oriented to capturing the existing consumer market—not in creating a mass market, which would entail increasing income and/or redistributing income toward the hundreds of millions with extremely limited consumer power. The tendency is to target the higher end of the market—the new bourgeoisie and the more affluent, upwardly mobile petit bourgeoisie. Cosmetics, brand name fashions, transport and electronics are already in high demand. Cheaper versions of the same goods follow, offering the MNCs mass-market shares among employed workers and salaried consumers in the interior and coastal regions.

On the horizon, foreign investors can be expected to use the new world trade agreements to penetrate Chinese communications and service sectors, especially the mass media, entertainment, advertising and marketing outlets, especially the major retail outlets.

The step-by-step gradualist takeover strategy of the 1990s and the first years of the new century will gain momentum in the following decade. The two-step approach of buying into national firms and accumulating shares and influence over time will be replaced by outright buyouts and direct investments in new monopoly firms. Chinese firms will still predominate in the highly competitive labor-intensive sectors. However they will be subject to a greater profit squeeze by the MNC subcontractors and subject to high rates of bankruptcy, opening the way toward greater concentration of ownership.

A "division of labor" between foreign and Chinese capitalists is already beginning to emerge. The MNCs will control marketing, financing, design, technology, R and D, and overseas sales. Their Chinese partners will be in charge of government relations (leveraging contacts, paying "commissions" or bribes, etc), labor relations, hiring of workers (but not necessarily hiring or firing middle and high level personnel, promotions and bonuses), public relations and engineering.

At some point, most likely in the second decade of this century, the cumulative power resulting from the dynamic growth of MNC power in finance, manufacturers, political influence and exports will result in a 'Great Leap Backwards'.

China will the leap from liberalism to neo-liberalism. The "Chinese" economy will lose its 'national identity' and become a territorial outpost for foreign controlled and operated banks and multinational corporations. Quantitative penetration will lead to qualitative change in the commanding heights of the economy and in the elite spheres of the governing class. China's bid to become a "world power" will be subverted. Instead China will become a gigantic proxy for imperial powers, who will increasingly compete for dominance, using different sectors of the political elite, military, students and so on.

The point at which China will be transformed from a burgeoning world power into a proxy for the imperial states depends on when the MNCs capture the means of production, finance and trade, and when this economic power is expressed within the Chinese state. There is a symbiotic relation between the growing presence of MNCs and the conversion of the Chinese state into a promoter of "free market" policies, each reinforcing the other. China's 'Great Leap Backwards' into an industrial outpost of empire will be consummated when the share of profits shifts from the national bourgeoisie to foreign capital, a process which accelerated in the first decade of the 21st century.

The Chinese bourgeoisie's lead role in retarding or deterring this capitalist transformation is based on two intertwining factors: its control over bureaucratic regulation and the residual nationalism of some political officials. Public officials undermine, delay and add costs to MNC entry. Additional impediments include the investment miscalculations which foreign investors make in terms of their choice of corrupt or incompetent 'strategic partners'. The Chinese bourgeoisie is strongest in the most labor-intensive industries drawing on the mass reserve army of rural unemployed. As this "reserve" is exhausted and urbanized workers demand higher salaries, the comparative advantages of the national bourgeoisie over foreign capital will decline. The national bourgeoisie most certainly will press for greater repression of labor unrest but as a result they will be caught between heightened workers' pressure and greater MNC competition. The future prospects of the national bourgeoisie will depend on their oligopolistic control of markets, the capacity to expand 'overseas' in search of cheap sites of low-wage exploitation, and their ability to upgrade their technology and internal organization. The likelihood is that large-scale global Chinese capitalists will expand into regions where they are competitive (like Africa) and will seek to find a modus vivendi with the ascending multinationals in areas where they risk military confrontation with western MNCs whose interests and access to resources they threaten. They will sacrifice a share of the Chinese market and expand overseas operations in the poorer African and Asian countries and into Latin American resource enclaves.

The Chinese approach to resource extraction has many similarities to their imperial predecessors—taking raw materials, processing them in China and selling finished goods to their "trading partner in Africa" or elsewhere. China provides aid with no political strings, avoids any critique of political rule, and provides large-scale infrastructure projects. Like other imperial countries, it convokes grand symbolic meetings in praise of international cooperation while pillaging the environment and exploiting labor. The history and logic of large-scale, long-term developments bears out the idea that each preceding social regime contains the transformative agents of the forthcoming regime. Just as "elite collectivists" (the "capitalist roaders") transformed China from a socialist into a state capitalist economy ("market socialism") so did the political officials and the emerging bourgeois lay the groundwork for the rise of liberal capitalism.

Foreign capital has grown into a dynamic force within the liberal framework, deepening its control within enterprises and banks and expanding across all sectors of the economy. Accompanying this non-violent transformation of China from a liberal to a neo-liberal capitalist state is a growing mass resistance. The reasons are obvious: the harshest exploitative work conditions in the world; the most arbitrary usurpation seizure of land; the most dangerous working condition anywhere; the greatest inequalities between the top one percent and the bottom fifty percent. Added to the Chinese bourgeoisie's brutal exploitation are their laissez faire agricultural import policies which are ruining millions of peasants and driving them to desperation. By the middle of the first decade of the 21st century, massive importation of heavily subsidized US cotton, rice and other grains had devastated sectors of the countryside. Increased competition by national and foreign private capital has set in motion close to 100,000 mass demonstrations[6] involving millions of workers and peasants protesting arbitrary firings, plant shutdowns, stolen pensions and arbitrary seizure of property without compensation.

The Deepening Social Crisis: The Return of Class Struggle

Between 2001 and 2004, major social protests rose from 4,000 to 72,000 a year, and in 2005 they increased to 91,000. Despite the formation of special military police units throughout the country, the rising tide of social protest, especially in the countryside, is threatening to destabilize the regime.

China's leadership has responded by announcing a series of new programs. In March 2006, at the annual session of the National Peoples' Congress, Prime Minister Wen Jiabao promised to build a "new socialist countryside", describing it as a "major historic task". Wen promised that the government would spend an extra $5.2 billion dollars on rural schools, hospitals, crop subsidies and other programs—a fifteen percent increase over the past year. A World Health Organization survey measuring the equality of medical treatment placed China 187th out of 191 countries. The regime's neo-liberal policies were reaping the whirlwind of mass rural protest against arbitrary land seizures by rapacious developers and corrupt officials. To head off the protests Du Ying, Deputy Minister of China's powerful National Development and Reform Commission, proposed 'reforms' based on 'market mechanisms' to provide 'just compensations' for land seized for commercial use. Over 133,000 hectares of Chinese farmland is converted to non-agricultural use every year leaving about 1 million farmers without land to farm. The leadership's 'new socialist countryside' proposal includes lower taxes and an end to extortionate payment demands by corrupt local officials. To fund these social reforms the leadership announced a slow down in the growth rate to eight percent and a plan to reallocate spending to encourage the growth of the domestic consumer market.

These measures, however, are too little and too late. In the first place the groups which are adversely affected by these reforms are the same people who are asked to implement the changes—a very dubious proposition. Secondly the additional spending of a few billion dollars will have a minimum effect on 800 million rural poor. The extension of free market policies to the countryside, especially in the context of the so-called leasehold system, will continue to concentrate landownership and increase the number of rural unemployed. The rich farmers, transport owners, commercial middlemen and informal money lenders, in alliance with urban land speculators, have a stranglehold on political power and will certainly ensure that few if any of the new rural funding reaches the most needy multitudes.

The regime's policy to promote domestic consumption requires a sharp increase in the minimum wage and regulation of highly skewed salary-profit ratios. This is not part of the neo-liberal agenda. Since most manufacturers are geared to the export market, the entire production structure would have to be adjusted to potential local market demand—again a costly process not currently on the screen for the new capitalist class. A substantial increase in the domestic consumer market means higher wages and products at affordable prices, both of which impinge on the profits of the new capitalists with the closest links to the leadership. The dilemma of power is that in order to contain rising social discontent by progressive structural adjustments, the regime would need to be transformed, a new social power configuration would have to come to power and restrictions in the 'open-door' policy to foreign investors would have to take place.

There are clear signs that the rapid national and foreign private takeover of strategic sectors of the economy has engendered sharp opposition even within the Party. A sharp ideological dispute over a new property law protecting private property in the National Peoples Congress took place in March 2006. Two sets of criticism arose in the debate: some argued that the property protections would shield the billionaires and millionaires who stole public assets or officials who took bribes; others claimed that the property law would obliterate the balance between state and private property in favor of the latter. While the debate is important in highlighting how China's foreign takeovers and rapid privatization has provoked vocal intellectual and public opposition, it is unlikely to have serious implications. The entire leadership of the regime is linked to the powerful expanding private sector elites who have become the essential motor force of growth. The social, familial and political overlap between the political leadership and the private economic elites and their support for the dominant neo-liberal model precludes any serious reforms. The class struggle will continue and probably deepen.

The old paternalistic communist and state capitalist bonds between directors and workers, cadre, collective farm leaders and peasants have been shattered. The spontaneous decentralized protests resulting from the first wave of liberal exploitation of mostly peasant workers is likely to be replaced by organized movements of the new urbanized workers. Angered by the grotesque class contrasts between a ruling class life style of conspicuous consumption and arbitrary power, the growing army of impoverished and unemployed urban workers, displaced peasants and exploited workers may set in motion a new rebellious period. The centralization of capital in large factories and concentrated in urban settings facilitates organization, exchange of ideas, sharing of experience and recollections of guaranteed employment without great class distinctions.

Past recollections of class solidarity and a grasp of workers interests could convince the massified concentration of highly exploited workers that a new type of 'Cultural Revolution' is the solution, one with a distinctly class and anti-imperialist orientation. There is an inverse relation between the rise and relative decline of the influence of the national bourgeoisie and the decline and rise of new working class consciousness. Mass opinion could shift from a 'consumerist ethic' to a fight for class and national dignity and freedom from the thousands of trials and tribulations imposed by the ruling class. The future ruling 'internationalized' Chinese bourgeoisie will lack the present national bourgeoisie's cultural ties, the 'national guise' and the messianic discourse of a Chinese 'world power' to mystify the workers. Worker-capital relations may increasingly be seen through the cash nexus only. Social relations based on foreign pillage may reawaken both class and national indignation and spread outward toward intellectuals, students, shopkeepers and peasants. The fusion of foreign and national capital could set in motion a new revolutionary struggle in the future decades.

CHAPTER 12

US-LATIN AMERICAN RELATIONS: RUPTURES, REACTION AND THE ILLUSIONS OF TIMES PAST

Introduction

Numerous writers, journalists, public officials and academics on the Right and Left have noted changes in relations between the US and Latin America. Those on the Right bemoan the 'end of US hegemony', the growth of a 'New Left', the 'revival of populism' and the 'loss of US influence'. Those on the Left herald the purported changes as a moment of progressive regional realignment. The Right speaks pessimistically of the threats to 'national security and democracy', and access to energy and other resources. One sector on the Left claims to perceive a new regional 'axis of counter hegemony' led by Cuba, Venezuela and Bolivia sweeping the continent, while other prudent conservative observers argue that a broad 'center-left' alternative headed by 'social democratic' regimes like Brazil, Chile, Argentina, Peru and Uruguay are replacing traditional US allies and challenging both the Leftist regimes and past US policies.

Inside the US Government, policymakers focus on isolating and destabilizing the Left, downplaying the challenges from the center-left, and emphasizing political continuities and economic opportunities with neo-liberal regimes.

Faced with radically different assessments of the strength and weakness of US influence in Latin America, an independent analysis of the *historic context* for measuring the rise or fall of US power is required. This requires a serious assessment, which avoids overblown generalizations, and examines specific issues, areas and particular conjunctures in which agreements or disagreements between the US and Latin America occur. This includes looking at how differences are resolved as well as the structural convergences and divergences.

Continuities and Expansion of US Influence

Contrary to many leftist and far-right pundits, there are several issue areas where *US influence has actually increased* over the past several years.

Bilateral Free Trade Agreements

The US has established bilateral trade agreements with Peru, Colombia, Central American nations, Mexico, Chile, Uruguay and most of the Caribbean states. What is significant about these agreements is that Washington did not have to make any concessions on its heavily subsidized agricultural export sector, nor lift its import quotas on over 200 products. Moreover, Washington secured free (non-reciprocal) entrance into its counterparts' financial, service, high tech, health, educational and media sectors. In a word the bilateral trade agreements were highly asymmetrical and more beneficial to US multinationals and non-competitive domestic producers.

Military Bases and Training Programs

Washington has expanded the number of military bases and joint military operations in Latin America over the past five years. In 2005 a large-scale military base and operations headquarters was established in Paraguay and a new military training program with local facilities has been agreed to in Uruguay. US military bases still operate in Ecuador (Manta), Brazil, El Salvador, Aruba and Colombia. Annual joint military operations and US training programs involve all Latin American countries except Cuba and Venezuela. Arms sales and military aid continue unabated to all the 'center-left' regimes except Venezuela. Drug Enforcement Agency personnel and US military advisers circulate throughout Latin America (except Cuba and Venezuela) and operate freely within security and intelligence offices.

Economic Presence

US business, banking and overseas investors continue to flourish undisturbed in Latin America, enjoying high rates of return, full and early payments of debt and new opportunities to bid on lucrative publicly-owned enterprises targeted for privatization. US energy and commodity enterprises in Latin America have had record profits from the historic high world prices of metals and oil products between 2003-2007. The US' relative share of Latin American exports, privatized firms, banks and profits has declined, but this is due to the increased presence of Latin American billionaires and European,

Chinese and other Asian investors and importers. Capitalist competition resulting in a 'relative decline' of US economic presence has not diminished its returns in absolute terms.

Ideological Conformity: The Neo-liberal Ascendancy
While most Latin American electoral parties on the campaign trail continue to criticize 'neo-liberalism', few, if any, renounce the free market doctrine once taking office. All regimes elected between 2005-2007 with the exception of that in Venezuela have yet to reverse the privatization process of the 1970-2001 period. All of these regimes have continued to follow or support lowering trade barriers — there is no increase of new protectionist legislation. In the current Doha World Trade Rounds, all the major Latin American countries have been pushing for greater trade liberalization, even more so than the United States.

Legislation privatizing pension funds, 'liberalizing' labor legislation (loosening labor employment protections), and facilitating the entry of foreign capital has been recently approved by most of the 'center-left' regimes. Fiscal and budgetary policies have been very much in line with IMF guidelines, much more so than in the United States, now due to ideological assent.

In conclusion there are substantial structural, ideological and policy continuities with the past which support continued US domination and elite hegemony throughout most, but not all, the Latin American countries.

New Realities: Relative Changes

To understand the exaggerated Left view, which claims to see a major decline in US hegemony, it is important to contextualize the present decade with the recent past. To correctly gauge the reality today, we need to compare three time periods: the 1960s to the early 1970s; the mid 1970s to 1999; the period 2000-2002 and the current period 2003-2006/7.

US-Latin American Relations in Historical Perspective—1960s to Early 1970s
This period was characterized by a series of serious challenges to US hegemony. Political regimes, socio-political and military-political movements challenged the structural (property) basis and ideological and foreign policy foundations of US hegemony throughout the continent for most of a decade. In many countries US power declined substantially, reducing its ability to mobilize the continent in defense of its global empire. In Chile, a socialist government was elected and proceeded to nationalize the US-owned copper mines with unanimous congressional approval. It accelerated an agrarian reform, which expropriated land from large landowners, historically allied with the US. It nationalized banks, factories and petroleum facilities owned by pro-US Chilean elites and US businessmen. Chile, under Socialist

President Allende, joined the non-aligned movement, broke the US embargo on Cuba and developed close working relations with other nationalist regimes in Latin America.

In Bolivia, Peru and Ecuador nationalist military regimes expropriated US petroleum and mining enterprises and adopted independent foreign policies, expanding relations with the Communist countries and seeking membership in the non-aligned movement. In Argentina, a nationalist Peronist Government, backed by sectors of the guerrilla movement, took power and adopted a nationalist foreign policy, while the radicalized Argentinian working class moved from nationalist populism to socialism. In Mexico, pressure from nationalist and agrarian movements blocked efforts to break relations with Cuba and to privatize public enterprises. In Cuba, the revolutionary government proceeded to expropriate all US firms, allied itself with the Soviet Bloc and supported revolutionary movements in Latin America, Africa and Asia. In Brazil, popular movements pressured the Goulart government toward radical nationalist and agrarian reform policies and an independent foreign policy.

A comparison between 1960-1975 and the present period, 2003-2006, demonstrates that the US has certainly strengthened its position in Latin America by practically any measure: neo-liberal regimes have replaced socialist and nationalist regimes throughout the region. What is considered 'nationalism' or 'radicalism' in Latin America today does not at all resemble its earlier counterparts. No major expropriation of US property has taken place. No 'center-left' regime has re-nationalized foreign firms, even those which were privatized under dubious circumstance. In terms of foreign policy, Cuba no longer supports revolutionary movements or even radical alternatives in most Latin American countries (it has excellent relations with the ultra-rightwing Colombian regime while opposing the FARC guerrillas; it supported the re-election of the center-right Brazilian President Lula da Silva against the leftist candidate Helena Heloisa).

Cuba and Venezuela have promoted a "Latin America only" integration plan or ALBA (as the integration program has been called) in which state enterprises in the energy sector would combine resources, a new development bank would finance projects, and a continent wide media would present news and programs to counter CNN. Apart from high levels of integration between Cuba and Venezuela, however, there are few indications it will succeed. Brazil under Lula looks toward big ethanol agreements with Washington, Cuba buys most of its foodstuff from the USA and not Bolivia, Argentina looks to greater trade with the European Union and Asia, and Bolivia retains all of its foreign owned petrol-gas MNCs, etc. What has emerged is a series of bilateral agreements to issue bonds between Venezuela and Argentina, oil for medical services between Cuba and Venezuela, and trade agreements between Venezuela to sell petrol at subsidized prices to a number of Caribbean, Central American and South American countries, including Colombia.

From a historical perspective it is factually and analytically false to say that US power in Latin America has declined *if we frame the discussion in the comparative terms of 1960-1975 and 2001-2006.*

Coup and Reversals: The Resurgence of US Power—1976-1980s

Beginning with the US-backed military coup in Brazil in 1964, the invasion of the Dominican Republic in 1965 and continuing with a series of CIA-backed military seizures of power in Bolivia (1971), Uruguay (1972/3), Chile (1973), Peru (1975) and Argentina (1976), Washington re-established its power and *reversed* the legislation and policies which adversely affected its big property holders and foreign policy. All the new dictatorships received large-scale funding from the US government, easy access to loans from the World Bank and IMF (thus starting the massive debt cycle) for many dubious ventures in exchange for repressing all nationalist, socialist, democratic and popular opposition.

Each and every regime broke relations with Cuba and the non-aligned movement, and lined up with the US in all international forums. The military regimes proceeded to denationalize the economy, abolish labor and social legislation favorable to workers, reverse land distribution programs, and promote 'free market' export-oriented growth at the expense of production for local markets. Large-scale, long-term US and European investments entered and in most cases proceeded to buy out local public and private firms. De-regulation of the economy led to the growth of easy inflows and rapid flight of speculative capital. In the deepest sense, these were more *free market* rather than *military* coups, the military being an instrument for the former.

The only point of contention was in Central America where the Sandinista National Liberation Movement in Nicaragua overthrew the long-standing US-backed Somoza dictatorship, and powerful guerrilla movements based on Indians and peasants in El Salvador and Guatemala challenged US domination. By the early 1990s, the US-backed political-military forces ousted the Sandinistas, co-opted the Salvadoran guerrillas into electoral politics and slaughtered the Indian insurgents in Guatemala.

The period 1976-1980s was the opening chapter of the 'Golden Age' of US power: With submissive dictatorial client rulers in control, policies were put in place which promoted large-scale openings to exploit minerals and energy under extremely favorable terms and imposed unquestioned obedience to US foreign policy positions.

The abrupt and massive shift of Latin American policies in favor of US economic and political interests led to greater social polarization, vastly increased inequalities, unemployment and poverty. Large-scale mass discontent broke out in Chile and Argentina in the mid eighties, in Bolivia during 1984-85, and elsewhere. The opposition to the military-authoritarian dictatorships was diverse and the demands varied. For the popular classes, the demands were for a return to democracy and the re-establishment of a social welfare nationalist regime. Among the middle class, the demands were for free elections, individual freedoms and greater power and income sharing between the upper and middle class. For the elite bourgeoisie, the demand was for free elections and accelerated liberalization and privatization including the many enterprises controlled by the military. As a result of mass pressure the military ceded power to elite-controlled electoral regimes in exchange for impunity, the irreversibility of the privatizations that had taken place, and the maintenance of existing property and class relations. While the impetus for regime change largely came from below (workers and the middle class), the leadership and direction of policy was vested in the hands of politicians beholden to the liberal bourgeoisie.

The Golden Age of US Dominance: 1990-2001

All the policy and structural indicators of the period 1975-1989 point to a substantial recovery and expansion of US power in Latin America over the previous decade. During the following decade (1990-2000), the restoration of electoral regimes, deepened, expanded and seemingly consolidated the ascendancy of US dominance. The anti-dictatorial popular movements were subordinated to electoral parties committed to liberal policies favoring US, European and Asian multinational corporations and banks. They were supportive of US foreign policy and closely aligned with the domestic financial and business oligarchies. Never in the 20th Century were so many lucrative public monopolies transferred to private national and foreign investors, in so many countries and covering such a vast an array of sectors in less than a decade. Never had so much wealth (amounting to over $900 billion dollars) in interest payments, profits, royalties and assets been appropriated by US, European and Asian MNCs in the course of a decade (1991-2001).

Washington and Brussels could cynically and literally claim that this was truly a 'Golden Age'. Since pillage was facilitated by electoral regimes, Washington and Brussels considered these massive transfers of wealth to derive from 'legitimate' policies of 'liberalization' no matter how asymmetrical were the benefits, no matter how great the emerging inequalities, no matter how great the growth of Latin American poverty and the exodus of professionals, skilled and unskilled workers, small farmers and peasants.

Several international factors favored this combination of free elections and private pillage. These included the collapse of communism in the former USSR and Eastern Europe, the annexation of East Germany and the conversion of their leaders into Western clients (Yeltsin, Havel, Walesa and others), which in turn eliminated alternative sources of trade and aid and skewed the balance of power toward the US. The resulting deep economic crisis in Cuba led to its sharp turn inward to stave off collapse. Cuba was forced to scale down its support for left movements in Latin America and its own poverty exacerbated by the US trade embargo further reduced its attraction as a developmental model. Low commodity prices weakened state revenues and strengthened the hand of the liberal advocates of privatization and the IMF. China was moving toward integration into the world market and was not yet in a position to provide an alternative market or source of external financing. The Middle East was 'under control'. Iran was weakened by Iraq's invasion, Saddam Hussein had been neutralized by the Gulf War. Israel was savaging the First Palestinian Intifada. The Central American guerrilla movements were domesticated and integrated into electoral politics dominated by US neo-liberal clients. Chavez was elected only at the end of the 1990s and was still several years from adopting his nationalist-welfare agenda.

Most important of all, Washington had successfully backed a string of *'ideal' clients* in the largest and economically richest countries in Latin America. Carlos Menem in Argentina privatized more public enterprises by executive decree (over a thousand) than any president in the country's history. Fernando Henrique Cardoso in Brazil privatized the most lucrative state enterprises, including the Vale del Doce iron mine for $400 million (its market value in 2007 is over $10 billion dollars with annual returns exceeding 25 percent), banks, telecommunications, oil and numerous other state enterprises, which were converted into foreign-owned monopolies. In Mexico, following his fraudulent election, Carlos Salinas privatized over 110 public enterprises, opened the borders to subsidized US agricultural exports—ruining over 1.5 million corn, bean, rice and poultry farmers and peasants—and signed the North American Free Trade Agreement. His policies facilitated the US takeover of Mexico's retail trade, real estate, agriculture, industry, banking and communications sectors. Similar patterns of foreign takeovers were evident throughout the region, especially in Ecuador, Chile, Peru, Bolivia and Colombia where lucrative gas, oil and mining firms were privatized and sold to foreign investors.

In their annual reports throughout the 1990s both the IMF and the World Bank described these regimes as 'exemplary and successful models' to be emulated throughout the world. Washington and the EU considered this period of exceptional revenue and profits, facilitated by extremely accommodating regimes, promoting unconstrained liberalization as the *norm for the future.* Anything deviating from the 'Golden Period' would be considered deviant, unacceptable, threatening, undemocratic and unfavorable to investors.

Crisis and Collapse of US-Backed Clients: The End of the Golden Era

Flush with the 'good times' and credulous consumers of their own rhetoric of 'free elections and free markets', neither the World Bank nor the IMF, Washington nor the EU anticipated the massive popular uprisings and electoral revolts of the late nineties through to the first half of the following decade (1999-2006), which overthrew or repudiated each and every US Latin American client.

In Ecuador, three popular uprisings replaced three consecutive neo-liberal presidents, blocked the privatization of gas, oil and petroleum, as well as the signing of the Latin American Free Trade Agreement. In Argentina, in December 2001, in the face of a financial collapse, the freezing of accounts of millions of bank depositors and a deep economic recession, a mass popular rebellion ousted the incumbent President De la Rua and three of his would-be 'successors'. In Bolivia, three bloody mass insurrections in January 2000, October 2003 and June 2005 led to the overthrow of two of Washington's most obedient and servile clients—Sanchez de Lozada and his Vice President Carlos Mesa, both notorious privatizers and lax regulators of tax, fiscal and contraband activities by foreign MNCs. In Brazil, mass pressure led by the rural workers movement (MST) and urban discontent led to the defeat of incumbent President Cardoso's party and the election of the apparently social democratic Lula da Silva.

Most important of all, Washington's efforts to destabilize Venezuela's President Chavez for objecting to the Bush Administration's Middle East war policy, and its subsequent backing of a failed coup, radicalized Chavez and his supporters.

Washington's 'Golden Age' led to massive popular hostility toward US clients and to the free market policies they pursued. The very conditions and policies that favored US business, military and banking interests, were precisely the ones detonating popular uprisings.

Throughout the region many of the leaders of the social rebellions and insurrections demanded the re-nationalization of privatized enterprises, the re-negotiation of contracts with multinational corporations, the return to state control of foreign owned banks and the prosecution of government officials complicit in privatization and the bloody repression of protestors. In Venezuela, the movements demanded the prosecution of US-backed coup makers and the 're-nationalization' of the state-owned petroleum company (including replacement of 10,000 public oil officials linked to US MNCs who had been complicit to Washington's efforts against Chavez).

The period 2000-2003 witnessed a sharp decline of US power, particularly the loss of vital client regimes. The popular uprisings represented a major threat to the privileged position of US and EU multinational banks, petroleum and telecommunication industries in the region.

In Colombia, US client ruler President Pastrana faced the advancing guerrilla armies of the Revolutionary Armed Forces of Colombia (FARC) and to a lesser degree the National Liberation Army. In addition there was a substantial increase in trade union and peasant-based opposition to the US authored and financed 'Plan Colombia' and free market policies.

Despite the scope and depth of mass protest and the success of the popular movements in overthrowing pro-US regimes, the political and economic foundations of US power in the hemisphere were shaken but not undermined. While sectors of the state apparatus associated with the discredited US client-regimes were forced to resign, the military, judicial, police and civilian ministries remained intact. While some of the leading kleptocratic capitalists moved their illicitly gained liquid assets abroad, most temporarily adopted a low profile, waiting for a more propitious moment to restart operations.

Most important for Washington's strategic interests, the powerful popular movements were not able or prepared to take state power and make a clean break with the neo-liberal, free market model. In each and every case in which an outstanding US client ruler fell, they were replaced by a new president who by necessity adopted anti-neo-liberal rhetoric; in some cases they even eliminated or replaced some of the most hated figures of the previous regime. But generally, all stayed within the class and political parameters of the previous regime. Particularly prior to and immediately after taking power, these new political elites adopted a posture positioning themselves on the 'center-left', not too dissimilar from the 'Third Way' position of their European counterparts.

Washington was caught by surprise by the ease and speed with which its clients were swept from power. Believing in their own triumphalist rhetoric about the 'end of history' with the collapse of communism in Europe and the advent of regimes embracing free markets and free elections, Washington was unsuccessful in defending its clients. In many cases Washington's favorite alternatives on the right, which were mustered to replace their fallen puppets, were themselves discredited. Lacking any political capital, they were not able to fill the political vacuum. Within the Bush Administration, particularly among the political appointees in the State Department (many of Cuban exile background), the initial response was generalized hostility and apprehension not only toward large-scale rebellions, but also to the emerging center-left regimes. The only exception was the ultra-neo-liberal 'socialist' Chilean regime, which even had the support of extremists like Otto Reich.

During the entire 2000-2002 period, Washington made few attempts to address the major political and economic changes that had taken place both internationally as well as in Latin America, in order to adjust the ambitions of the US Empire to the new realities. The 1990s Golden Era of pillage had blinded Washington to the new political and social polarization it engendered. As a result most of its political clients were isolated. Having grown accustomed to easy access to its client rulers and dependent on intelligence garnered from complacent Defense Ministry and CIA, Washington was unprepared to change horses before they fell.

More seriously, the deep economic crisis and collapse of 2000-2002 shifted the balance of forces within the Latin American countries in a way that made it practically impossible to continue with the politics, ideology and economic policies of the 1990s.

The New Realities of the 21st Century

Washington and its business partners refused to recognize that the 1990s were an exceptional period based on a particular constellation of circumstances, which were transitory and not entirely replicable.

The fear generated by the military dictators in the 1970s no longer paralyzed mass movements. The new generation had not suffered torture, prison and mass murder. Their primary formative experience was downward mobility, financial collapse, unemployment, loss of savings and dim prospects for the future.

The beginning of the 1990s had witnessed the introductions of deep neo-liberal policies. US clients had made grandiose promises of shared prosperity, entry into the First World markets, access to cheap credit, and inexpensive low-cost consumer imports. By the end of the decade, none of the promises of rising living standards came to fruition for the great masses of the working and salaried classes. Free market policies bankrupted millions of peasants and small farmers. Over half the manufacturing workers were shoved into the informal sector. Deregulation led to bank failures, fraud and the massive loss of middle class savings. Privatized state enterprises fired workers, closed unprofitable subsidiaries and replaced most permanent workers with temporary 'contract workers'.

The mass illusions about 'prosperity and free markets' turned into a bitter, angry sense of deliberate mass deception. Washington, however, continued to live with the illusion that the masses were still enthralled with the neo-liberal promises and that outside extremists were responsible for the unrest—though it might be hard pressed to say where those "outside" extremists were now coming from. Washington's most bizarre expression of denial was found in the IMF and World Bank appraisals of the collapse of client regimes and mass popular uprisings. According to their economists the reason for the collapse was that the 'economic reforms' were not fully or correctly implemented in a timely manner! The message to the Latin American clients was to 'carry on'. The only problem was that there were no viable local pro-US political agencies available to restart the politics of the 'Golden Era'.

Parallel with the vast political and economic changes within Latin America that made 'Golden Age' politics no longer practical, significant changes were taking place outside of Latin America, namely the opening of the huge Asian market and demand for Latin American agro-mineral exports, the rise in world liquidity, the massive rise in exports and earnings and the huge trade surpluses accruing to Latin America. Washington refused to accept the tax, welfare and foreign policy changes in Venezuela. Instead it backed a military coup in April 2002 and a business/oil lockout in late 2002 to early 2003. Oblivious to President Chavez' mass support, the White House, far from accommodating to the initial limited range of changes proposed by Chavez, resorted to financing and promoting electoral fronts and NGOs to defeat President Chavez. Each of Washington's failed attempts further radicalized the government's domestic and foreign policies while eliminating important US political assets. Chavez took his case to Latin America. Popular approval skyrocketed. The new 'center-left' regimes signed on to lucrative energy and trade investment deals. Washington's failed destabilizing programs extended Venezuela's influence and strengthened the appeal of its welfare-statist policies throughout Latin America. The Chavez factor was in great part an influential counterweight to the US because of the vast increase in petroleum prices during the period 2002. Between the mid-1990s to the early 2000s oil prices rose by a multiple of five.

Equally important, the new millennium saw a vast increase in all major commodity prices. Copper, nickel, iron, soya, beef, grain, gold and silver, as well as other raw materials doubled and tripled in prices. In large part this resulted from the dynamic double-digit growth of Chinese industry. In fact, demand boomed throughout Asia as importers of raw materials recovered from the crisis and recession of the late 1990s. India grew over six percent, Japan pulled out of its 'lost decade', South Korea overcame its 1997 economic crisis even though much of its industry that had been de-nationalized during this period did not return to domestic ownership, and China grew by over ten percent.

The US, in part, lost its economic leverage based on debt refinancing, trade dominance and its technological monopoly. Trade and investment diversification by the new 'center-left' regimes was based on retaining the neo-liberal framework but working through it with new Asian partners. Washington's attempts to use the 'economic stick' of the 1990s were less effective in dictating policy to the large Latin American nations. Yet Washington persisted in applying pressure.

The new more diverse trading patterns, the economic crises in Latin America and the rising popular movements meant that Washington's attempt to impose a privileged position in Latin America via the so-called Latin American Free Trade Area (FTAA)[1] was doomed. Brazil, Argentina, Venezuela, Ecuador and Bolivia rejected the ludicrously one-sided nature of FTAA in which Washington insisted that Latin American countries lower all trade barriers in all economic sectors while the US would continue providing $21 billion dollars in agricultural subsidies to US producers, while maintaining quotas on over 200 exportable commodities from Latin American and the brazen use of other 'non-traditional' barriers on trade.

Clinton initiated FTAA and signed Mexico to NAFTA during the early 1990s—the Golden Age of Pillage. Bush, facing continent-wide resistance, turned toward *bilateral free trade* agreements with client rulers in Central America, the Caribbean and in Latin America with Peru, Colombia and Chile. Instead of recognizing the new realities and the need to develop trade agreements based on more symmetrical relations with the new neo-liberal center-left regimes, Washington persisted in sacrificing vast economic opportunities for non-agricultural exports, especially toward Brazil, Argentina, Bolivia and Ecuador.

Washington singularly failed to take account of the extensive changes in the international environment. Russia was no longer ruled by its drunken client, Boris Yeltsin, surrounded by kleptocratic gangsters hell-bent on pillaging the country and accommodating each and every policy emanating from Washington. Under President Vladimir Putin, Russian capitalism was normalized. Growth, investment, improved living standards and national interests were pursued in a systematic and coherent fashion. The Russian state petrol and gas MNC renationalized a majority of the illegally privatized enterprises. The boom in world prices for gas, oil and other raw materials fueled the recovery of Russian industry and its pursuit of overseas markets. Russia once again emerged as a potential alternative investment and trading partner for Latin American countries, especially in the fields of energy development, arms purchases and joint ventures.

As was mentioned above, China's voracious appetite for raw materials opened alternative trade and investment opportunities for Latin American agro-mineral industries. Washington failed to recognize that the expansion of the Russian and Asian countries weakened US economic hegemony in Latin America and persisted in pushing outmoded 'integration' proposals that failed to take account of the new global economic dynamics.

Even US military options, frequently wielded in the past, as threats or actual interventions, were severely weakened by the Bush Administration's involvement in the prolonged and unending wars in Iraq and Afghanistan. The US invasion and occupation of Iraq and Afghanistan led to massive resistance, which tied down the great mass of its active combat troops and reserves. The cumulative losses in dead and injured reached 3368 killed in action, and over 24,314 wounded;[2] the financial cost soared to over $423 billion dollars by mid-2007.[3] Over seventy percent of Americans opposed the war. The erosion of support for Bush's Middle East and Asian military agenda and the depletion of active military forces sharply weakened Washington's capacity to engage in new interventions to forestall credible threats to US imperial interests in Latin America. Unlike the 1990s when Bush Sr. defeated Iraq, withdrew the troops and declared a New World Order with some credibility, Bush Jr.'s declaration of 'permanent war' rings hollow as US forces are driven from the streets of Baghdad to their reinforced concrete sanctuaries.

While the Bush Administration *could* resort to the military option in Latin America, the prospects of securing Latin American, European, Asian and even public backing in the US (especially if it became a prolonged operation with losses) is dubious. The very *generality* of the so-called War on Terror and the extreme colonial strategies adopted in Iraq have severely weakened Washington's capacity to intervene in particular adversarial countries in Latin America. The regional and international changes since the 'Golden Age' of US dominance have heavily influenced discussions about the 'decline of US power'.

Fluidity of Hegemony: Relative Losses, Relative Gains (2003-2007)

If we consider the power of the US in Latin America, there are certainly clear signs of declining influence evident in the diversification in sources of export earnings, investments and joint ventures. Yet none of the US MNCs within Latin America have been adversely affected. The worst that can be said is that they may pay higher taxes to the Venezuelan government. In part this is simply because the prior taxes were so low. For example, in the Orinoco tar field, taxes rose from one percent to 15 percent and now approach 33 percent— a change, yes, but not reflected in a loss of profits given current high oil prices. All the big US oil companies, Chevron, Exxon, etc, continue to operate in Venezuela and harvest windfall profits even as they lose shares to the Venezuelan government. All the major oil companies continue to profit in Venezuela as minority shareholders. But perhaps not for long: as the *International Herald Tribune* reported on March 7, 2007: "Venezuela's state oil company said Thursday that ConocoPhillips Co. and Chevron Corp. have agreed to discuss handing over their heavy oil projects to the government by May 1."

However, the US has lost influence in most (but not all) of the top government circles in Venezuela. However Washington still has numerous clients in the private sector, including the private mass media. It finances and backs a large array of self-styled non-governmental organizations, a dozen electoral parties, a highly bureaucratic trade union apparatus and sectors of the Catholic hierarchy. Washington's clients include large sectors of the business, financial and service elite, important sectors of the private and public professional class (doctors, professors, consultants, public relations agents and lawyers). Despite some losses, the Pentagon retains influence among sectors of the National Guard, secret police (DISIP) and Armed Forces. In other words, despite Washington's failed policies of confrontation (coups, electoral boycotts, lockouts), which have resulted in the loss of key allies, it still retains formidable assets to influence domestic and international policy in Venezuela. If it discarded its '1990s ideal' and adapts to the new realities of nationalism and social welfare, Washington's clients could make a comeback of sorts as an opposition.

Throughout Latin America, the center-left regimes in Argentina, Brazil, Bolivia, Uruguay and elsewhere have severely weakened the mass movements, de-radicalized the demands of social struggles and, at least, partially re-legitimized the privatizations, which took place in the 1990s.

If we compare 2004-2006 to 2000-2003, it is clear that US power has not declined overall; it is not facing radical challenges to its extended military and economic presence in Latin America. Argentine President Kirchner has tamed and co-opted many of the insurrectionary leaders, channeled the rebellious lower middle class into electoral politics and the trade unions into commonplace 'wages and salary' struggles or at best toward 'reformist' programs. Even more striking, Brazilian President Lula da Silva has fully embraced the free market-free elections doctrine of the 1990s, and has deepened and extended the preceding Cardoso regime's restrictive budget, salary, and pension policies while extending its privatization program. No previous elected Brazilian president has been as successful as Lula in *demobilizing* mass movements and trade unions and even turning them into transmission belts for his pro-MNC, pro-international finance policies.

However Lula's embrace of the free market via an agro-mineral export strategy has set him on a collision course with the US protectionist-subsidized agro-export policies. It was Washington's intransigent belief that the US could 'have it all'—like in the 1990s—that undermined Brazil's willingness to sign onto FTAA. Today the same class forces rule Brazil's economy as in the 1990s. The same macro-economic stabilization policies are currently pursued as in the 1990s. The same Central Bank high interest-budget surplus policies are practiced as in the 1990s. While Brazil, *as in the past*, has diplomatic relations with Cuba and Venezuela, Lula's Foreign Minister, Celso Amorin, is a liberal, pro-Washington, former-Ambassador to the US under Cardoso. He is staunchly in favor of 'symmetrical free trade' and has dissociated Brazil from most of Chavez' criticisms of US imperialism. Brazil is proceeding to diversify its exports to Asia, pursue lucrative joint energy ventures with Venezuela and criticize one-sided trade agreements. This is part of the new reality that Washington has failed to grasp.

Lula could be a strategic asset in Washington's agenda of furthering opportunities for business and minimizing challenges from the nationalist and socialist forces in Brazil and throughout Latin America. In Brazil during the period of 1999-2001 (prior to Lula's election) there was a robust extra-parliamentary and Congressional opposition to neo-liberalism, a badly discredited US client regime, and widespread political demands to reverse Cardoso's privatizations. During the six years of Lula's regime, he has re-enforced the neo-liberal economy, favored US financial and business interests, and pursued greater integration into the world market. The attempt by the US to pressure Brazil into even further ideological conformity and into unacceptable one-sided trade agreements is the principal obstacle to its gaining greater influence in Brazil.

Empire-building in a Time of New Political and Economic Realities

Power does not simply flow from the structures of US collaborators whether they include big business groups, client regimes, and US trained economists embedded in Ministries. Power also emanates from organized classes, ethnic communities and quasi-spontaneous popular uprisings. The latter can, in certain circumstances, challenge or overthrow client regimes, and in exceptional periods abolish institutions that collaborate with US imperialism.

As we have seen over the past half-century, US-Latin American relations are not fixed in time and place. They are fluid and reversible (in both directions) within decades or shorter time frames. The frequent impressionistic commentaries by discursive writers of a long-term decline of US power or hegemony or that speak of 'five-hundred years of domination' fail to account for the changing correlations of forces within Latin America and in the world, the shifts in global markets and the rise and fall and re-emergence of US adversaries both in Latin America and the world.

In recent history we have witnessed alternative periods of high levels of US influence over Latin America and other movements of declining power and the emergence of significant counter-hegemonic regimes and movements. The strategic basis of US power in Latin America is structural. It is located among the peak business, agro-mineral and banking elites, backed by collaborator regimes and state institutions (military, judicial, central banks, intelligence agencies and mass media). From 'the outside', US influence is exercised via its military programs and through the IMF and World Bank, the OAS and the IDB. US intelligence operations and political front groups provide additional institutional leverage over Latin American decision-making. The principal strategic weaknesses of US power in Latin America is found in client rulers who, in pursuit of US interests, quickly lose legitimacy, public support and are vulnerable to overthrow. Their 'free market' and structural adjustment policies favor US business and banks, but prejudice wage and salaried workers, peasants, small business and public employees and professionals. As a result the great majority of organized social movements are opposed to US policies. There are virtually no mass pro-US movements. Latin American historical experience and consciousness, particularly nationalist sentiment, is deeply suspicious of and predisposed to question the US motivations, presence and policies.

The Shortsightedness of Historical Projections

Linear views of long-term tendencies in the exercise of US power in Latin America are almost always shortsighted and have repeatedly over the past 50 years been demonstrated to have been wrong. Even a cursory view of the dramatic shifts in power in the most recent six years provides ample evidence that power shifts can be abrupt and profound.

The fall of client regimes and the wave of insurrectionary and anti-neo-liberal movements during 2000-2002 were followed by five years of relatively stable neo-liberal regimes. Their rulers defend established US and EU business and banking interests, make early payments on foreign debts, allocate budget surpluses to pay the debt and neutralized anti-imperialist movements in Argentina, Brazil, Uruguay, Peru and elsewhere. The 'new reality' is a *partial* recovery of the power and dominance exercised by the US during the Golden Age of the 1990s.

While ill-informed and ideologically driven policymakers in the Bush Administration and among US and European progressives emphasize the nominal 'left' credentials of the new regimes especially in Argentina, Brazil, Uruguay and Bolivia, the reality is that little has changed in the basic property, class and income structures of those countries. Small recoveries in wages and salaries have been matched by losses in pensions or other social benefits. The changes initiated by some of these regimes have in some cases even been in the direction of furthering US interests. In 2007 Uruguay signed an unprecedented bilateral free trade and investment agreement with the US which will favor a few Uruguayan beef and mutton exporters while opening up lucrative financial, banking and tourist facilities to US MNCs . Brazil is pursuing labor and pension 'reform' programs to lower the cost and increase the ease of firing workers, while further reducing spending on public sector pensions. In Argentina a number of corrupt Supreme Court Justices, police and military officers were retired without facing charges, although some senior military officials, implicated in mass killings and torture during the dictatorship, are facing trial.

In Bolivia and Venezuela (to date at least), only moderate increases in royalty and tax payments by US, Brazilian and EU multinationals have taken place. Bolivia has secured modest increases in the price of gas charged to Argentina. Even in these so-called 'radical regimes' basic US and EU interests have not been expropriated, though again, it seems that Venezuela is heading in this direction. In Bolivia new invitations for further investments have been tendered under terms only slightly less favorable than occurred during the 1990s. Bolivia and Venezuela, by substituting profit sharing agreements for naked pillage, are modifying—not ending—US operations in Latin America. Venezuela has succeeded in implementing and enforcing its new contracts with the MNCs far more effectively than the inept regime of Evo Morales. Even in Cuba, large-scale, long-term foreign investments are found in various economic sectors ranging from joint ventures with Israeli-managed citrus plantations, to Spanish-owned tourist hotels and resorts, Mexican and Chinese-owned manufacturing and mining operations, and French and Venezuelan-owned petroleum exploration, biotechnology and pharmaceutical ventures. As of 2006, US agro-business exporters from 34 states have sold over $1 billion dollars in farm products to the Cuban market in the past decade. Cuban foreign policy has moved toward closer ties with Colombia's rightwing President Uribe, supports Brazil's incumbent neo-liberal President Lula da Silva and purchases many times more agricultural commodities from the US than from its radical ally, Bolivia.

The failure of Washington to exploit the favorable conjuncture of 2003-2006 is a result of its own ideological extremism, based on unrealistic criteria. This includes the idea that the servility of Latin American regimes in the 1990s and their full compliance with US demands can be replicated. The neo-conservative and anti-Cuba policymakers cannot adapt to the new realities and exploit the new opportunities. The politics of confrontation with Venezuela and Cuba under highly unfavorable domestic and international circumstances has led Washington into a blind ally. Today it is Washington which is isolated from the great majority of the non-aligned countries, as well as from its allies in Europe and Latin America regarding its economic embargo. The real issue facing US policymakers is not whether to continue a losing confrontation with pragmatic regimes like Cuba, Venezuela and Bolivia in the hope of precipitating their immediate collapse but whether to recognize that mutual accommodation can lessen international hostility and safeguard strategic US economic interests.

For the Left, the possibility of radical change in Latin America is largely dependent on continuing US intransigence and insistence on a return to the 'Golden Age of Pillage'. Advances by the Left can begin by recognizing that a minority of trade unions and some movements are challenging the neo-liberal presidents in Brazil, Argentina and Uruguay. The Left needs to recognize that in both Bolivia and Venezuela there are deep social fissures within and between the governing parties and between the latter and the working class. It is insufficient to merely focus on the conflict between Chavez and Morales on the one hand and the right-wing opposition from the upper classes and the US on the other.

Four Competing Blocs of Power

In reality there are four competing blocs of nations in Latin America, contrary to the highly simplistic dualism portrayed by the White House and most of the Left. Each of these four blocs represents different degrees of accommodation or opposition to US policies and interests. Moreover much depends on how the US defines or re-defines its interests under the new realities.

The *radical left* includes the FARC guerrillas in Colombia, sectors of the trade unions and peasant and barrio movements in Venezuela; the labor confederation CONLUTAS and sectors of the Rural Landless Movement in Brazil; sectors of the Bolivian Labor Confederation (COB), and the Andean peasant movements and barrio organizations in El Alto; sectors of the peasant-indigenous movement CONAIE in Ecuador; sectors of the teachers and peasant-indigenous movements in Oaxaca, Guerrero and Chiapas in Mexico; sectors of the nationalist-peasant-left in Peru; sectors of the trade union and unemployed workers in Argentina. In addition, there are numerous other social movements in Central and South America and a plethora of small Marxist groups in Argentina, Bolivia, Chile and elsewhere. Together these organizations form a heterodox, dispersed political bloc, which is staunchly anti-imperialist, rejects any concessions to neo-liberal socio-economic policies, opposes debt payments and generally supports a socialist or radical nationalist program.

The *pragmatic left* includes President Chavez in Venezuela, Morales in Bolivia and Castro in Cuba as well as a multiplicity of large electoral parties and major peasant and trade unions in Central and South America. Included here are the left electoral parties, the PRD in Mexico, the FMLN in El Salvador, the left electoral bloc and the labor confederation (CUT) in Colombia, the Chilean Communist Party, the majority in Peruvian nationalist Humala's parliamentary party, leadership sectors of the MST in Brazil, the MAS governing party in Bolivia, the second largest labor confederation (the CTA) in Argentina, and a minority of the Broad Front and the labor confederation (PIT-CNT) in Uruguay. The great majority of left Latin American intellectuals are found among this political bloc.

It is worthwhile to examine why this bloc is referred to as the 'pragmatic' left. First of all Venezuela, Bolivia and the entire spectrum of above-mentioned social movements, trade union confederations, parties and fractions of parties do not call for or practice the expropriation of capitalism, the repudiation of the debt, the complete expropriation of US or EU banks or multinational corporations, or any rupture in relations with the US.

For example, in Venezuela, private national and foreign banks earned an over thirty percent rate of return in 2005-2007. Foreign-owned oil companies reaped record profits between 2004-2007. Less than one percent of the biggest landed estates were fully expropriated and titles turned over to landless peasants. Capital-labor relations still operate in a framework heavily weighted on behalf of business and labor contractors who rely on subcontractors who continue to dominate hiring and firing in more than one half of the large enterprises. The Venezuelan military and police continue to arrest suspected Colombian guerrillas and activists and turn them over to the Colombian police. Venezuela and US-client President Uribe of Colombia have signed several high-level security and economic co-operation agreements. While promoting Latin American integration (excluding the US) Chavez has looked toward greater 'integration' with neo-liberal Brazil and Argentina, whose oil production and distribution is controlled by European MNCs and US investors.

While Chavez attacks US attempts to subvert the democratic process in Venezuela, it still provides 12 percent of total US petroleum imports (not counting oil at reduced prices to benefit low income Americans in the Bronx and elsewhere), and owns 12,000 CITGO gasoline stations in the US and several refineries. Finally Venezuela's political system is wide open to influence by the private mass media, which are overwhelmingly hostile to the democratically elected president and Congress. US-funded NGOs continue to act on behalf of US policymakers, as do a dozen pro-US political parties and a trade union confederation. The majority of pro-Chavez congressional members and officials are of very dubious nationalist credentials, having jumped on his political bandwagon more for personal advancement than from any populist loyalties. Many emigrated from defunct pro-US right wing political parties. In a word, Venezuela's pragmatism spells out a very lucrative field for US investors, a reliable supplier of energy and alliances with the US's major client (Colombia) in Latin America. The essence of the matter is that Chavez's radical rhetoric and discourse on 21st century socialism does not now or in the proximate future correspond to the political realities. If it were not for Washington's intransigent hostility and continued confrontation and destabilization tactics, even Chavez's discourse would likely be moderated. That sectors of big business complain about increased royalty payments, profit sharing and taxes is to be expected, but hardly the basis for Washington to engage in arms boycotts, cheap rhetorical shots and undercover subversion.

US-Venezuela relations embody what is wrong and has failed in Latin America. By comparing Chavez' policy with that of the previous Venezuelan client regimes during the 1990s, Washington is painting Chavez as a 'dangerous radical'. Taking into account the changed international environment of the 2000-2007 period, the limited social welfare, tax and other reforms, and taking Chavez' foreign policy pronouncements with a grain of salt, the US is in fact dealing with a pragmatic radical who can be accommodated. But that presumes that Washington rejects the 1990s as a standard for measuring friends and enemies. It presumes that Washington realizes that the favorable international conjuncture of the 1990s is gone and that it must accommodate moderate reforms and foreign policy differences to avoid a social revolution.

The same is true regarding US policy toward Cuba and Bolivia. Cuba has established diplomatic ties with almost all US clients and allies in Latin America, further undermining the US boycott of Cuba. It has explicitly extended a friendly diplomatic hand to US-backed Colombian President Uribe, rejects the revolutionary left (FARC) in Colombia, gives public support to neo-liberals like Lula of Brazil, Kirchner of Argentina and Vazquez in Uruguay and has signed a wide range of purchasing agreements with big US food exporters amounting to over $500 million dollars a year despite onerous terms.

Cuba has provided free health services to a large number of US client regimes ranging from Honduras and Haiti to Pakistan. This aid frees the reactionary regimes of any responsibility for taking care of their own people and allows them to continue allocating resources to the rich, and the police and military buttressing the status quo. So far, Cuban health programs have had zero effect on improving the political situation inside the recipient countries, and have not improved state-to-state relations. And equally important, this has deflected tens of millions of dollars and thousands of professionals from the urgent tasks of rebuilding and improving Cuba's own dilapidated hospitals and diagnostic services, not to speak of the crumbling housing in central Havana, the 1 million housing deficit and the horrendous public transport system. It is training thousands of doctors and educators from the poorest of US client states and has opened the door to foreign investors from four continents in all its major growth sectors. Paradoxically as Cuba has deepened its integration into the world capitalist market leading to the emergence of a new class of market-oriented elites, Washington has increased its ideological hostility because it sees the ideological merit in Cuba's extensions. By issuing military threats and exercising diplomatic pressure and provocations, the White House has strengthened radical tendencies in Cuban society. Washington has adopted a similar extremist posture toward the pragmatic-leftist Morales regime in Bolivia, whose 'nationalization' has not and will not expropriate any foreign-owned enterprise. One of Morales main purposes is to stimulate trade agreements between Bolivia's agro-business elite and the US.

The third and most numerous political bloc in Latin America are the *pragmatic neo-liberals* which includes Brazil under Lula, Kirchner's Argentina and the major trade union confederations in Brazil and Argentina, sectors of the big business and financial elites and the principal provincial political bosses handing out subsistence unemployment doles and food baskets. There are numerous imitators of these regimes among left-liberal opposition groups in Ecuador, Nicaragua (the Sandinistas and their split-offs), Paraguay and elsewhere. Both Kirchner and Lula have defended the entire gamut of legal, semi-legal and illegal privatizations, which took place in the 1990s. Both have prepaid on their official debt obligations (though Argentina imposed a sixty percent discount on private debt holders). Both have pursued agro-mineral export growth strategies. Both have vastly increased financial and business profits while restraining wages and salaries. There are also differences between the two. Kirchner's pro-industry strategy has led to a growth rate over twice that of Lula and he has reduced unemployment by fifty percent (from a high base figure) compared to Lula's failed employment policies. In other words, the investment environment for US business-people and bankers in Argentina and Brazil is as favorable to profit making (or even more so for US bankers in Brazil) as it was during the 'Golden Years' of the 1990s.

The major changes in relations between the pragmatic neo-liberals and Washington are in the negotiations over a free trade agreement. The vast increase in global trade opportunities and the stronger market position of elite export producers and manufacturers within Latin America gives them a stronger negotiating position. Both Lula and Kirchner will have nothing to do with extremist-militarist US efforts to overthrow or boycott Chavez *because* they have growing and lucrative market investments and joint oil/gas projects in the works. They recognize the basically capitalist nature of the Chavez regime even as they reject most of his radical anti-imperialist discourse. Likewise both presidents are diversifying trading partners and pursuing markets with US competitors in China and Asia because it is lucrative, revenue generating and *part of their neo-liberal practice.*

There is a clear difference between the market-oriented and free trade-driven policy of Argentina and Brazil and the militarist, ideologically driven US policy toward Venezuela, Cuba, the Middle East and elsewhere.

While Washington is not hostile to Argentina and has a friendly working relation with Brazil, it has failed to fully exploit the possibilities of extending influence because of its refusal to recognize the emergence of a kind of 'nationalist' free trade regime. Measuring Argentina against the 1990s 'Golden Age of Pillage' under President Carlos Menem, Kirchner's pursuit of negotiated agreements, regulated investments, tax collection and debt re-negotiations is seen as 'nationalist', 'leftist' and barely tolerable. Likewise Washington, accustomed to Cardoso's role as a Washington client, is disturbed by the fact that Lula's free market policies include a demand that the US end agricultural subsidies and quotas *as well as Brazil.* Once again Washington's extremism sacrifices large-scale, long-term US entry into Brazil's industrial and service sector in order to defend uncompetitive US farm enterprises. Washington's attitude is more akin to a 19th century colonial (or mercantile) power than a 21st century market-based empire-builder, especially when faced with pragmatic rulers looking to build their own regional power bases.

The fourth political bloc is the doctrinaire neo-liberal regimes, parties and elite associations, which closely follow Washington's dictates. This includes the Calderon regime in Mexico, preparing to privatize the lucrative public petroleum and electrical firms, the Bachelet regime in Chile—the perennial agro-mineral-exporter, and the countries of Central America—the tropical fruit and assembly plant exporters (El Salvador, Nicaragua, Honduras, Costa Rica and Guatemala). The latter were brought into the US orbit subsequent to the killing of over 300,000 people between the late 1970s and early 1990s. Colombia, another member of the hard-line neo-liberal bloc, is recipient of $5 billion dollars in US military aid since the late 1990s. Peru, which over the past twenty years has privatized almost all of its mineral wealth, is governed by US client President Alan Garcia who continues the same policies. Paraguay has become the biggest military base for Washington. In Uruguay, a regime of ex-leftists has signed onto a new free trade agreement with the US and agreed to a military training base.

In the Caribbean, the US occupies Haiti via the UN after overthrowing and abducting the elected President Bertram Aristide, and has a loyal ally in the Dominican Republic (President Leonel Fernandez). In other words,

Washington dominates a 'Pacific Arc' of loyal clients extending from Mexico, through Central America down the Southern Pacific coast, including Colombia, Peru and Chile. While the political labels, rhetoric and degree of stability vary, these regimes all embrace US-backed doctrines of the free market, mostly follow the US lead in regional and international forums and in one degree or another openly or surreptitiously oppose Venezuela and Cuba. Powerful pragmatic leftist movements challenge these client regimes, especially in Mexico, El Salvador, Peru and Colombia (including the radical left in the latter). Nevertheless for the immediate future, Washington has a loyal bloc of follower regimes even as, over the middle course, this could change abruptly.

Conclusion

Claims by Washington and right-wing ideologues that 'radical populism' is sweeping the region are self-serving and gross simplifications of a complex reality. Instead there is a 'quadrangle of competing and conflicting forces' within Latin America. There are also new and changing international scenarios, which complicate any attempt to pigeonhole policies with either/or choices. Washington has emphasized the subversive influence of Venezuela and Cuba in weakening US dominance in Latin America. A far more important factor is the across the board rise in commodity prices of goods which are major export earners for Latin America. This means that the Latin American countries have less need to rely on IMF 'conditions' for securing loans, thus severely limiting US political leverage. Secondly the greater liquidity means that commercial loans can be secured without resorting to the World Bank, another instrument of US influence in Latin American political and economic policy making. Thirdly the rapidly expanding markets in Asia and particularly the growth of Asian investment in Latin America's extractive industries have further eroded US market leverage in Latin America over and above what Washington possessed in the 1990s. Fourthly with the slowdown of the US economy in 2007, the US is expected to lessen its investments and trade with Latin America. In other words, Washington has less market leverage over pragmatic leftists and neo-liberals than it possessed during the 1990s. To continue to act in the late-2000s as if Washington's relative loss of influence reflects the ebb and flow of political forces (radical populism) within the region is to pursue failed policies. Mislabeling regimes and exaggerating the degree and kind of opposition leads to the exacerbation of conflicts. Furthermore Washington's persistence in believing that it can secure continent-wide free trade agreements based on non-reciprocal concessions (particularly in agriculture) could cause it to lose out on opportunities for trade deals.

Washington's over-politicization and ideological labeling of changes in US-Latin American relations is a result of the ultra-conservative configuration of policymakers and their principal advisers in Washington.

If Washington has grossly misrepresented Latin American political reality and misreads the current regional and international context, the Left is hardly more prescient. Leftist intellectuals exaggerate the radicalism or revolutionary reality of Cuba and Venezuela. They overlook the contradictory realities and their pragmatic accommodations with neo-liberals of all stripes. The Left, with little historical perspicacity, continues to categorize pragmatic neo-liberals like Lula, Kirchner and Vazquez as 'progressives', lumping them together with pragmatic leftists like Chavez, Castro and Morales. In many cases they characterize parties and regimes based on their past leftist political identities prior to coming to power, rather than their current free market, pro-agro-mineral elite policies once in government. The Left confuses the pragmatic neo-liberal regimes' efforts to negotiate symmetrical free market trade agreements with the US as some sort of 'anti-globalization' policy or as a 'counterweight' to US power.

The Left has to face up to the fact that while US power has declined relative to the 'Golden Age of Pillage' during the 1990s, it has *recovered* and *advanced* since the mass rebellions and overthrow of client regimes of 2000-2002. The hopes that the Left had that the presidential victories of former center-left electoral parties in Brazil, Uruguay and Argentina, would augur a reversion of the neo-liberal policies of their predecessors have been demonstrably dashed. The attempt to redefine the conversion of the ex-leftist-turned-pragmatic neo-liberals into something progressive or as a 'counterweight' to US power is disingenuous at best and at worst compounds the initial error. The Left's lack of political clarity regarding political changes has led it into a blind alley as damaging to its future growth as are Washington's failed efforts to recognize the new realities.

The only consistent and consequential allies and forces for change are found among the radical left. Tactical and selective alliances between the radical and pragmatic left are necessary and important, but only if they are based on retaining organizational and political independence. For the Left there needs to be a critical analysis and vigorous debate on the disastrous consequences of subordinating their activities to the electoral campaigns of what are now dominant pragmatic neo-liberal regimes. A review of the strength of the social movements in toppling doctrinaire neo-liberal US client regimes is as necessary as a critical analysis of the incapacity of these same movements to block the re-emergence of new 'pragmatic' neo-liberals. Above all the social movements need to discuss strategies for taking power. This implies a program for governing, transforming the economy and state as well as a leadership responsive to the radical demands of the social bases of the movement and an organization capable of organizing the ouster of the old regime and transforming the state.

While US power over Latin America has declined since the 1990s it has not been a linear process; a sharp fall has been followed by a partial recovery. The decline of the US has not been matched by a sustained rise in the power of the radical left. The real 'gainers' have been the pragmatic leftists and neo-liberals who rode to power with the demise of the doctrinaire neo-liberals and the favorable expansive conjuncture in world market conditions. There are neither inherent long-term 'laws of imperial decline' as some Leftist historians claim, nor 'an end of the revolutionary left' as their neo-liberal counterparts claim. Rather a realistic analysis demonstrates that political interventions, class conflict and international markets will continue to play a major role in shaping US-Latin American relations and more particularly the ascent and decline of US imperial power, social revolutionary forces and the other political variants in between.

CHAPTER 13

NEW WINDS FROM THE LEFT OR HOT AIR FROM A NEW RIGHT?

Introduction

Several years ago I asked an editor of a leading US business journal (*Forbes*) about a Mexican President (Echevarria) who was speaking at a Leftist conference commemorating Chilean President Allende.

He answered, "He talks to the Left and works for the Right".

A factual review of the performance of the recent "center-left" presidents in Latin America fits very well with the comment of that *Forbes* editor, and goes contrary to much of the opinion of the European and US Left.

What is "Left": Method

Prior to any discussion of the "center-left" regimes in Latin America today, it is important to review exactly what it means to be left—from a historical, theoretical and practical perspective. The method for determining "What is left" is based on analyzing the substance of a regime or politician and not the symbols or rhetoric. The practical measures include budgets, property, income, employment, labor legislation, priorities in expenditures and revenues. The key is to focus on the *present* social referents, social configurations of power and alliances—not those of the past—given the changing dynamics of power and class politics. The third methodological issue is to differentiate between a political campaign and the policies of a political party once in power, as there is a well-known enormous discrepancy between them.

What is Left: Criteria

Historically and empirically there is a consensus among academics and activists as to what constitute criteria and indicators for defining Left politics. These include:

1. Decreasing social inequalities,

2. Increasing living standards,

3. Increasing public and national ownership over private and foreign ownership,

4. Instituting progressive taxes (income/corporate) over regressive taxes (VAT, consumption),

5. Prioritizing greater budgetary social expenditures and public investments in jobs rather than subsidies to business elites and foreign debt payments,

6. Promoting and protecting national ownership of raw materials over foreign exploitation,

7. Diversifying production to value-added products as opposed to selling unprocessed raw materials,

8. Subordinating export production to the development of the domestic market,

9. Enhancing popular participation and power in decision-making as opposed to elite decision-making by businesses, international bankers (IMF) and political elites,

10. Consulting with mass movements in the selection of key cabinet ministers instead of with local and foreign business elites,

11. Adopting an anti-imperialist foreign policy rejecting free-markets, military bases and imperial wars and occupations,

12. Reversing prejudicial privatizations / against extending and consolidating privatizations,

13. Increasing the minimum wage,

14. Rejecting excessive foreign debt payments and

15. Promoting labor legislation facilitating trade union organization, and universal free public education and health services.

With these criteria in mind we can proceed to analyze and evaluate the contemporary "center-left" regimes to determine whether "*new winds from the Left*" are sweeping Latin America.

Brazil: President Lula to 2007

Even prior to his election, Lula signed a letter of understanding with the IMF (June 2002) to pay the foreign debt, to maintain a budget surplus of four percent (up to 4.5 percent subsequently), to maintain macro-economic stability and to continue neo-liberal 'reforms'. It was a political agreement intended to pacify and assure international finance capital that he was eager and ready to betray millions of supporters to satisfy the interests of finance capital—and he spent the next five years proving it

Lula had a mandate to recover the billion-dollar Vale del Doce iron mine, and Petrobras (main stock holders private mostly US), and to carry out an agrarian reform. He had a clear majority, mass backing and a disoriented opposition—a capitalist system on the defensive. The context was most propitious for radical changes or positive reforms, but Lula did the opposite—not because he was "forced" but because he was convinced that was the way to go.

Upon election he slashed public employee pensions by thirty percent (and bragged that he had the "courage" to carry out IMF "reforms"[1] where previous right-wing presidents failed). Agrarian policy was directed toward financing and subsidizing agro-business exports, while the agrarian reform program stagnated and even regressed. Lula's promise to his "ally", the Landless Workers Movement (MST), to distribute land to 100,000 families a year was totally disregarded.[2] To "promote" capital investment, Lula introduced labor legislation increasing the power of employers to fire workers and lowering the cost of severance pay. Social programs in health and education were sharply reduced by over five percent during the first three years, while foreign debt creditors received punctual (and even early) payments of $150 billion dollars—making Brazil a "model" debtor. Lula extended past privatizations of dubious legality in such lucrative sectors as petrol (Petrobras), mining (Vale del Doce), and banks, to public infrastructure, services and telecommunications—reversing seventy years of history and making Brazil more vulnerable to foreign owned re-locations of production.

Brazil increasingly took on the profile of a primary producer, as its exports of iron, soya, sugar, citrus juice, and timber expanded. Its industrial sector stagnated due to the world's highest interest rates of 18.5 percent and the lowering of tariff barriers to imported products. Over 25,000 shoe workers lost their jobs due to cheap Chinese imports. Brazil, after Guatemala, remained the country with the greatest inequalities in Latin America. Lula's pro-agro-export policy led to accelerated exploitation of the Amazon rain forest and deep incursions into Brazilian Indian territory, thanks to budget cuts in the Environmental and Indigenous Affairs Agencies.

In foreign policy, Lula sent troops and generals to occupy Haiti and defend the puppet regime resulting from the US orchestrated invasion and deposition of elected President Aristide. Lula's differences with the US over FTAA were clearly over US compliance with "free trade" and not over any defense of national interests. As Lula stated, "Free trade is the best system, providing everyone practices it"—meaning his *opposition* revolved around US subsidies and protection of agriculture.

Lula's key *economic* ministers and central bankers were primarily right-wing bankers, corporate executives and neo-liberal ideologues linked to the IMF and multinational corporations. They occupied the Finance, Economy, Trade, Agriculture Ministries and the Central Bank.

While Lula opposed the US-sponsored coup against Venezuela in April 2002 as well as other extremist measures and spoke for greater Latin American integration via MERCOSUR, in practice his major trade policies focused on deepening Brazil's ties outside the region—with Asia, Europe and North America.

The empirical data on all the key indicators demonstrate that Lula now fits the profile of a right-wing neo-liberal politician, not a "center-leftist" president. Intellectuals and journalists who classify Lula as a leftist rely on his social, trade union and occupational background, twenty to thirty years earlier and his theatrical populist symbolic gestures.

Argentina: President Kirchner, 2003-2007

Under President Kirchner Argentina has grown at a rate of 8.5 percent per year, substantially increased export earnings, reduced unemployment from over twenty percent to approximately fifteen percent, raised pensions and wages, re-negotiated a portion of the private foreign debt and rescinded the laws granting impunity to military torturers. Compared to Lula's ultra-liberal policies, Kirchner appears to be a progressive leader.

Looked at from a leftist perspective, however, the regime still falls far short. Kirchner has not reversed any of the fraudulent privatizations of Argentina's strategic energy, petroleum and electrical industries. Under his regime, profits of major agro-industrial and petroleum sectors have skyrocketed with no commensurate increases in salaries. In other words, inequalities have either increased or remained the same depending on the sectors. While Kirchner has financed and subsidized the revival of industry and promotion of agro-exports, salaries and wages have barely reached the level of 1998—the year before the economic crisis. Moreover while poverty levels have declined from their peak of over fifty percent in 2001, they are still close to thirty percent—for a country which produces enough grain and meat to supply a population six times the size of Argentina. While unemployment has declined, one out of seven Argentines is still out of work. The unemployment relief remains at $50 per family per month. While nominal salaries have increased, growing inflation of over ten percent has reduced real earnings for the majority of public employees. The structures of socio-economic power remain in place—in fact Kirchner has played a major role in restoring and consolidating capitalist hegemony after the mass popular uprisings of December 2001. He has redistributed neither property, income nor power—except among the different segments of the capitalist class.

Kirchner's central banker and economic and finance ministers have long-term ties to international capital and banks. While economic growth and some social amelioration have taken place, much of it can be attributed to the favorable world commodity prices for beef, grains, petroleum and other prime materials. In foreign policy, Kirchner, like Lula, opposes FTAA because the US has refused to reciprocate in lowering its tariff barriers.

Kirchner's foreign policy is hardly anti-imperialist: Argentine troops occupy Haiti at the behest of the US and engage in joint maneuvers with the US. While Kirchner repudiated the law of impunity, few new trials and punishments have been meted out. While Kirchner opposes US attacks on Venezuela, he supports the US proposal to refer Iran to the Security Council of the UN. His criticism of Washington only extends to the most extreme interventionist measures which prejudice Argentine big business and convert it into a powerless client—a reason why Argentina opposes the State Department's attempt to form an *anti-Chavez bloc*. Kirchner's rejection is assuredly colored by the facts that Argentina has secured a major shipbuilding contract and has signed lucrative trade agreements with Venezuela to market its agricultural and manufactured products. With regard to Cuba, Kirchner opened diplomatic relations but has maintained his distance. While on excellent diplomatic terms with Chavez, he shares none of his redistributive policies.

Kirchner's agreement with private debt holders, which originally was presented as a substantial victory in debt payment reduction, has turned out otherwise. A clause in the agreement increased payments in accordance with Argentina's growth rates—which have been over eight percent. As a result, billions of dollars have flowed to debt holders.

In conclusion, Kirchner meets none of our criteria as a leftist. He is more clearly a pragmatic conservative willing to dissent from the US when it is profitable for his agro-business and industrial capitalist social base. At no point has Kirchner shifted any of the budget surplus now used to pay the foreign debt to fund the deteriorated health and educational facilities and to provide better salaries for personnel in those vital public sectors.

Uruguay: President Tabare Vazquez

Tabare Vazquez was elected by an electoral coalition (The Broad Front and Progressive Encounter), which included Tupamaros (ex-guerrillas), Communists, Socialists and an assortment of Christian Democrats and social liberals. However his key appointments to the Central Bank and the Economic Ministry (such as Danilo Astori) are hardline neo-liberals. They defend budgeting constraints on social spending while generously financing the agro-export elites.

During the Economic Summit in Mar de Plata, Argentina, in November 2005, while tens of thousands protested against Bush, and Chavez declared FTAA dead, Tabare Vazquez and Astori signed a wide-reaching 'investment protection' agreement with the US, which embraced the major free market principles embodied in FTAA. Astori, with Tabare Vazquez' backing, has not only rejected re-nationalization of enterprises, but has proposed to proceed to privatize major state enterprises including a water company, despite a popular referendum vote which exceeded 65 percent in favor of maintaining state ownership. The Tabare Vazquez regime has taken no measures to lessen inequalities and has put in place a paltry "job creation" and emergency food relief program which covers a small fraction of the needs of poor, indigent and unemployed Uruguayans.

Meanwhile the government has laid down the royal carpet for a Finnish-owned, highly contaminating cellulose factory which will prejudice fishing communities and perhaps even the important tourist facilities downstream. Tabare Vazquez and Astori's unilateral signing off on the controversial factory has resulted in a major conflict with Argentina which borders the Uruguay River where the plant will be located.

The Tabare Vazquez regime has repudiated every major programmatic position embraced by the Broad Front (Frente Amplio) in its 35 years of existence: sending troops in support of the occupation of Haiti, privatizing public properties, embracing free trade, welcoming foreign investment and imposing moderate wage and salary increases on the working class. Tabare Vazquez, like Kirchner, re-established diplomatic relations with Cuba, but he avoids any close relationship with either Cuba or Venezuela.

Probably the most bizarre aspect of the Broad Front government is the behavior of the leadership of the Tupamaros, the former urban guerrilla group, now converted into Senators and Ministers. Minister of Agriculture Mujica supports agro-business and foreign investment in agriculture while upholding the law on evicting landless squatters. Senator Eleuterio Huidobro attacks human rights groups demanding judicial investigations against military officials implicated in assassinations and disappearances of political prisoners. According to Huidobro, the "past is best forgotten". He embraces the military and turns his back on scores of his former comrades who were tortured, murdered and buried in unmarked graves.

Bolivia: President Evo Morales

Probably the most striking example of the "center-left" regimes that have embraced the neo-liberal agenda is the Morales regimes in Bolivia.

Between October 2003 and July 2005, scores of factory and unemployed urban workers and Indian peasants were killed in the struggle for the nationalization of petroleum and gas, Bolivia's most lucrative economic sector. Two presidents were overthrown by mass uprisings in two and a half years for defending foreign ownership of the energy resources. Evo Morales did not participate in either uprising; in fact he supported the hastily installed neo-liberal President Carlos Mesa until he, too, was driven from power.

As president, Evo Morales has totally and categorically rejected the expropriation of gas and petroleum. He has provided explicit long-term, large-scale guarantees that all the facilities of the major energy multinational corporations will be recognized, respected and protected by the state. As a consequence, the MNCs have expressed their support for Morales-style 'nationalizations'. Through a not-too-clever semantic manipulation, Morales claims that "nationalization" is not expropriation and transfer of property to the state. According to Morales' "new" definition, private-public ownership of shares, tax increases and promises to "industrialize" the raw materials are equivalent to nationalization. While the exact terms of the new contracts have yet to be published, all the major MNCs are in agreement with Morales policies. The proof is that Petrobras, the primarily privately-owned Brazilian oil and gas giant, is prepared to invest $5 billion dollars over the next six years in the exploitation of gas and petroleum and in the construction of a petrol-chemical complex. Repsol (the Spanish MNC), promises to invest $150 million dollars, Total (French MNC), BP (British MNC) and every other major energy and mining MNC are prepared to expand investments and reap billions in profits under the protective umbrella of Morales and his MAS (Movement to Socialism) regime. No previous regime in Bolivian history has opened the country to mineral exploitation by so many MNCs in such lucrative fields in such a short period of time. In addition to oil and gas sell-offs, Morales has declared he will proceed to privatize the Mutun iron fields (60 square kilometers with an estimated 40 billion tons of iron with an estimated worth of over $30 billion dollars), following the lead of his neo-liberal predecessors. The only changes which Morales will introduce in the bidding is to raise the share of taxes Bolivia will receive from $0.50 (US cents) a ton to an undisclosed "but reasonable" (according to the MNCs) amount.

Contrary to his promises, Morales has refused to triple the minimum wage. His Minister of the Economy is prepared to retain the previous regime's policies of fiscal austerity and "macro-economic stability" while the increase in the minimum wage will amount to less than ten percent. The Morales government raised the teachers' base salary a meager seven percent, which in real terms amounts to less than two percent. The teachers' base salary is $75 US dollars a month, so their net gain under the new 'revolutionary' Indian president is less than $2 dollars a month (and this at a time of record prices for Bolivian raw material exports)…at a time of a budget surplus, no less.

Evo Morales, the *cocalero* (cocoa farmer) leader, declared his support for the continued presence of the US military base at Chapare, and the intrusive presence of the US Drug Enforcement Agency. Morales supports the reduction of the areas of coca production to less than half an acre for medical uses, in keeping with US policy demands, though enforcement is lax.

Morales' appointments to the economic, defense and other ministries have been linked to the IMF, World Bank and to previous neo-liberal regimes.

Morales and his Agricultural Minister are opposed to any expropriations of any large landowners, "whether they are owners of…5,000, 10,000, or 25,000 or more acres as long as they are productive". This has effectively put an end to the hopes of millions of landless Indian peasants for a "profound agrarian reform" as promised by the Indian President. Instead Morales is promoting agro-export agriculture with generous subsidies and tax incentives. Whatever land redistribution may occur in the future will occur with regard to public lands in inhospitable regions.

Most indicative of Morales' pro-big business policies was the February 2006 signing of a pact with the Confederation of Private Businessmen of Bolivia, in which he promised to maintain "macro-economic stability" and the "international credibility" of the country. This, in effect, meant curtailing social spending, promoting foreign investment, prioritizing exports, maintaining monetary stability and above all, promoting private investors. Morales' abject servility before the Bolivian capitalist elite was evident in his decision to re-activate the National Business Council which will analyze and take decisions on economic and political issues. Morales said, "I am asking the businessmen to support me with their experience" (forgetting to add their experience in exploiting the labor force). He went on to ask the businessmen to advise him on "FTAA, MERCOSUR… on agreements with China, the USA…as to their benefits for the country". The president of the Business Confederation, Guillermo Morales, immediately emphasized the importance of signing the free trade agreement.

While Morales was signing a business pact he refused to meet with the leaders of FEJUVE (The Federation of Neighborhood Councils of El Alto), the biggest, most active democratic urban organization in Bolivia which had played a primary role in the struggle overthrowing the previous neo-liberal presidents and demanding the nationalization of gas and petroleum. Morales received 88 percent of the vote in El Alto, which suffered scores of deaths and injuries in the run-up to his election. Morales named two ministers from FEJUVE, Mamani (Water Minister) and Patzi (Education Minister) but without consulting FEJUVE, which takes all decisions via popular assemblies. Both Ministers were forced to resign from FEJUVE, Patzi in part because he rejected the longstanding demand of creating a teacher's college for the 800,000 residents of El Alto, claiming it was an "unacceptable cost for the system" (given Morales' selective austerity budget). Equally reprehensible, Mamani has refused to expel the foreign multinational Aguas del Illimani, which overcharges consumers and fails to provide adequate services. (Subsequently, under mass pressure, Aguas was forced to leave.)

According to FEJUVE the Morales regime has failed to deal with the most elementary problems such as the exorbitant electricity rates, the absence of any plan to provide and connect households with heating gas and water lines. The major trade union confederations and federations (COB, Miners and others) have protested Morales' refusal to abrogate the reactionary labor laws passed by his predecessors which "flexibilized" labor"—empowering employers to hire and fire workers with impunity. In two years, Morales has raised the minimum wage on average only six percent, or $4 USD per month. In reward for his pro-business policies, Japan, Spain and the World Bank have "forgiven" Bolivia's foreign debt.

Morales has excelled in "public theater", adopting a "populist" folkloric style which engages the lower classes. He delivered part of his Presidential Speech to Congress in the indigenous Aymara language. He dances with the crowds during carnival. He declared a reduction of his presidential salary… as part of an austerity program lowering living standards for millions of poor Bolivians. He announced a "plot" against him by unspecified oil companies to rally support among his followers, while he signed away the country's energy resources…to the oil companies. Needless to say, neither the Defense or Interior Ministries were aware of the "plot", nor was any evidence ever presented. But the non-existent "plot" served to distract attention from his energy sellout. While Morales has spoken of his dear friend Hugo Chavez and embraced Fidel Castro, he has conceded US military bases and offices to the US Drug Enforcement Administration and signed off multi-billion dollars of Bolivia's energy and mining resources to the US, European and Brazilian MNCs. While Morales has improved diplomatic relations with Cuba and Venezuela and secured generous social and economic aid, the economic foundations of his policies and the dominant economic institutions are oriented toward integration with the Western imperial countries.

Empirical analysis demonstrates that the Morales regime is following in the footsteps of his neo-liberal predecessors in terms of his big business outlook and his obedience to IMF fiscal, monetary and budgetary policies. His policies, appointments, institutional ties and big business beneficiaries link him closer to the Center-Right than to any "Left-Wing".

A Note on Peru and Ecuador

At an early point in their taking office, the Left hailed the election of Toledo in Peru and Gutierrez in Ecuador, citing their plebian beginnings, their alliances with Indian organizations (such as CONAIE in Ecuador) or Indian origins (Toledo spoke Quechua and wore a poncho during his election campaign). Notwithstanding the fact that Toledo was a graduate of Stanford's neo-liberal graduate program and a functionary in the World Bank, the Left hailed his opposition to the Fujimori dictatorship (with US backing) as a sign that "change would come".

Indeed change did come, in the form of intensified privatizations of mining, water and energy, subsidies for agro-mining exporters, lifting of trade barriers and declining living standards for the poor and middle class. For the last three years in office Toledo's opinion ratings never exceeded 15 percent and mostly hovered below ten percent.

Gutierrez, once in office, embraced IMF doctrines, extended support to the US' Plan Colombia, backed the US military base in Manta, proposed the privatization of the state oil and electrical companies, jailed protesting trade union leaders, divided the Indian movement through selective funding and ties to right wing evangelical leaders. Eventually he was ousted in a popular uprising in 2005. The legacy of having supported Gutierrez was a much-weakened Indian social movement (CONAIE), the discrediting of Pachacutik, its fraternal party, and a decapitated trade union movement.

It was only after the political damage was an accomplished fact that the Left belatedly recognized the reactionary nature of the Gutierrez and Toledo regimes, dissociated themselves from them, and stopped referring to them as part of the "New Left Winds".

The Misleading Acclaim of Left Intellectuals

Great majorities in Latin America—workers, peasants, unemployed and poor have—have suffered grave consequences from their movements' support for "center-left" parties and coalitions. Much of the blame must fall on their immediate leaders, some of whom were co-opted, and others deceived, manipulated or self-deceived.

But part of the fault also lies with Leftist intellectuals, journalists, NGOs, and academics who wrote and spoke in favor of the "center-left" politicians and parties. They promoted their virtues, their histories and their promises. They lauded their electoral promises, plebian backgrounds, and probity—in a vastly uninformed, uncritical and superficial manner. The list of Leftist intellectuals covers three continents and reads like a 'Who's Who' of the Left: Emir Sader, Michel Lowy, Heinz Dietrich, Perry Anderson, Atilio Boron, Raul Zibechi, Frei Betto, Noam Chomsky, and Ignacio Ramonet, among others. All to one degree or another, over a longer or shorter time, sang to the chorus of "New Left Winds are blowing in Latin America". A close reading of their writings reveals that the Left intellectuals were more influenced by the text and rhetoric of the "center-left" personalities and parties and less by their *class practices*, economic policies, strategic political appointments and their elite linkages prior to and after being elected.

In general, the Left intellectuals were seduced by political symbols, political forms and identity politics (especially the presence of "Indians" and women in positions of power) to the neglect of scrutinizing the socio-economic content and class nature of their policies. They made much of the "Indian", ethnic identity or social origins of the party or personality while failing to draw attention to their neo-liberal transformation, business elite reference groups, and their current socio-economic elite associates. They played into the political gestures and theater: the promises to reduce presidential salaries (Morales), ceremonies paying homage to past struggles (Tupamaros), weeping or 'feeling' for the poor (Lula) rather than to the selling off of strategic raw materials to foreign multinational corporations.

In part the Left intellectuals' judgments were impaired by a nostalgic remembrance of years past—when they knew Lula as a militant trade union leader (25 years before), the Frente Amplio as resisting the military dictatorship in Uruguay in the 1970s, Evo as the militant coca farmers leader in the 1990s, Kirchner as a sympathizer to the Montoneros in the 1970s. Writing on the basis of out of date identities, the Left intellectuals failed to intuit, analyze, understand or pursue the vast transformation from left to right. Instead they invented a non-existent but hospitable "Center-Left" which fit in with their wishes and desires to be 'against' the system while still being part of it.

Not a few left intellectuals were heartened by the "Center-Left's" diplomatic gestures of friendship to Cuba and Venezuela, the warm reception of Hugo Chavez, even the occasional embrace of progressive leaders. Perhaps they confused Cuba's and Venezuela's favorable diplomatic gestures toward the "center-left" regimes (understandable from the view of their state policies aimed at countering US pressures) as a general endorsement of their internal policies. Independent from the reasons for Cuban and Venezuelan support, the Left intellectuals purported to see a 'common purpose' within the "center left". Some even fantasized about a new 'left bloc' (Dietrich) based presumably on their policies deepening foreign ownership of strategic materials, widening social inequalities and promoting free trade...

Symbolic politics is usually visually accessible on the front pages of the mass media—it does not require a capacity to research, collect and analyze date. Insofar as the Left intellectuals have substituted the 'symbolic left" for the real existing converts to neo-liberalism, they are at ease in accepting invitations to presidential inaugurations, imbibing cocktails at receptions. They are enticed by their chance to be close to power—for many a new experience. The "Left Winds" blow through the empty space between their ears…

This would not matter—were it not for the fact that their writings, their prognostications, their affirming and accrediting of a co-opted Latin American leadership, echo through the concerned global public's understanding of current trajectories in Latin America, misleading (even disarming?) local and global supporters, while inciting imperial enemies, and depriving the "center-left" political leadership of the benefits or the lash of a meaningful critique.

Conclusion

There are powerful left-wing forces in Latin America and later or sooner they will contest and challenge the power of the neo-liberal converts as well as their allies in Washington and in the multinational corporations. Sooner, in the case of Bolivia, where the scale and scope of Morales' broken promises and embrace of the business elite has already provoked the mobilization of the class-conscious trade unions, mass urban organizations, Indian (Aymara) communities and the landless peasants. The insurrectionary movements on whose back Morales rode to office are completely intact and their co-opted leaders replaced by new militants. The populist 'gestures' and 'folkloric' theater have only a limited time span for diversion in the face of the grinding poverty of class-conscious miners and the Indian militants in El Alto. The insurrectionary forces that brought Morales to power can also bring him down.

In Ecuador in January 2007, a massive popular demonstration led by trade unionists, Indian organizations, students and leftist coalitions seized the Congress in support of President Correa's demand for a new Constituent Assembly with legislative power to enact new socio-economic reforms.

In the past 4 years over $3 billion dollars of US military assistance has been spent on Plan Colombia by the Uribe state terrorist regime which includes 1,500 US Special Forces 'advisers'. Not only has the Washington-Uribe axis failed to defeat he Revolutionary Armed Forces of Colombia (FARC), they suffered major defeats between 2005-2007 in the face of a guerrilla offensive. Uribe was re-elected as president but at best he rules less than half of the country.

In Brazil, the Lula regime and its control and co-optation of the class collaborationist labor confederation (CUT) has led to the formation of a new militant confederation, ConLuta (founded in May 2006). The MST's critical collaboration with the Lula regime has led to a political impasse, provoking internal debates and a sharp decline in support within and outside of the organization. Following his re-election and embrace of the right, the MST is pursuing re-orientation toward class politics. The Brazilian left faces a "long march" to regain its former formidable presence. The case is similar in Uruguay and Argentina. The new "center-left" neo-liberal regimes, unlike the old right, have co-opted many of the leaders of the major trade unions and some of the unemployed workers groups through awarding them government posts, inclusion in Congressional electoral slates and generous stipends.

Venezuela's President Chavez stands as the major political figure representing a real *governmental* challenge to US imperialism. He has led the fight against FTAA and the US invasion of Haiti; he defeated a US-sponsored coup attempt and has demonstrated that social welfare, nationalism and political independence is viable in the Hemisphere. But as in Cuba, Chavez faces not only US aggression from the outside but contradictions from within. Many officials in his party (The Fifth Republic), the state apparatus and sectors of the military are not in favor of his proposed Twenty-First Century Socialism. Between Chavez and the 10 million voters who support him is a political apparatus of dubious political credentials with notable exceptions.

Likewise, Fidel Castro has spoken of a profound internal threat from a 'new class' of rich emerging from the scarcities of the Special Period (1992-2000) and the opening to tourism. He has called for a new revolution within the revolution. If there are 'New Left Winds blowing in Latin America' they come from Fidel's call for a new revolution within the Left, from Chavez insistence that socialism is the only alternative to capitalism, from the new mass leaders in Bolivia, Brazil and elsewhere as well as from the advancing 20,000-member guerrilla movement in Colombia.

The center-left regimes and their Left intellectual supporters represent a sad epitaph on the radical generation of the 1970s and 1980s. They are a spent force, lacking critical ideas and audacious proposals for challenging imperialism and capitalist rule. They will not fade away—they now have too much of a stake in the current system. A new generation of popular self-didactic leaders and young intellectual-militants is emerging in the urban councils of El Alto, in the new class-oriented trade unions of Brazil, and among the students joining the peasant fighters in the jungles of Colombia.

They are the "Left Winds" of Latin America.

.

CHAPTER 14

FOREIGN INVESTMENT IN LATIN AMERICA: SOCIAL COSTS AND POLITICAL RISKS

Introduction

This chapter focuses on the role of foreign investment in the development of Latin American countries. We challenge many of the arguments propounded by neo-liberal economists about the necessity for large-scale foreign investment in order to modernize and develop the forces of production and distribution. The first section of this chapter demystifies the impact that the entry of foreign investment has on the economy. We examine its role in the takeover of existing national firms, in increasing the competitiveness of the economy, and generating foreign exchange surpluses. The second section deals with the social and economic costs of state incentives to attract foreign investment. We discuss the perverse consequences privileging foreign investment has on state revenues as well as on social and public investments. We argue that there are real and tangible political risks in attracting foreign investment insofar as they limit future local development as well as invite imperial intervention in any disputes between foreign investors and the local state. In Chapter 15 we will set out a number of domestic sources for financing development which have fewer political risks, a more positive social impact on the work force, provide greater stability and increase indigenous innovative capacities. We argue that in limited circumstances of time and space foreign investment can play a complementary role under strict public oversight.

Part I: Six Myths about the Benefits of Foreign Investment

There are several myths about foreign investment propounded by orthodox economists and publicists for multinational corporations (MNCs), which are repeated and widely circulated by mass media journalists and editorial writers.

Myth #1: Foreign Investment (FI) creates new enterprises, gains or expands markets, and stimulates new research and development of local technological 'know-how'.

In fact most FI is directed toward buying privatized and profitable existing public enterprises and private firms, taking over existing markets and selling or renting technology designed and developed at the "home office". Since the late 1980s over half of FI in Latin America was directed toward purchasing existing enterprises, usually at below market valuation. Instead of *complementing* local public or private capital, FI "crowds out" local capital and public initiative and undermines emerging technological research centers.

With regard to market expansion, the record is mixed. In some sectors where public enterprises were starved for funds, like telecommunications, the new foreign owners have expanded the number of users and enlarged the market. In other cases, like water, electricity and transportation, the new foreign owners have reduced the market, especially to low-income classes, by raising charges beyond the means of most consumers.

The experience with FI and technological transfers is largely negative: over eighty percent of research and development (R&D) is carried out in the main office. The "transfers of technology" is the *rental or sale* of techniques developed elsewhere, rather than the development of local design. MNCs usually charge subsidiaries excessive royalty fees, service and management costs, to artificially or fraudulently lower profits and taxes to local governments.

Myth #2: FI increases the export competitiveness of a country and stimulates the local economy via secondary and tertiary purchases and sales.

In reality FI buy up lucrative mineral resources and export them with little or no value added. Most of the minerals are converted into semi-finished or finished value-added goods—processed, refined, manufactured—in the MNCs' home countries or elsewhere. Little is accomplished in creating jobs, diversifying economies or increasing skills. The privatization of the lucrative giant iron mine Vale del Doce in Brazil in the 1990s has led to huge profits for the new owners and the sale of raw ore overseas, particularly to China, where the iron ore is converted to steel for transport, machine industries and a host of job-generating metallurgical enterprises. In Bolivia, the privatization of the gas and petrol industry in the mid 1990s has led to billions in MNC profits. Few if any jobs were created in the processing of petroleum and gas into value added goods. In addition by exporting oil and gas and insisting on international market prices for sales in domestic producer countries, the MNCs fail to supply local low-income consumers with inexpensive energy. The extraction of raw materials is capital intensive using few workers. Processing and manufacture is more labor intensive and job creating.

Myth # 3: Foreign investors provide tax revenue to bolster the local treasury and hard currency earnings to finance imports.

In reality FI usually enjoy lengthy tax exemptions or reduced tax rates for periods between 10 to 40 years on imports, exports, corporate earnings and foreign executives salaries—or even operate tax free as part of the enticement to invest, or as a result of their leverage in contract negotiations. Despite these numerous taxation advantages, they are given to perpetrating massive tax frauds. Even as they swoop in to scoop up lucrative public enterprises forced onto the market by political fiat, they cannot resist a further sweetening of the pie through swindles in the purchasing process. The structural relations of branch industry to MNC headquarters directly, or even transversely through other branches, facilitates large scale money laundering.

In May 2005, the Venezuelan government announced that a billion-dollar tax evasion and fraud had been committed by major overseas petroleum companies who signed on to service contracts since the 1990s. The entire Russian petroleum and gas sector was literally stolen by a new class of billionaire robber oligarchs associated with foreign investors, who subsequently evaded taxes. The trial and conviction of two oligarchs, Platon Lebedev and Mikhail Khodorkovsky, for $29 billion tax evasion was facilitated by US and European banks.

The impact of the MNCs on the local state's balance of payments over the long run is largely negative. For example, most assembly plants in export zones *import* all their *inputs*, machinery, design and know-how, and export the semi-finished or finished product. The resulting trade balance depends on the cost of the inputs relative to the value of exports. In many cases the imported components charged to the local economy are greater than the value added in the export zone. In any event, because most of the export platforms operate tax free and pay low wages, local revenue is minimal.

The Brazilian experience over the past decade and a half is illustrative of how negative external balances rather than hard currency earnings result from FI and externally funded investment. In 2004 Brazil paid foreign bankers $46 billion (USD) in interest and principal while receiving only $16 billion dollars in new loans, leading to a net outflow of $30 billion dollars.[1] Between January and April 2005 Brazil was bled for $4.6 billion (USD) in interest payments, $3.7 billion in profit remittances by MNC, $1.7 billion for 'external

[2] The total drain of $17.3 billion dollars far exceeded the positive commercial trade balance of $12.2 billion dollars.[3] In other words, the FI-led export model led to new indebtedness to pay for the shortfall, the loss of employment by small and medium farmers at the mercy of the agro-business elites.

Myth #4: Maintaining debt payments is essential to securing financial good standing in international markets and maintaining the integrity of the financial system. Both are crucial to sound development.

The historical record reveals that incurring debt under dubious circumstances and paying back illegally contracted loans by non-representative governments jeopardizes the long-term financial standing and integrity of the domestic financial system and leads to financial collapse. The Argentine experience between 1976-2001 is illustrative.

A substantial part of the public external and internal debt was illegally contracted and had little development utility. A lawsuit launched by an Argentine economist against payment of the Argentine foreign debt revealed that the foreign private debts of Citibank, First National Bank of Boston, Deutsch Bank, Chase Manhattan Bank and Bank of America were taken over by the Argentine government.[4] The same is true of debts of subsidiaries of overseas banks. The economist's lawsuit also documented how the Argentine dictatorship and subsequent regimes borrowed to secure hard currency to facilitate capital flight in dollars. The foreign loans went directly to the Central Bank, which made the dollars available to the rich who recycled the dollars to their overseas accounts. Between 1978-1981 over $38 billion USD fled the country. Most of the foreign loans were used to finance the "economic" openings, luxury imports and non-productive goods, especially military equipment. The evidence pointed to a perverse source of greater indebtedness: the Argentine regime borrowed at high interest rates and then deposited the funds with the same lender banks at lower interest rates leaving a net loss of several billion dollars, added to the foreign debt.

The pursuit of 'low risk' status by many Latin American regimes in order to attract FI undermines sovereignty in several ways. In the first place, it opens the country to international judicial processes, embargoes and heavy fines. If and when a future government decides that the privatization agreements violated the country's laws or were signed under duress or lacked transparency or simply gave undue privileges to FI, it faces international institutional hostility. In other words, the pursuit of 'low-risk' status sacrifices future options and raises 'risks' for future governments intent on restructuring or transforming the country or merely altering the balance between public, private and foreign investment. 'Low-risk' agreements for investors may close the book or make it costly or 'high-risk' for future regimes designing new strategies, as the economy outgrows the FI-dependent stage.

Myth # 5: Most Third World countries depend on FI to provide needed capital for development since local sources are inadequate or not available.

Contrary to the opinion of most neo-liberal economists, most of what is called *foreign* investment is really *foreign borrowing of national savings* to buy and profit from local enterprises and finance investments. Foreign investors and MNCs secure overseas loans backed by local governments, or directly receive loans from local pension funds and banks—drawing on the local deposits and worker pension payments. Rather than bringing new resources to the table, the FI has interjected itself into what could have been a local process. Recent reports on pension fund financing of US MNCs in Mexico shows that Banamex (purchased in the 21st century) secured a 28.9 billion peso (about $2.6 billion USD) loan; American Movil (Telcel) 13 billion pesos ($1.2 billion USD); Ford Motor, 9.556 billion pesos in long term loans and one billion pesos in short term loans; and General Motors (financial sector) received 6.555 billion pesos.[5]

This pattern of foreign borrowing to take over local markets and productive facilities is common practice, dispelling the notion that foreign investors bring "fresh capital" into a country. Equally important it refutes the notion that Third World countries "need" FI because of capital scarcity. Invitations to FI divert local savings from local public and private investors, crowd out local borrowers and forcing them to seek 'informal' moneylenders charging higher interest rates. Instead of *complementing* local investors FI compete for local savings from a privileged position in the credit market, bringing to bear their greater (overseas) assets and political influence in securing loans from local lending agencies.

Myth #6: The proponents of FI argue that the entry of FI serves as an anchor for attracting further investment and serves as a 'pole of development'.

Nothing could be further from the truth. The experiences of foreign-owned assembly plants in the Caribbean, Central America and Mexico speak to the great instability and insecurity that has been engendered there. With the emergence of new sources of cheaper labor in Asia, especially China and Vietnam, the MNCs moved their assembly plants, decimating local economies. Foreign investors are more likely than local manufacturers to relocate to new low-wage areas, creating a "boom and bust" economy. The practice of FI in Mexico, the Caribbean and Central America, faced with competition from Asia is to relocate, not to upgrade technology and skills or to move up the value-added ladder. Finally a long-term study of the impact of FI on development in India has found no correlation between growth and FI.[6]

Conclusion

Reliance on FI is a risky, costly and limiting development strategy. The benefits and costs are unevenly distributed between the "sender" and receiver of FI. In the larger historical picture it is not surprising that none of the early, late or latest developing countries put FI into the center of their development scheme. Neither the US, Germany and Japan in the 19th and 20th century, nor Russia, China, Korea and Taiwan in the 20th century depended on FI to advance their industrial and financial institutions. Given the disadvantages cited, the way ahead for developing countries is through *minimizing* FI and *maximizing* national ownership and investment. Local financial resources and skills, and enlarging and deepening local and overseas markets through a diversified economy, can best be achieved through national ownership and direction.

Because the negative economic, social and political costs of FI are evident to increasing numbers of people in Latin America, it is a major detonator of mass social movements, and even revolutionary struggles, as was the case in Bolivia in 2003 and 2005. Since the large-scale entry of FI is a direct result of *political* decisions adopted at the highest level of government, mass social struggles are equally directed against the incumbent political regime responsible for promoting and mollycoddling FI. The increasing turn of social movements toward political struggles for state power is directly related to the increasing recognition that political power and FI are intimately connected, and that FI entry represents a policy choice, not an inescapable policy imperative. In the 21st century in Latin America, all of the electoral regimes that have been overthrown by popular majorities had deep structural links to FI: Gutierrez in Ecuador (2005), Sanchez de Losada (2003) and Mesa (2005) in Bolivia, and De la Rua in Argentina (2001) were overthrown by mass uprisings protesting their giveaways to MNCs.

The leader with the greatest sustained support in Latin America, President Chavez in Venezuela, is precisely the only one who has nationalized and increased regulations and taxes on multinationals and redistributed the increased revenues to the poor, working class and peasants. The question still remains whether this new infusion of mass energy and class awareness can go beyond defeating pro-FI regimes to constructing a state based on a broad alliance of class forces, which combines selective 'nationalizations' with a strategy for a socialist transformation.

Part II: Foreign Investment's Prejudicial Incentives

Foreign investments by MNCs are highly prejudicial to the interests of most Latin American countries, because of the non-market incentives that they demand. Much of what passes as favorable "market conditions" are in large part brought into being by political decisions which maximize benefits to the MNC at the cost of the local economy, its taxpayers, consumers and workers. Investments are not merely market transactions in which MNCs justify their profits on the basis of the risks they run, the innovations they introduce, the capital they invest. Contrary to these claims commonly proclaimed as legitimizing capitalist profit, most foreign investment is subsidized and risk-free, and relies on securing monopoly profits based on the appropriation of existing national (state) enterprises and control of strategic markets.

Privatized Lucrative Public Enterprises

A great deal of foreign investment adds little to new productive or distributive systems since it is directed at purchasing existing privatized public enterprises directly or via the takeover of the same from original private national capitalists. The transfer of ownership from the state to private/ foreign capital increases the outflow of profits, which previously accrued to the national treasury or were reinvested in the local economy. Privatization is part of the structural adjustment policies imposed by the IMF and World Bank as conditions for refinancing debt payments. The sale of national assets more often than not is hardly transparent and the sales take place at far below market value or prejudice the local investors. In other words, privatization has served to create a class of capitalists or 'oligarchs' who performed none of the 'tasks' associated with capitalist enterprises: they neither invested in training labor, invested capital in infrastructure, innovated nor located new markets. Privatization in the context of the ex-communist and nationalist countries most closely resembles *pillage* rather than *investment*. The process of privatization follows one of two paths: either direct buyouts by foreign capital or the theft of public properties by former state managers and/or oligarchic-gangsters (dubbed by the media as an emerging 'national bourgeoisie'). During a second phase many of the national oligarchs sell part or all of their shares to foreign capitalists/MNCs. These political "incentives" for foreign capital and oligarchic groups are justified by the "free-market" ideological dogma of the governing elite.

The infamous author of Russia's disastrous privatization (Anatoli Chubais), which led to the massive disarticulation of the economy and the impoverishment of the Russian people, justified his "shock" policy by citing the need to *make capitalism irreversible*, to undermine any effort to sustain a mixed social economy. In other words, privatization was an ideological decision. Corruption, vast concentrations of wealth, and a vertical fall in living standards, including an unprecedented decline in life expectancy, were the accepted costs of establishing capitalism.

De-Nationalization of Natural Monopolies

One of the key justifications used by ideologues of FI is that it encourages "competition" with local monopolies, and thereby increases productivity, lowers costs and prices, and increases employment. Most of the available data would argue otherwise.

One of the favorite targets of foreign investors and one of the prime incentives offered by neo-liberal regimes to attract foreign investment in the economy in general is their willingness to put public utilities—electricity, power, energy, gas, and communications, which are 'natural monopolies'—on offer. The real effect is to convert public monopolies to foreign-owned private monopolies. This usually results in an increase in charges, a decline in services for less profitable regions or low-income consumers, and an end to subsidized rates for emerging domestic industries and the impoverished urban and rural poor.

One of the most powerful 'incentives' which FI demand and pliable regimes offer is the privatization of energy sources. Once held up as strategic national assets, FI have successfully secured control over some of the most lucrative oil and gas fields from compliant rulers.

The obvious result has been a huge transfer of wealth from the national economy to the MNCs under the assumption that new investments and foreign 'know-how' will provide compensatory benefits. The problem is that energy corporations are notorious for not fulfilling their investment obligations. They charge international prices to local consumers, pricing endogenous producers out of international markets and impoverishing low-income energy users. The *privatization* of energy and utilities attracts foreign investors; indeed it is one of the most favored incentives for FI. It has several strategic drawbacks. Higher charges make local competitive firms less competitive. It deprives the revenue-starved state of a source of public funding. It heightens inequalities between the foreign rich and their local associates and the rest of the population.

Three other economic areas are targeted by FI. Telecommunications (especially cell phones), transport and raw materials, such as iron and cobalt, and agricultural products, like soya and forest products were especially sought. Telecom sell-offs to FI has frequently led to the demise of local hi-tech enterprises and virtual monopolies, rather than to heightened competition. This leads eventually to monopoly profits. FI has also targeted all the transport sectors: railroads, airlines, ports, and highways. Once again FI gains monopoly control and increase rates.

Preceding privatization, FIs demand that the state pay the costs of the 'transition' period—firing workers, paying pensions or severance pay—and provide guarantees of higher rates. To create the political climate for privatization, complicit client states usually disinvest in public enterprises and run deficits via high tax rates, thus worsening public services in order to provoke popular discontent with the public sector. Given government-induced debts and deficits, the public transport systems can then be sold at low prices to FI. Subsequently the new owners secure rate increases, tax concessions, reduce staff and cut less profitable routes. Most importantly, no independent regulatory system is put in place to check the violations of contracts by the FI.

The result is the disarticulation of the transport system. Only major routes to large metropolitan centers are kept operating while the outlying regions suffer severe reductions in transport, undermining local economies. Privatization and de-nationalization of airlines has led to the stripping of assets, decline of services and, in some cases, the bankruptcy of the firm. As an instance, Iberia's purchase of Argentine Airlines resulted in the stripping of assets and the airlines being run into bankruptcy.

Foreign investors have shown little interest in maintaining and upgrading railroad lines and port facilities that fail to generate the profit ratios that their shareholders demand. Where regulators are in place, they either lack authority to enforce contract obligations on FI, or are co-opted or subject to political pressure to overlook FI failures to comply with investment agreements.

When foreign investment in infrastructure, for example highway construction and toll roads, fails to provide the necessary profits or their high rates force users to secondary roads, they frequently demand compensation or re-purchase by the state at inflated prices. In the cases of Mexico, public highways were privatized and went bankrupt. The state took over, paid the private debts—and then re-privatized them—all in the course of a decade!

The most highly publicized and disastrous privatization in which FI has been involved was in water distribution in Bolivia (Cochabamba and El Alto) and in Peru. Mass popular uprisings protested the high rates and the failure to connect the majority of working poor with water lines, forcing public authorities to cancel the private contracts.

While FI has been deeply involved in most of the disastrous privatization activities in Latin American countries, many similar experiences have taken place in the imperialist countries. The privatization of the power and electricity sector in California led to major blackouts and exorbitant price hikes due to corporate malfeasance. The privatization of the passenger rail services in Great Britain led to safety hazards, exorbitant rates and unprecedented delays due to ancient equipment. The privatization of water in England led to health problems, forcing public investigations and a move to re-nationalize.

In summary, by offering choice profitable economic sectors as incentives to FI, Latin American regimes have fostered private monopolies, not competition, and a high-cost infrastructure that fails to integrate regions because of narrow corporate calculations of cost-benefits. Incentives to MNCs have prejudiced long-term, large-scale industrial diversification by offering raw materials, energy and natural resources as incentives to attract FI.

Using privatization as an incentive for attracting FI has had an extremely harmful impact on the deep structures of the economy, polarizing society by privileging elite enclaves, local oligarchs and influential politicians.

Subsidies

Many foreign investors demand and obtain, from pliable neo-colonial and/or neo-liberal regimes, direct and indirect subsidies in the form of lengthy tax exemptions or reduced tax rates for periods between ten to forty years on imports, exports, corporate earnings and foreign executives salaries. In addition, regimes provide land for enterprise free of cost or at minimum prices, subsidize utility and energy prices, build infrastructure, and finance labor training and policing. The net result is that Latin American countries pay to be exploited. Frequently the only 'benefit' to the country is a minimum tax, and low wages to highly regimented workers confined to export processing zones. By not paying appropriate taxes—or sometimes any taxes at all—the FI deny states revenue for public investment in education, health and skills upgrading. States lacking tax revenues frequently resort to borrowing, setting in motion new concessions to FI as a condition for receiving loans from the international financial institutions (IFI).

Export Processing Zones

The most striking development in FI has been the massive growth of export processing zones (EPZ). By 2005 there were 5000 EPZ employing forty million workers, throughout the world. Employment in the EPZs takes place under the most arduous repressive work conditions with the lowest pay in absolute and relative terms (output/productivity to wages). The EPZ are not a first step toward higher skill, higher wage, or technically advanced industrialization. That takes place outside of or parallel to the EPZ. The EPZ are attractive to FI because owners and managers have absolute control over labor and the environment, free of environmental, health and safety regulations. Many regimes which conceived of EPZ as the first stage of a process of 'deeper industrialization' have been disappointed: EPZ are simply 'pieces' in the MNC global production strategies—a locus for cheap labor in the labor intensive 'assembly stage' of manufacturing.

Tax Privileges

The tax incentives for the MNCs means a higher tax burden on local workers, peasants, professionals, public employees, and small- and medium-sized businesses, if their children are to receive an adequate education and health care. The people pay to produce healthy, literate workers to be exploited at low wages by tax-exempt MNCs who then transfer their untaxed profits to millionaire (billionaire) CEOs, stockholders and speculators. The list of tax "incentives" or privileges is lengthy and extremely costly to the countries and working population.

The better known and most common tax privileges extended to foreign investors include exemptions on imports of parts and other inputs as well as exports, low or non-existent property taxes, minimal profit and revenue taxes, generous depreciation allowances and tax holidays of between five and twenty years. In addition, expatriate managers and CEOs receive their salaries, bonuses and stock options tax-free. If we add the cumulative sum of tax losses to the state to the vast expenditure of state resources invested in infrastructure, severance pay, and 'restructuring' costs to attract FI, it is clear that the *total cost* of attracting FI far exceeds the benefits in employment and future taxes which might accrue over the foreseeable future.

If we add the loss of tax revenue from displaced local businesses driven to bankruptcy, we face even fewer benefits resulting from FI. Finally it is a common practice of foreign investors to relocate their enterprises when their tax holidays expire, or when workers' salaries begin to increase. The idea propounded by FI apologists that 'present sacrifices' are for future gains is an illusion—an ideological ploy to secure current privileges.

Market Liberalization

Under conditions of total liberalization, the strategy advocated by the IFIs and followed by many Latin American states, all barriers to foreign investors entering the local economy have been lifted. Studies have demonstrated that where local establishments go head to head with large MNCs, they almost always lose out; they either go bankrupt, are bought out by the bigger firm or become a satellite supplier. Since most employment in Latin America takes place in small and medium size enterprises, the entry of FI leads to an increase of unemployment as millions of firms providing jobs go bankrupt.[7]

FI relies in part on suppliers, experts and consultants from their home base to externalize costs (and maximize profits) and to maintain control. This cuts out existing local suppliers who were mostly local small- and medium-size producers. Only a small number of local firms survive the large-scale entry of foreign-owned MNCs. The emergence of a minority of locally owned competitive firms is commonly publicized by neo-liberal ideologues as part of their success story, excluding the much bigger story of the extent of failed enterprises and the foreign takeovers of majority shares of the local market, and the other attendant negative effects.

The invasion of local economies by foreign investors seriously compromises efforts to promote 'regional integration' because the principal beneficiaries of broader markets are precisely the large foreign-owned enterprises, not the national firms. This is particularly evident in MERCOSUR (the regional trade agreement of Brazil, Argentina, Uruguay, Venezuela, and Paraguay). By locating in the country with the lowest labor and tax costs, the MNCs dominate regional markets, undermine protected industries in neighboring countries, and generate severe and destabilizing trade imbalances between different members of the regional integration pact.

Contrary to most 'progressive' opinion, far from being a nationalist or regionalist alternative to imperial domination, regional integration becomes a FI *launching pad* for entry into broader markets. What gives a particular reactionary cast to "regional integration" proposals is that they skip over the more obvious problems of the lack of *national integration* within the participating countries. The decline of the domestic rural market because of inequalities of land tenure, the concentration of wealth in the urban central cities and the vast impoverishment of sprawling suburban slums undermine the internal market. What emerge are dynamic enclaves in a sea of low paid, precarious, informal economic activities.

"Regional integration", which is anchored in large-scale foreign and national owned MNCs, simply becomes a strategy to expand sales overseas without changing the national class structure and the unequal distribution of land and income.

Opening the economy to FI is almost always accompanied by the "de-regulation" of the economy, or more accurately, a change in the rules that facilitate the movements of capital in and out of the country. The 'liberalization' of financial markets means the decline of public oversight of financial transactions, allowing FI to 'launder' unreported revenues and profits and transfer funds overseas.

The net effect of increasing market access for FI is to replace a market attuned to transactions between local producers by a market constructed in the image of FI—with a heavy import content and deleterious nutritional effects (like soft drinks and fast foods) accompanied by colonial ideological-cultural propaganda.

Cheap Labor: Unskilled, Skilled and Professional

One of the most striking incentives to FI offered by Latin American regimes is state-promoted cheap labor in manufacturing, services and the primary sector. In order to attract FI, Latin American regimes, frequently following IFI directions, have initiated a whole series of decrees and laws dramatically favoring capital over labor. Wages and salaries were reduced, frozen or kept below the rate of inflation. Job protection legislation has been abolished or severely modified to allow investors to hire and fire without any restrictions or due process. Severance pay has been eliminated or reduced. The workday and working conditions have been revised, extending and intensifying exploitation. Pension and health benefits have been reduced, eliminated and privatized. Trade unions were repressed or incorporated into state-run, investor-dominated 'tri-partite' pacts and have effectively lost the right to strike.

By concentrating power in the hands of capital (euphemistically called "labor flexibility") the neo-liberal regimes compete with each other in bidding for FI. Favorable anti-labor legislation and draconian restrictions on trade unions have lowered labor costs and have favored foreign investors in labor-intensive manufacturing.

Since the 1990s, FI has increasingly looked toward 'outsourcing' skilled jobs to low-wage/salary regions. This requires state promotion of an educated low-paid work force and financing of local business elites to act as recruiters and point men for the FI. Overseas relocation—the reality and the threat—is a common policy to lower wages, pensions, health benefits and job security in the imperial countries. Foreign investors benefit from both ends: exploiting skilled and unskilled labor in assembly plants and manufacturing industries in Latin America while reducing labor costs within the United States. The MNCs play one against the other and secure labor-related incentives in both. The net effect is to increase profitability by squeezing out greater productivity per worker at lower costs, expanding market shares and creating lucrative export platforms to sell back into the "home market".

The same practice and logic which applied to the outsourcing of unskilled labor to low-wage areas has been extended to high end skilled labor in an array of activities—specialized software programming, accounting, engineering, research and development, and design. The notion propagated by neo-liberal apologists that the loss of manufacturing jobs would be 'compensated' by the growth of skilled service positions fails to recognize that corporations would follow the same exploitative logic with regard to skilled service jobs.

The net result of low-cost labor incentives to attract or retain FI has been to widen the economic gap between labor and capital, and deepen the inequalities in political and social power. In the process the MNCs dissociate growing productivity and profitability from wage payments. Wages and salaries increasingly lag behind capital gains in productivity, profits and export earnings largely as a result of the vast and profound labor incentives to FI. Under the rule of labor incentives to FI, growth of GNP spreads few positive effects to the rest of society, creating highly polarized growth.

One of the primary concerns of FI is securing ironclad legal guarantees against nationalization, expropriation or new regulations, no matter what the circumstances or non-compliance of MNCs. To attract FI, neo-liberal regimes legislate or decree measures that override constitutional, health, environmental and other laws, in order to provide the absolute security which FI demands.

In practice, there cannot be any durable investment 'guarantees' against expropriation, new regulatory or tax regimes, or even confiscation because the conditions for FI vary with the fortunes of the class and national struggle. In addition global economic conditions and the changing priorities and internal dynamics of MNCs affect compliance with agreements. The 'low-risk' agreements between a neo-liberal regime and FI will last only as long as the regime can silence or co-opt the opposition.

Elected regimes which single-mindedly provide generous contracts and opportunities to FI while imposing prejudicial austerity programs on working majorities have damaged the more highly developed Latin American economies. Argentina, Mexico and Brazil, all countries with a highly trained labor force, a developed home market, reasonably sound infrastructure, and a modicum of a social welfare net, have witnessed a brain drain, weakened domestic demand and the growth of severe poverty.

Over a twenty-year period (1980-2000) living standards have plunged, with over one third of the workforce unemployed: over half fell below the poverty line. The ranks of the truly indigent climbed to over fifteen percent. Pension plans, advanced medical systems, educational and scientific facilities crumbled and skilled professionals fled the country in droves. Foreign investors initially prospered with their privileged access to the economy, but uncontrolled plunder led to a general crisis, which eventually engulfed the very speculators who brought it about.

PART IV
AN AGENDA
FOR MILITANTS

CHAPTER 15

ECONOMIC ALTERNATIVES

Countering FI Strategies to Counter Social Reform

For policymakers intent on constructing an alternative development model to the FI centered approach, it is important to *anticipate* the strategies that FI will adopt, and be prepared to put in place timely countermeasures.

Countering the Threat of Disinvestment

The most likely first move of FI to counter policies designed to enhance the national economy and popular living standards is to threaten or practice disinvestment in local facilities. This involves lowering production, closing facilities, and reducing or withdrawing capital in order to destabilize the economy and force the government to rescind or not implement legislation or executive rulings. Disinvestment can be accompanied by the threat of an "exit strategy"—putting in jeopardy the employment of local workers, suppliers and other satellite enterprises.

Knowing this is a real probability, the state can raise the stakes by insisting that disinvestment can lead to the cancellation or re-negotiation of the original investment agreement and/or to state intervention into the enterprise. If this fails to stop MNC investment strikes, it can be followed by outright state takeover in the public interest to safeguard employment, production, maintenance and shares of export markets. In other words, firm assertion of state purpose makes FI disinvestment a two-edged sword. It allows the state to put some teeth into its reform proposals by telling the MNCs to either abide by the new legislation or lose access to the local market, exploitation of local resources and supply of strategic goods. The state can also affirm that there is 'no return' once an "exit strategy" is adopted.

To back up the counter-strategy and make it more credible, the state should be ready to replace senior corporate personnel with local specialists from within the plant, or from other agencies, or hire foreign experts. Negotiations with suppliers and purchasers should be in place. Most of all the employees, workers and professionals in the affected economic sector should be mobilized, consulted, and organized by the state to respond favorably to the impending confrontation. They and the larger public—the workers, peasants, lower middle class, and professionals—should be informed and prepared for a period of transition to the new socio-economic model, in case there are dislocations and temporary hardships.

Preventing Capital Flight

A reduction or the elimination of the privileged place of FI in the economy will likely lead to a run of liquid assets and will certainly cause financial disruption. Here decisive and rapid action is essential—including the freezing of assets, capital controls and other restrictive measures on the movement of capital. The state should sponsor policies to maintain levels of credit and production even if it means a spike in inflation and monetary emissions. These can be compensated by price controls or subsidies on basic items of popular consumption.

Countering Systemic Pressure

Failing to intimidate the progressive regime through economic threats or actions, FI will turn to their imperial state to exert bilateral or multilateral pressures. These can range from threats to cut off loans from IFI and restrictions on imports and exports, to destabilization efforts and/or threats of military intervention. Several contingencies may influence the effectiveness of these political pressures. Competing imperial countries may not be in agreement on these measures, especially if they affect mostly one or another imperial power. The global economy is neither homogenous nor 'unipolar' in trading or military policy: losses by one imperial power can be gains for another.

Again, threats to cut off financing by the IFI is a two-edged sword. Resisting states too can threaten the mobilization of systemic pressure—from below. Ending of new financing can be met by debt default, setting a precedent for other debtor countries, and escalating the conflict to the global level. Once debt payments are suspended, the 'extra revenues' can be used to compensate enterprises prejudiced by IFI cut-offs. The larger the debt, the greater the destabilizing impact of a debt moratorium or repudiation on the international financial markets.

Promoting and Implementing a New Developmental Model

In anticipation of the escalation of the conflict with FI, the state can view the problem through a *political* lens in order to best prepare its counter-attack. Imperial threats usually radicalize and mobilize popular movements, isolate elite allies of the imperial power, and polarize the country in a way favorable to the regime. This is especially the case if the resisting state government has clearly defined and demonstrated the socio-economic advantages of pursuing its new development model. If the imperial state pursues a military-political interventionist strategy, the regime in consultation with its mass constituency can pursue a multi-layered national defense strategy, which can range from anti-terrorist measures to legislation outlawing imperial funding of political parties, NGOs and media outlets.

Significant changes in one vital sector of the economy can imply changes in the totality of the society and state. In redefining the state-FI relationship, new political actors are drawn in. As the conflict spills over to other sectors of the economy and across frontiers, pressure builds for further changes in the economy and state security structure. Looking at the problem of state-FI conflict in narrow economic terms of a state-investment framework can lead to unanticipated attacks and likely defeats and retreats.

Engaging in the Battle of Ideas

FI can rely on their associates in the mass media to launch "scare propaganda campaigns", which demonize progressive governments, labeling them terrorists, rogue states and communists. This becomes part of the battle of ideas. A progressive government can counter elite propaganda warfare through its own mass media within the country and via solidarity social movements and alternative media throughout the world. Internet sites, community radios, videos and international solidarity organizations can be effectively mobilized to reach active populations who may respond to and provide support for the positive changes. What is essential for the survival of the progressive regime is to move beyond "critiquing" the power of the adversarial corporate media and toward the creation of multiple mass outlets and activities to gain political support. If the progressive government cannot secure a mass support with some politicized understanding of the nature of the attacks to be faced, it will be unable to implement its policies in the face of FI resistance. The role of the Venezuelan masses not just at the ballot box but on the street has proved to be key, to date, to the survival of the Chavez government. Indeed, much of the dramatic impact surrounding Chavez' role—his comments at the UN, his "shadow-tour" of Latin America during the Bush visit—indicate an awareness of the need to create and deepen the counter-climate of opinion that makes political action possible.

Countering Corruption

Another strategy to undermine progressive legislation, which is almost always adopted by FI, is the corruption of government officials—especially regulators, trade union officials and the political elite. This involves cash payoffs in foreign accounts, job offers to relatives or promises of managerial positions after serving office, visiting professorships to prestigious universities with lucrative stipends, and a host of other pay-offs. Judges appointed by pliable executives can be expected to rule against state measures to revise FI contracts or to rule in favor of lawsuits in imperial jurisdictions.

While "international" and NGO investigatory agencies have established "transparency" ratings for countries, few if any have examined or established corruption ratings for MNCs and FI, despite their widespread use of bribes and illicit activities. Nor have they evaluated the devastating effects corruption has in undermining progressive changes. In fact the tendency has been to discuss corruption in developing countries in terms of the corrupted, not the corruptors— as if the condition were somehow endemic to these states, and divorced from the interventions of imperialist powers.

Corruption by FI can be limited by introducing a number of institutional changes. The creation of workers, consumers and environmental oversight committees with open access to all accounts, transactions and especially government contracts would be a first step. Secondly, corruption can be limited by publicizing all stages of negotiations between states and MNCs. Legislation could make it obligatory for all contracts to be subject to scrutiny by the employees and consumers most affected. Auditors and investigators who have no ties to FI interests can serve a technical advisory role in preparing evaluations of contracts and state-FI agreements. Reform of the public administrative structure is essential and should include deep ethical changes, inculcating members with a commitment to national and class or collective values. Ultimately technical and ethical/political commitments are the best safeguard for neutralizing the MNCs' corruption of government officials designed to undermine the implementation of progressive legislation.

Addressing Labor Legislation and Price Constraints

FI may accept regulations and reforms, but resort to increasing prices and lowering labor costs to maintain profits. State intervention fixing rates is an obvious counter-measure, along with threats to re-nationalize if FIs decide to hold back on promised new investments. Enforcement of labor legislation and price constraints monitored by trade unions and organized consumers can block corporate efforts to "pass the costs" of state reform to the consumer.

Incentives to FI usually come at an unacceptable cost to workers, consumers, taxpayers, local producers and environmentalists in the way of higher taxes, lower social services, scarcer and more expensive credit, and higher prices. Alternatives to incentives and privileges to FI are readily available, feasible and beneficial when a popular government is prepared to withstand the inevitable threats, pressures and propaganda, which emanate from Washington and Wall Street. Taking a broad strategic approach prepares the state to develop effective countermeasures to the possible reprisals taken by the FI.

Is Anti-Imperialism Compatible with Foreign Investment?

Over the past forty years, many "socialist" and nationalist regimes attempted to combine public enterprise with private investments, including foreign investment. In the beginning, decisions were made to limit the scope of foreign investment to particular sectors and in some cases to a limited time frame via "fade-out formulas" (over time the foreign shares would be bought out by the public sector).

In the last decade of the "socialist" regimes, the governing elites widened the scope of private and foreign capital and, in some cases, signed agreements with the IMF, which accelerated the process. With the collapse of the "socialist" regimes in the former Soviet Union and Eastern Europe and the ascendancy of pro-capitalist policies, the ruling elites and foreign capital proceeded to pillage the public sector to an unprecedented degree. Foreign capital and newly minted local oligarchs ran amok, grabbing and stripping public assets, raiding the public treasury, seizing natural resources, public utilities, the mass media and energy resources. This led to unprecedented and rapid impoverishment of the great majority of the working population, stripped of social wages (the termination of free health, education, cultural and other social benefits) and the growth of monstrous socio-economic inequalities between the upper one percent of multi-millionaires and the lower eighty percent of the population. Large-scale emigration, corruption on a scale never experienced in modern history, and powerful murderous international gangs organized and traded in hundreds of thousands of women and girls (sex slaves for international brothels), narcotics and illicit arms sales.

Similar sell-offs of public assets in Latin America were also accompanied by large-scale corruption, and in many cases long-term loss of state leverage over their economies, resulting in economic stagnation and unprecedented social inequalities.

By the end of the nineties, the disastrous political and socio-economic consequences of the rapid and massive conversion to capitalism and the unregulated invasion of foreign capital in the former "socialist" and nationalist countries was recognized by several progressive and nationalist regimes which had not taken the leap into the abyss of "free market" capitalism. Debates and discussions about the role of foreign capital emerged within and between the rulers of these regimes and a wider public of intellectuals, workers, and political activists. One group calling itself "Pragmatic Progressives (PP)" argued for a greater or lesser role for foreign capital, while others, referred to as "Radical Leftists (RL)" citing the debacle in the ex-USSR, argued against any large-scale, long-term openings.

The debate has continued, the issues shifting with circumstance and context. The "PP" emphasize a new dimension—"globalization"—which they argue "demands" greater responsiveness to 'market signals' (competitiveness) through 'links' with foreign capital. In contrast the "RL" reject foreign investment and point out the increasing threats from the links between FI and "militarist imperialism". They cite the US-EU's Balkans Wars, the US-led invasions of

Yugoslavia, Iraq, Afghanistan, and Haiti as well as the US-sponsored attempted coup in Venezuela and the overt military threats against Iran, Syria and Cuba. For reasons of national security, the "RL" argue for fewer openings to foreign capital.

The "pragmatists" have been unable to effectively counter the facts about imperialist aggression, except to cite the possibility of "separating" the role of foreign capital from the behavior and interests of the bellicose imperialist state—an argument not without merit under certain circumstances. Nevertheless the *economic* arguments of the "PP" still carry weight and have had considerable influence over state policies, leading to 'piecemeal' adaptation by the "RL".

Arguments for Foreign Investment

The seven most common arguments in favor of foreign capital usually base themselves on the following propositions:

1. There is a *shortage of capital*, therefore foreign capital needs to be attracted in order to develop the economy and encourage foreign lending.

2. The country needs foreign capital as a *source of "know how"*—providing management and marketing skills—to secure export markets and competitive advantages.

3. Foreign investment provides *advanced technology* to modernize the economy and upgrade productivity and therefore competitiveness.

4. Foreign capital will increase the competitiveness of local producers, driving out the inefficient firms while encouraging local firms to become more efficient.

5. Foreign capital will lower prices, extend and improve services to consumers.

6. Foreign capital will increase *competitiveness* in global markets, increase exports and secure overseas market shares.

7. Foreign capital pays *better wages*, provides *better working conditions* and *pays more taxes* than local producers.

A Regulated FI

There are differences among the publicists advocating foreign investment. The points of differences include:

1. Whether foreign capital should be allowed the same terms as local enterprises, or whether there should be differential tax rates, restrictions in areas of investments (some argue 'strategic areas' like energy should remain under state or national ownership) etc. In the case of export processing zones, advocates of FI encourage lower tax rates, rents and labor standards for FI.

2. Whether foreign-owned enterprises should only produce for the export market or for the internal market as well (export trading zones).

3. Whether foreign capital should be obligated to reinvest a percentage of its profits into the domestic economy or whether it can remit all its profits to the home office.

4. Whether foreign-owned firms should be obligated to invest substantial sums to upgrade firms and modernize production.

5. Whether foreign firms can own majority, minority or all shares in an enterprise. Similar differences exist on management rights between foreign and national owners.

6. What kinds of incentives to offer foreign firms, in terms of tax concessions, land grants, infrastructure investment by the state, job training by the local government, etc.

7. The longevity of foreign ownership especially of mineral and subsoil rights; should it be in perpetuity, or leased over extended or shorter time periods; should contracts allow for renewal and options, sanctions for non-compliance, etc..

In other words among the advocates of foreign investment there is a range of positions on the scope and depth of concessions which accompany the promotion of foreign capital. During the 1980s the general tendency was for governments to expand concessions to foreign investors. Since the 1990s, as public regulations were severely weakened, the rules governing the entry and operations of foreign capital have been relaxed.

As a result the debate on foreign investment today has generally followed the lines of how many and what types of incentives to offer foreign capital, without evaluating whether foreign capital brings in its wake greater development problems than it is purported to overcome, or seeking to make its entry into the country more beneficial through judicious and enforced regulation.

Arguments Against Foreign Investment

The decision to open a country to foreign investment raises profound political, economic, social and cultural questions that go beyond short-term calculus of the costs and benefits that accrue to a firm or even an economic sector. In most cases the initial "openings" lead to subsequent large-scale, long-term strategic invasions resulting in a whole series of unanticipated but predictable outcomes.

First and foremost foreign ownership of strategic industries and resources leads to the states' loss of decision-making in shaping investment decisions, pricing, production, and future growth. The foreign owners decide which enterprise in their business empire will expand, stagnate or decline depending on the labor costs, taxes, transport and communication networks. The new owners decide whether to conduct research locally within the enterprise or at the 'home office'. Foreign investment, especially large-scale buyouts of strategic enterprises, severely compromises national sovereignty and converts political regimes into 'hostages' of the foreign owners. No doubt prior agreements between foreign investors and regimes have sought to establish rules that may be applied to each case in the future, but these are subordinated to and conditioned by both the state's willingness and ability to enforce them and the foreign investors' willingness to abide by them. Experience tells us, however, that in most Latin American states the initial agreements to privatize are rife with corruption and the subsequent presence of large-scale foreign enterprise can easily lead to influencing administrators and regulators into lax enforcement of whatever contractual protections might have been instituted.

Foreign investment brings initial capital, but leads to long-term, large-scale outflows of profits to the home office, contributing to the de-capitalization of the economy and balance of payments problems. Turning over state enterprises to foreign investors (or local oligarchs) leads to a decline of state revenue, increased unemployment and in some cases to plant closures in regions where the rates of return to the company are below expectations.

Foreign capital's "rationalization" and "restructuring" may increase enterprise profits but activate a *negative multiplier effect* in the primary and tertiary sectors. For example, when private firms took over the railroads, they closed down rail lines and their attendant machine and maintenance shops because of their low rates of return in order to increase overall profits. These closures however led to a steep decline in commercial, industrial and agricultural production in the provinces adversely affected. Provincial enterprises went bankrupt and unemployment increased. The net *gain* by the MNC was an absolute loss to the region and its labor force.

Foreign investment leads to unbalanced and overly specialized production, principally the expansion of highly volatile commodities at the expense of a diversified economy with a broader production and trade base. Most foreign investment in Latin America seeks to earn hard currency by betting on commodities with a high export component, like oil, soya, iron, copper which complement their domestic requirements or those of industrializing economies. For Latin America the net result is a 'boom and bust' economy in which exports and revenues from high-priced commodities inflate regime revenues and imports temporarily, prior to a harsh fall in commodity demand leading to serious trade deficits, sharp cuts in spending, rising unemployment and increased indebtedness.

Foreign capital tends to create "enterprise enclaves" that import technology (charging royalty fees) and are linked to outside production and distribution networks, thus having a minimal impact on the local economy. There are numerous examples: the better known are assembly plants in which the manufacturing and distribution is done elsewhere, by other subsidiaries of the MNC, and the only contribution to the local economy is the payment of subsistence wages. Primary materials exporters extract iron, copper and soya and it is processed overseas where value added and jobs accrue to the recipient country. The raw material exporters employ few workers, the countries are converted into 'monocultures' and their economies are subject to volatile shifts in their revenue base. Dependence on income from a few exports or a single export (like oil) and overseas remittances does not bring about a developed and integrated economy.

Foreign investment has captured the important banking sector in Mexico, Brazil, Chile, Argentina and elsewhere, shaping state credit and interest policy and, more importantly, deciding what sectors and enterprises receive credits and at what interest rates. Foreign ownerships of banks leads to lending to and privileging foreign-owned firms ("most creditworthy"), those which earn hard foreign currency (agro-mining export firms) and to systematically excluding small businesses, farmers and peasants producing for the local market and employing the majority of the labor force. This leads the latter to depend on usurious moneylenders or to divert capital from production to speculation.

Moreover, given the preference of foreign capital for extractive industries, their influence among local government elites and their backing by the IFI, foreign investors have been at the forefront of polluting the environment. Timber barons and soya exporters are demolishing the Amazonian rain forest. Oil and mining companies devastate the land and water in Ecuador and Peru. The increase in revenues to the federal state is hardly ever used to compensate for the destruction of the local agricultural and fishing economy. Instead state revenues are recycled to build roads and ports linking environmental predators' pillaged resources to external markets.

The local political influence of foreign investors increases with their greater presence in the local market, their control of strategic sectors of the economy and the emergence of western-trained local political leaders promoting "free enterprise". Equally important, foreign-owned enterprises employ local executives, managers, lawyers, publicists and economists, with linkages to the political elite, who frequently move into key political positions (presidents of the central banks, Ministers of Economy and Finance) and implement macro-economic neo-liberal policies that maximize benefits to the foreign investors at the expense of the local labor force and treasury. Furthermore, executives from foreign-owned enterprises play a lead role in local banking, industrial and other business associations, leveraging them to secure policies favorable to their interests.

Foreign-owned firms, especially US MNCs, frequently act as conduits for imperial state policies. They do so by *disinvesting* in countries, which are on the US State Department blacklist, and *relocating* productive facilities to pro-US countries. US MNCs *'house'* and provide a false cover to intelligence agents, pass on economic intelligence to the CIA, and refuse to supply repair parts to countries in conflict with the US. US bank subsidiaries facilitate capital flight, tax evasion and money laundering for wealthy elites.

It is only infrequently that 'marginal corporations' or even subsidiaries of major corporations do not follow the line of the imperial state—either because the profits are too lucrative to overlook, competitive pressures from other MNCs are intense, and/or because the long-term incentives offered by the targeted state offset the risks of antagonizing imperial policymakers. While Washington attacks Venezuela and Bolivia, US oil and gas companies have signed new agreements and joint ventures. They are perhaps more astute readers of the malaise in the Middle East, and its import for Washington's capacity to enforce its will in its own back yard, than is the current Bush administration.

Foreign-owned firms are at least initially run by expatriates, at least at the most senior positions. 'National' executives are usually hired to handle (1) links with the local regime, (2) labor relations, (3) tax evasion or exonerations from payments and (4) public relations campaigns and political advice.

In summary foreign investment has strategic disadvantages, endangering national independence and popular sovereignty, and severely compromising the capacity of the state to represent its citizens, especially the working class and the peasants. Foreign investment increases inequalities and produces a polarized social structure as a result of the low tax rates, the high rates of return and the pro-foreign-investor outlook of the state. The "residual benefits" to the "receiving country" are usually concentrated in the hands of local "political facilitators", top and middle management, and subcontractors and distributors.

Alternatives to Foreign Investment

Foreign investment in the broadest sense is incompatible with any notion of an independent, socially progressive country—which is not to say that in *limited* circumstances (in time and place) under *specified political* conditions, under *particular* sets of regulations, administered by select groups of regulators, foreign investment cannot be useful.

In the face of the overwhelming economic constraints and regressive social outcomes of FI, its advocates resort to the argument that "there are no alternatives". They argue that without FI there can be no development, access to markets or technological advance.

On the contrary, there are very solid empirical and historical grounds for arguing that there are substantial financial and economic resources available to popular regimes, which are more efficient in producing positive growth and have none of the negative social and political outcomes and accompaniments of FI.

1. *Reinvest profits* from lucrative export industries and strategic domestic enterprises via public ownership back into the domestic economy. Profits, which would be remitted abroad by foreign capital, can be channeled inward to expand local production, producing a 'multiplier' effect and increasing local consumption, in a virtuous circle.

2. *Control foreign trade* to increase retention of foreign exchange in order to avoid overseas seepage. Allocating hard currency to priority enterprises would increase local production, employment and popular consumption.

3. *Invest pension funds* in productive activities and distribution rather than holding them in private banks or trust funds.

4. *Create development banks* to channel overseas workers' remittances into productive, job-creating activities. In many countries overseas remittances are a leading source of hard currency. Most are used for local family consumption and marginal economic activities. The neo-liberal state uses the hard currency to service the foreign debt.

5. *Impose a moratorium on debt payments* based on the need to investigate whether earlier loans took place within a legal framework, whether they resulted in productive activity or whether they financed

corrupt practices and unproductive uses (military expenditures). Economic studies should be made to determine whether the original principal has been paid. If debts were the result of borrowing by private firms, payments should be cancelled or referred back to original borrowers. The state should not accept socializing the bad debts of private firms. Mismanagement and poor judgment by private sector investors and careless loan decisions by creditor institutions should not be paid for by the taxpayers. Past lenders and borrowers should assume the risks of losses, rather than saddling the populace with payment for loans concerning which they were neither consulted nor benefited.

6. *Recover funds stolen from the public treasury* and property illicitly privatized by previous regimes. Overseas accounts based on illicit transfers especially by local business and political elites should be impounded as part of an anti-corruption commission headed by independent tax lawyers and representatives of the mass organizations. Such a pursuit of transported Marcos wealth was undertaken to some effect by the Philippines. Enterprises privatized under dubious circumstances should be re-nationalized.

7. *Recover unpaid taxes,* especially state losses through tax evasion by MNCs and international firms. Offenders should be prosecuted and forced to pay back taxes. The state should demand full recovery of back taxes or undertake seizure of physical and liquid assets of the delinquent firms should a payback schedule fail to be negotiated. The state can demand that the accounting sheets of MNCs be open to public inspection to foil the common practice of intra-firm "transfer pricing", thus artificially and illegally lowering profits and income to evade adequate tax payments.

8. *Graduate land taxes and expropriate underutilized or speculative land* to provide land for agrarian reform and low-income public housing. This will increase agricultural productivity and food for local consumption as well as exports. Extensive estates and plantations illegally occupying public lands should be expropriated without compensation. Compensation for expropriated private estates should be paid in long-term bonds based on past tax-declared value (or at market value, if the estate owners are willing to pay back taxes on the difference between the declared and market value.)

9. *Liquidate overseas holdings or investments by public firms* and reinvest the revenues in upgrading national productive infrastructure and

processing industries. Excessive foreign reserves should be downsized and put to work in diversifying the economy. Reserves should be held in diverse currencies but not deposited in overseas banks, where an imperial adversary could freeze national holdings. Efforts should be made to avoid holding reserves in dollars since these are losing value against other currencies.

10. *Maximize employment of under-employed labor.* In some cases up to eighty percent of the labor force is in the informal sector. Putting the under-employed to work in large-scale infrastructure projects can compensate for "scarce capital" and become a source for initial capital accumulation. Likewise organizing public projects can employ underutilized, educated, skilled workers and professionals to lead to innovations and organizational breakthroughs.

Any serious examination of the social economy of most countries would discover there are multiple *national* sources of capital without the need to rely on foreign capital. These sources have all the advantages of raising the rates of capital investment with none of the political uncertainty, economic vulnerabilities and social inequalities associated with foreign capital.

Alternative FI Management Strategies Where FI Is Unavoidable

Let us assume that a Third World country receives few overseas remittances, possesses sparse or non-existing pension funds and few taxable sources. On the other hand it possesses valuable resources which require high initial capital investments and new technology. External financing or expertise will be required. The question then becomes: what are the optimal short-term and strategic contracts that will minimize the negative effects, enumerated above.

The optimal approach is to disassemble the "foreign investment packages" to minimize direct foreign ownership and long-term management control. To maximize strategic national ownership and control, it is preferable to sign short-term management contracts which include training of national replacements over a fixed period, preferably from countries with less intrusive imperial states. Likewise where technical assistance is necessary, for lack of know-how of specific processes, it is preferable to contract technical advisers to work in tandem with local specialists, training them for a future takeover. If foreign MNCs are required to construct local productive facilities, "turnkey contracts" should be signed in which the MNCs are guaranteed a certain rate of profit over a specified time period after which ownership is handed over to national owners. It is possible to contract for construction without ceding ownership, with payment to be guaranteed as a percentage of profit, until fee for service is paid up. Specific contracts with *time* limits allow the nation to maximize the employment of national skilled professionals, managers and workers. The widening pool of available high-skill specialists in the global market provides a variety of choices, eliminates dependence on any single country (particularly imperialist countries) and avoids depending on foreign investment with the long-term loss of ownership, control and strategic investment planning.

To limit entanglement with foreign capital, it is essential for the country to invest in professional and technical training, research and development, all of which can be done through sending students abroad or by contracting foreign specialists.

Advantages of Worker-Engineer Public Control (WEPC)

There are a number of significant advantages to relying on 'Worker-Engineer Public Control' or WEPC over foreign-owned MNCs in pursuing a development strategy.

Tax Evasions and Tax Revenues

The multinational corporations are masters in the art of evading taxes and corrupting local regulators. WEPC, operating with "open books" and independent auditors responsive to workers and consumers, can minimize tax evasion, leading to increases in revenues, sound fiscal balances and low levels of corruption.

Social Investment versus Profit Remittances and Privileged Salaries

Profits under the MNC-dependent strategies are largely invested overseas. Exorbitant salaries, bonuses and expenses are paid to the CEOs and other management elites. Under the WEPC model, profits are reinvested in expanding local production, social development programs and improvements in working conditions.

Capital Flight versus High Reinvestment Ratios

The MNC model is based on volatile movements of capital, including capital flight, leading to greater investment instability and fluctuations in state revenues. The WEPC leads to higher and steadier re-investment ratios, and greater stability in employment, investment and public revenues.

Speculative Investment versus Long-Term Investment in Research and Development

One of the basic demands of the MNCs is the deregulation of financial markets, in order to be able to move capital back and forth between fixed and 'liquid' investments. This has led to the growth of speculative investment, which has provoked severe crises throughout the capitalist world. Under the WEPC model, highly regulated financial transactions minimize the flow of capital into speculative activity and maximize financing of product innovations, research and development.

Capitalist Privileges versus Social Welfare

Under the MNC model, the state provides enormous subsidies to foreign investors, in the way of tax exonerations, rent-free land, state-funded infrastructure, low interest loans and de-regulation of labor and environmental laws. Under the WEPC model, both costs and profits are socialized—providing free health services, guaranteed employment, livable and fixed pensions, childcare, safe work conditions, adequate vacations and continuing education to upgrade skills and productivity to increase leisure and study.

Mobile Capital/Fixed Labor versus Fixed Capital/Mobile Labor

Under the MNC model capital 'relocates' to maximize profits, lower taxes, undermine working conditions, and avoid health and pension obligations. Under the WEPC model, "capital" is fixed to a specific location and labor is trained and mobile, moving up in skill level, employment, and possibly assuming leadership roles. Labor can be engaged in lifetime education and job training. Under WEPC there is no 'contracting out' or 'outsourcing' or 'temporary work contracts'. This model takes advantage of a stable skilled work force applying its knowledge and experience to improve production without the frequent disorganization caused by worker turnover.

Potential Problems in the WEPC

There are several problems that can occur under the WEPC. These include:

1. Decisions favoring greater consumption over productive investment

2. Bureaucratization of organization

3. Worker indiscipline (tardiness, absenteeism etc.) leading to a decline in production and innovation

4. Loss of competitiveness due to state protection

5. Either excess or insufficient taxes to the central government

6. Inter-sectoral inequalities due to differential rates of productivity or prices

7. Over-emphasis on social benefits as opposed to individual consumption

8. Failure to deal with issues of gender, race and ecology

For the WEPC model to be effective, its leaders and popular supporters must have a long-term 'holistic' view of the development process, in order to balance the demands for immediate consumption with investment in medium- and long-term production. Inevitably, especially in the initial phase of the model, there will be strong pressure to 'make a difference' with regard to past capitalist approaches which perennially postponed popular satisfaction in order to 'increase the pie'. The new government will have to adjust to this political demand by initially providing significant social impact programs. Free medical care and higher education, rent reductions and debt forgiveness can gain the confidence of the working classes and demonstrate that the new government represents a break with the past. The social impact programs will also secure the loyalty of the popular classes and give them a stake in defending the regime, an important issue given the likely hostility of the imperial powers and the defeated local ruling class.

The new model needs to guard against tendencies toward bureaucratization based on the delegation of power, differential expertise and the prestige of particular leaders. Formal mechanisms including popular workplace and neighborhood assemblies, popular access to the mass media, referendums on strategic socio-economic decisions and, above all else, a politically educated working class which is exposed to public debate—these are the best antidote to incipient bureaucratism.

Worker indiscipline "should" not occur under WEPC but it does or it will: some workers will try to lessen their official workload in order to carry on with "under the table" jobs. Others will take advantage of a lax regime or the apparent lack of sanctions, and increase absenteeism or fake illness. Some workers may be perennially late or fail to adequately perform duties and neglect quality control. Social education on rights and responsibilities can be inculcated in all workers, backed by sanctions including loss of pay, benefits and layoffs without pay for chronic offenders. A combination of rewards and penalties will continue for an indefinite time, otherwise most workers will have to carry extra societal burdens because of a minority of slackers.

While the WEPC economy functions in a world capitalist market place, the enterprises must combine humane social relations of production with improving competitiveness. All WEPC of whatever size and resource base will need to invest in research and development (R&D) to encourage innovations in new technologies and quality commodities, and be able to have marketable products at competitive prices. Specialized production can take place in countries with favorable endowments in locations, resource bases and skills. Productivity gains can reduce working hours and years of work, extend time for rest and recreational activities, provide opportunities for continuing education as well as quality time for personal and family relationships and friendships. Without constant innovations and competitiveness, market losses will severely hinder the growth of humane social relations.

The socialization of production will not automatically change inequalities in racial and gender relations among workers and professionals. A concerted 'cultural revolution', based on legal, educational and government initiatives will be necessary to begin the process of reversing institutional and attitudinal racism and sexism in all spheres of production, consumption and cultural representations. Representatives of racial minorities and women in political and social leadership roles are key. Likewise the socialization of production requires the direct presence of representatives of environmental organizations to minimize the excess exploitation of non-renewable resources, environmental pollution, and chemical agricultural abuse.

Finally the WEPC faces the problem of inequalities generated by different levels of productivity and market demand leading to inequalities between factories, sectors and regimes. Decentralized control will accentuate the advantages of some to the disadvantage of others, leading to the reproduction of class and regional inequalities. A system of progressive taxes, wage and social subsidies, as well as increased investment in upgrading less developed industries and regions can lower the inequalities.

Conclusion

The historical and empirical evidence demonstrates that the political, economic and social drawbacks of foreign investment far exceed any short-term benefits perceived by its defenders. Research has demonstrated that most economies possess the financial and capital resources and underutilized human productive capacities to undertake successful development without the high political costs that FI brings to bear. As an alternative model, the WEPC provides numerous advantages over dependence on international finance and investor capital. While FI has a general negative role, the WEPC model does not totally exclude FI in specific sets of circumstances, limited in time and location, to implement endogenous development. A strategy that is directed toward drawing on international assistance to complement endogenous growth would emphasize contracts with a variety of providers, particularly with those not linked to the imperial state.

While the WEPC model provides an alternative approach that maximizes national and working-class interests, it has potential drawbacks and internal contradictions, which require constant reflection, deliberation, debate and reforms. Nonetheless the model provides the surest and most direct road to development with democracy, social justice and national independence. The success of the WEPC model, its introduction and sustainability, does not depend merely on its socio-economic viability but also on appropriate and supporting national security and cultural policies and institutions..

CHAPTER 16

LATIN AMERICA: THE MIDDLE CLASS, SOCIAL MOVEMENTS AND THE LEFT

The political and social behavior of the middle class is determined by its class position and interest and the political-economic context, which it confronts. In the context of a right-wing regime, which is expanding, providing cheap credits and importing low-priced consumer goods, the middle class is attracted to the right. In the context of a right-wing regime in deep economic crisis, the middle class can be part of a broad popular front, seeking to recover its loss of property, savings and employment. When there is a popular anti-dictatorial, anti-imperialist populist government, the middle class supports democratic reforms but opposes any radicalization that equalizes conditions with the working class.

Three examples in Brazil, Argentina and Bolivia illustrate the shifting orientation as well as the internal divisions of the middle class. In Brazil, upwardly mobile middle class functionaries, professionals, labor lawyers and trade union bureaucrats took over the Workers Party (PT) led by Lula da Silva. With 75 percent of the delegates, they supported an electoral alliance with the big business Liberal Party, and the financial sector. But once in power, they moved from social democratic to neo-liberal politics. The social movements, including the Landless Rural Workers Movement (MST) and the Urban Homeless Peoples Movement (MSC) supported Lula's election on the basis of pre-election promises, failing to apply a class analysis to either predict or then accept the fact of his changes in policy, leadership and program.

As a result, the social movements spent five wasted years arguing that the Lula regime was 'contested terrain' that could be pushed to the left. As a consequence the MST lost political ground, was organizationally weakened and its membership disoriented for nearly five years. In the meantime, Lula cut the pensions of the public sector workers unions (teachers, post-office employees, health workers, functionaries, etc.) by 30 percent, increased the age of retirement, and privatized public pension funds. As a result, the public employees unions broke with the government and the pro-government labor confederation (CUT) and joined with other independent unions to form a new confederation, CONLUTA, which includes student, ecologists and other groups.

By 2007 CONLUTA was joined in a national assembly by the MST and sectors of the CUT in organizing a general strike on May 23 2007. The social movements' links to the electoral politics of social democratic parties, which were moving toward neo-liberal policies, was a political disaster. The social movements' lack of an *independent class-based political program* and leadership oriented toward *state power* forced them to subordinate to the former social democratic Workers Party, which was tied to imperialism, finance and agro-mineral capital. On the other hand, the public employees trade union and the public sector of the middle class were forced to break with Lula and to seek allies in the radical left, including social movements, and to reject ties with the big and petit bourgeoisie.

In Argentina, the middle class, especially the private petit bourgeoisie, supported the neo-liberal Menem regime in the 1990s. Their support was based on cheap credit (low interest rates), cheap imports of consumer goods, a dollarized economy and an expanding economy based on overseas borrowing. With the economic crises (1999-2002) and collapse in the economy (December 2001-December 2002), the middle class saw their banking accounts frozen, their jobs lost, their businesses bankrupted and poverty affecting over fifty percent of the population. As a result, the middle class 'radicalized': they took to the streets in a mass rebellion protesting in front of banks, the Congress and the Presidential palace. Throughout the major cities, middle class neighborhoods formed popular assemblies and fraternized with the unemployed workers organizations (*piqueteros*) in blocking all the major highways and streets. This spontaneous middle class rebellion adopted the apolitical slogan "Que se vayan todos!"— All Politicians Out!—reflecting a rejection of the neo-liberal status quo but also of any radical solution.

The official 'left' public employees trade union (CTA) and the right-wing private sector union (CGT) provided little in the way of leadership—at best individual members played a role in the new social movements in the 'villa de miseria'—the vast slums. The left and Marxist parties intervened to *fragment* the mass unemployed workers movement while over-ideologizing and dissolving the middle class neighborhood assemblies. By the middle of 2003, the middle class shifted to electoral politics and voted for Kirchner who campaigned as a 'center-left' social democrat. Beginning in 2003 world commodity prices rose significantly, Argentina postponed and later lowered its debt payments and Kirchner stabilized the economy, unfreezing the bank accounts of the middle class who then shifted toward the center.

Meanwhile Kirchner took advantage of the fragmented unemployed workers movement and co-opted many unemployed workers' leaders, provided $50 monthly subsidies to each family and began a process of selective exclusion followed by repression, isolating the radical from the reformist left. By 2007, the major class struggles involve the public sector employees of the middle class and the Kirchner regime over wages and salaries. The occupied factory movement has been co-opted into the state. The unemployed workers movement still exists but with much reduced strength. The private middle class, having recovered and enjoying high growth, is moving from the center-left to the center-right.

Argentina illustrates how middle class politics can shift dramatically from conformity to rebellion but lack any political direction. With stabilization, the private middle class splits from the public employees, with the former backing neo-liberals and the latter social democracy.

The MAS (Movement toward Socialism) government in Bolivia has a mass electoral base of urban and rural urban poor but its cabinet ministers are all bourgeois professionals, technocrats and lawyers with a few co-opted movement leaders. Evo Morales combines political demagogy for the masses, like 'nationalization of petrol and gas' and 'agrarian reform' with liberal practices, such as signing joint ventures with all the major international oil and gas companies and excluding 'productive' large plantations owned by the oligarchy from expropriation for land reform. In the meantime, the private petit bourgeois, who initially supported Evo Morales to avoid the rebellion of the Indians and workers, subsequently turned to the right. In addition, as Morales supports IMF-type austerity macro-economic stabilization policies, he has provoked the major public employee unions (notably teachers and health workers) to go on strike.

The consequence for the Bolivian movements, as in Brazil and Argentina, includes the fragmentation and the return of the private middle class to the center-right. The social movements are de-mobilized and there is increasing discontent among the public sector middle class over pay increases that barely exceed the rise in the cost of living, despite the vast increase in government revenue due to the high price of mineral exports.

The new center-left (CL) programs regimes are in reality the new faces of the neo-liberal right. The CL regimes have followed the same macro-economic IMF policies, refuse to reverse the illegal privatizations from previous regimes and have maintained the gross inequalities of classes while weakening the social movements. The CL regimes have been stabilized by the boom in commodity prices, budget and trade surpluses, which allow them to provide minimal poverty alleviation programs. Their main success has been to demobilize the left, restore capitalist hegemony and to gain a relative degree of autonomy from the US by diversifying markets to Asia.

Towards an Alternative Orientation

The main problem of the social movements was the failure to develop a political leadership and program for state power and therefore depending on the electoral politicians of the upwardly mobile professional middle class. As soon as the movements subordinated extra-parliamentary politics to the electoral parties, they became enmeshed in electoral alliances between the middle class leaders and big capitalists.

The center-left, taking advantage of favorable international economic conditions (high commodity prices, high liquidity), can stabilize the economy, lower unemployment and reduce poverty, but cannot solve the basic problem of uneven development, under-employment, concentration of wealth and power, and exploitation and inequalities.

The relation of the Left to the middle class has a right and left wing approach. The right-wing approach is to drop the anti-capitalist, anti-imperialist demands in order to gain the support of the private sector of the middle class. This meant sacrificing *structural changes*, favored by the working class, peasants and unemployed, in favor of vague promises of employment, stability, protection of local business and growth.

The left-wing approach is directed at supporting the *public sector* of the middle class opposing neo-liberal measures like privatization, supporting the re-nationalization of basic industries, mining and energy and supporting wage and salary increase for workers and public employees. The Left also supports public employee demands for pensions and social security guarantees including state-subsidized public health and higher education. The key challenge for the Left is to convert the public sector middle class from anti-neo-liberalism to anti-capitalism and anti-imperialism, and to combine urban, welfare to agrarian reform.

CHAPTER 17

THE CENTRALITY OF IRAQ AND AFGHANISTAN IN DEFEATING THE EMPIRE

Washington outlined in explicit language its plans to engage in sequential wars in the Middle East, Southwest and Northeast Asia and the Caribbean. Under the offensive military doctrine of Pre-emptive Wars and the Global War against Terrorism, the United States pursuit of military conquest was backed by Israel, Great Britain and several newly incorporated client states from Eastern Europe. The White House's grandiose scheme of world conquest was orchestrated and pre-maturely celebrated by top Zioncon (Zionist Conservative) officials embedded in the Pentagon, White House and the National Security Council.

The imperial wars of conquest however were stopped literally dead in their tracks at their starting point: Iraq and Afghanistan. Subsequent to the US invasion and occupation of Iraq and Afghanistan, a formidable mass armed resistance emerged from the underground, aided by widespread civilian support. Large majorities of public opinion, major religious communities, trade union militants , small business associations and neighborhood-based community organizations actively and passively opposed the US-led occupation forces at every turn, providing logistical support and intelligence to the armed and non-violent resistance. Similar developments took place at a later stage in Afghanistan.

Despite draconian military measures, including the bombing of population centers, systematic mass round-ups of civilians followed by brutal torture, the US military failed to consolidate its rule via puppet regimes. As the resistance grew, Washington's efforts to foment ethnic-religious sectarian warfare and territorial fragmentation failed. By late 2006 it was clear that the imperial army's only territorial conquest was the bunkers in the so-called Green Zone. In 2007 Washington escalated its troop commitments in a desperate effort to fend off impending defeat and to recover the massive loss of domestic support

From a world historical perspective, the Iraqi and Afghan resistance has successfully stymied Washington's military pursuit of world domination through a series of offensive wars. The success of the national liberation movements led to the over-extension of the US imperial armed forces, thereby weakening efforts to launch pre-programmed ground wars against Iran, Syria and elsewhere. The prolonged resistance led to wholesale domestic opposition in the face of never-ending US casualties and skyrocketing financial costs.

The demoralization of the US infantry and National Guard prevented Washington from following up its failed coup against Venezuelan President Hugo Chavez with a direct military invasion.

The prolonged and deteriorating war in Afghanistan, with the advances of the re-grouped guerrilla fighters especially among the civilian population, has led the US-controlled colonial coalition to engage in indiscriminate bombing of civilians, adding to the growth of the anti-colonial resistance.

The success of the resistance movements in Iraq and Afghanistan and the appeal of their examples has encouraged new formidable anti-colonial struggles, led by Hezbollah in Lebanon, Hamas in Palestine, the Islamic Courts Union in Somalia and has stiffened the resolve of Iranian leaders to resist US demands to unilaterally suspend their nuclear programs.

Further abroad, the weakening of US global military interventionist capacity has taken the heat off of progressive governments in Venezuela and revolutionary Cuba. The consolidation of the Venezuelan nationalist-populist government has had a powerful demonstration effect throughout Latin America, encouraging new anti-imperialist movements and dissident governments in Ecuador and beyond. In an all-out battle of ideas, programs, foreign aid and solidarity, Bush is losing out to President Chavez. Unable to launch a full-scale military invasion, to eliminate the Chavez government, Washington has failed to match Venezuela's vast petrol subsidies and promising alternative integration proposals: ALBA, the Bolivarian alternative for the Americas, has prevailed over ALCA/FTAA.

The failure of Washington's will to a world empire has led to the shrinking of its power relative to its global situation prior to 2001. And in large part that is due to the fighting capacity and organized resistance in Iraq and Afghanistan. It is the fighters in Iraq and Afghanistan, and indeed in Lebanon, who have demonstrated once again for the 21st century, that despite the great store of modern technological warfare and monopolies of media propaganda, wars are decided on the ground, by the popular majorities directly affected. It is they who set in motion the conversion of enthusiastic domestic majorities for the US war to demoralized minorities; it is they who have given backbone and resiliency to the Middle Eastern governments who vacillate between collaboration and rejection with the colonial powers.

ENDNOTES

PART I: THE US EMPIRE AS A SYSTEM

Chapter 1: WHO RULES AMERICA?

1. In November 2002, voters in San Francisco rejected a local public power system, which proponents said would bring cheaper rates and more reliable service to ratepayers. "The business community spent more than $2 million to defeat the measures, outspending advocates more than 10 to 1. Rachel Gordon, "S.F. Voters Turn Off Public Power Bid,"*San Francisco Chronicle*, November 10, 2001.

2. See my recent work, *The Power of Israel in the United States*, Clarity Press, Inc., 2006.

3. See Financial Times, April 24, 2007, and its special report, "Hedge Funds", April 27, 2007, pp. 15. Also see Associated Press, "Goldman Breaks Wall Street Bonus Record", December 20, 2006.

4. Ben White *"Megabucks Deals for an Elite Few"*, *Financial Times*, January 3, 2007, p.15.

5. See Morningstar.com for the end of the year summary of leading stock market stars.

6. On concentration of wealth see: *"Richest 2% Own Half the Wealth"*, BBC December 5, 2006) quoting from World Institute of Development Economics Research at the United Nations. The study demonstrates that two percent of the adults in the world own more than fifty percent of all household wealth, while the lowest 50% of the population own one percent. The study was based on data from 2000, before the rise of over 200 new billionaires in China, Russia and India, which would further heighten inequalities.

7. David Brown, "Richest Tenth Own 85% of World's Assets", *The Times*, December 6, 2006.

8. *Financial Times*, December 13, 2006 p.15.

9. *Financial Times,* December 15, 2006 p.11.

10. Goldman Sachs signed a strategic co-operation agreement with National Commercial Bank, Saudi Arabia's largest lender. Lloyd Blankfein, Goldman's chairman and CEO stated regarding the agreement: "We are focused on building a broad business in the region and see this initiative as a big part of our strategy." *Financial Times*, February 5, 2007, p. 14. On Wall Street's trading in Islamic bonds, see *Financial Times*, January 18, 2007 p.17.

11. The increasing link between Wall Street finance capital and US overseas expansion is found in the fundamental importance of overseas profits. See "Wall Street Banks Earn More Abroad", *Financial Times,* January 21, 2006, p.1.

12. *Financial Times*, November 2, 2006, p.11.

13. *Id.*

14. *Financial Times,* November 3, 2006, p.13.

15. *Financial Times,* December 21, 2006.

16. *Financial Times,* November 2, 2006, p. 11.

17. *Id.*

18. *Id.*

19. *Financial Times,* November 3, 2006, p. 13.

20. According to the United Jewish Communities website, Rahm Emanuel, head of the Democratic Congressional Campaign Committee (or DCCC) for the US House of Representatives, "served a noncombat stint as a volunteer in the *Israeli* [italics added] army during the first Gulf War". See http:/www.ujc.org/content_display.html?ArticleID=68298

21   As head of the Democratic Congressional Election Committee in the 2006 Congressional elections, Israeli-American Congressman Rahm Emanuel ensured that 20 of the 22 Democrats running in closely contested House races were 'pro-war' Democrats, see John Walsh's "Emmanuel's [sic] War Plan for Democrats: The Book of Rahm", http://www,counterpunch.com. Congressman Rahm Emmanual now heads the Congressional Caucus and is a committed member of the Zionist Power Configuration and eminent self-promoting warmonger to the right of President Bush. In his book *The Plan: Big Ideas for America* (2006), the Zionist zealot writes "We need to fortify the military's 'thin green line' around the world by adding to the US Special Forces and the Marines and by expanding the US Army by over 100,000 more troops...we must protect our homeland and civil liberties by creating a new *domestic* [my emphasis] counter-terrorism force like Britain's MI-5." This leading Democrat and Israel-Firster wants to escalate the number and activities of the US' foremost international death squads and US combat forces for new wars in the Middle East, and increase the number and activities of our secret police to further curtail domestic democratic freedoms.

22   Zionlibs are politicians and citizens who support progressive political causes and rightwing pro-Israel war aims, including billion dollar foreign aid grants to Israel.

23   See Jim VandeHei and Jonathan Weizman, "Republicans Split With Bush on Ports: White House Vows to Brief Lawmakers On Deal With Firm Run by Arab State", *Washington Post*, February 23, 2006, p. A01.

24   This caused the Chinese government-controlled company, CNOOC, to withdraw its bid for the US company. Both the Port and the Unocal attempted acquisitions made clear the limits of trade liberalization that lawmakers (with the apparent assent of the Bush administration) were prepared to accept, as it related to takeovers which had a national security dimension.

25   *Financial Times*, December 4, 2006, p.3.

26   *Financial Times*, December 4, 2006.

Chapter 2: CRISIS OF US CAPITALISM OR CRISES OF US WORKERS?

1   *Financial Times*, July 12, 2006, p.4.

2   *Financial Times*, July 5, 2006.

3   *Financial Times*, June 21, 2006.

4   *Id.*

5   *Financial Times*, June 5, 2006, p.3.

6   *Financial Times*, June 10, 2006, p.6.

7   *Id.*

8   *Id.*

Chapter 3: MARKET LIBERALIZATION AND FORCED EMIGRATION

1   Cited in "Immigrant Workers in the United States Meat and Poultry Industry" submitted by Human Rights Watch to the Committee of Migrant Workers, Office of the High Commissioner for Human Rights, December 15, 2005

2   The Mexican National Population Council December 2001 report "concluded that 400,000 Mexicans a year would migrate to the US through 2030 if Mexican economic growth averaged five percent a year, and that 500,000 Mexicans a year would migrate if economic growth averaged 1.5 percent a year." Cited in "Mexico: More Migrations, Remittances", *Migration News*, Vol. 9 No. 1, January 2002.

Chapter 4: ECONOMIC EMPIRE-BUILDING AND THE CENTRALITY OF CORRUPTION

1   *Financial Times*, October 11, 2006, p. 24.

2   See "Past, Present and Future of China: From Semi-Colony to World Power?" herein.

3   *Financial Times*, October 9, 2006, p. 15.
4   *Id.*
5   The impetus for so doing, however, came from external sources who awaited
        (even guided) the actions of their domestic counterparts.
6   *Financial Times*, October 9, 2006, p. 15.
7   Id.

Chapter 5: THE SYSTEMIC APPLICATION OF FORCE:
HIERARCHY, NETWORKS AND CLIENTS

1   James Petras and Morris Morley, *Empire or Republic,* Routledge, New York,
        1995; J. Petras and M. Morley, "The Role of the Imperial State", in *US Hegemony
        Under Siege*, Verso Books, London, 1990.
2   James Petras and Morris Morley, "The US Imperial State", in James Petras *et al
        Class State and Power in the Third World,* Allanheld, Osmin, Montclair, NJ, 1981.
3   The 10 main troop-contributing countries to UN peacekeeping operations as of
        February 2006 were Bangladesh (10,126), Pakistan (9,797), India (9,290), Nepal
        (3,510), Jordan, Ethiopia, Uruguay, Ghana, Nigeria, and South Africa. See UN
        Document, Ranking of Military and Police Contributions to UN Operations, July
        31, 2006, http://www.un.org/Depts/dpko/dpko/contributors/2006/july06_2.pdf.
4   In 2006 Israel ranked behind US, Russia and France. See Barbara Opall, "Israeli
        Arms Exports Set Record in 2006", *Defense News* http://www.defensenews.com/
        story.php?F=2395124&C=mideast
5   See James Petras, *The Power of Israel in the United States, supra.*
6   See Congressional Research Service Issue Brief for Congress titled "Israel:
        U.S. Foreign Assistance" by Clyde R. Mark, updated July 12, 2004. Order code
        IB86055.
7   James Petras and Morris Morley, "The US imperial State", in James Petras et al.,
        Class State and Power in the Third World, supra.
8   See Andrew England "Spectre of Rival Clans Returns to Mogadishu", *Financial
        Times,* December 29, 2006, p. 3.
9   *Financial Times,* December 29, 2006.
10   William Church, "Somalia: CIA Blowback Weakens East Africa", *Sudan Tribune*
        Feb 2, 2007.
11   *Financial Times,* December 29, 2006, p. 3.
12   *Financial Times* January 31, 2007 p. 2.
13   Stephan Shalom "Gravy Train: Feeding the Pentagon by Feeding Somalia", *Z
        Magazine*, February 1993.
14   In fact, Clinton claimed the pharmaceutical plant was producing biological and
        chemical weapons—a story which was refuted by scientific investigators.
15   Shalom, supra.
16   *Financial Times,* December 31, 2006, p. 2.
17   *Financial Times,* January 5, 2007, p. 4.
18   William Church, supra.
19   "Somalia: Another War Made in the USA" interview with Mohamed Hassan
        (Michel.Collon@skynet.be)
20   Id.
21   *Financial Times,* January 5, 2007 p.5; *Financial Times,* December 29, 2006 p.
        3.
22   BBC News, "US Somali Air Strikes 'Kill Many'", January 9, 2007; aljazeera.net,
        "US Launches Air Strikes on Somalia", January 9, 2007
23   *Financial Times,* February 5, 2007, p. 5 "...there has been no confirmation yet
        of targeted al-Qaeda suspects according to Meles Zenawi, Ethiopian Prime
        Minister."
24   aljazeera.net December 29, 2006; aljazeera.net January 6, 2007; BBC News
        January 26, 2007; aljazeera.net January 28, 2007, aljazeera.net February 11,
        2007

25   "Looting and shooting broke out as soon as the Islamic fighters left the crumbling capital as militias loyal to the local clans moved on to the streets." *Financial Times*, December 29, 2006.

26   id.

27   BBC News January 25, 2007; BBC January 30, 2007; BBC January 5, 2007.

28   "Ugandan Parliament halts bid to rush deployment of peacekeepers to Somalia". *People's Daily Online* February 2, 2007.

29   *Financial Times* January 26, 2007, p.6.

30   aljazeera.net, February 7, 2007.

Chapter 6: IMPERIALISM: THE DRIVING FORCE OF GENOCIDE

1   As per the definition of the Convention on the Prevention and the Punishment of the Crime of Genocide. The Convention excludes from the definition of genocide the killing of members of a social class, members of a political or ideological group, and that of cultural killings.

2   Mike Davis, *Late Victorian Holocausts*, Verso, London, 2001.

3   Yehuda Bauer, *A History of the Holocaust,* Franklin Watts, New York, 1983; Mitchell Bard, *The Complete History of the Holocaust,* Green Haven, California 2001.

4   Alexander Dallin, *German Rule in Russia, 1941-45*, MacMillan, London,1957; Harrison Salisbury, *The 900 Days: The Seige of Leningrad*, De Capo Press, New York, 1969; Arno Mayer, *Why Did the Heavens Not Darken: The Final Solution in History*, Pantheon Books, New York, 1988.

5   James Fenby, *Generalissimo: Chiang Kai-Shek and the China He Lost,* Free Press, London, 2003.

6   On Vietnam see Francis Fitzgerald, *Fire in the Lake: The Vietmanese and the Americans in Vietnam*, Little, Brown and Co., New York, 1972; Edward Herman, *Atrocities in Vietnam: Myths and Realities*, Pilgrim Press, 1971; Noam Chomsky and Edward Herman, *The Washington Connection and Third World Fascism: The Political Economy,* South End Press, Boston, 1979, Ch. 5; Richard Falk, *Crimes of War*, RH Press, New York, 1971; The Dellums Committee Hearings on War Crimes in Vietnam, Vintage, New York, 1972. On Cambodia, see Center for Genocide Studies (Yale University). The website states: "For US bombing points, attributes of a site's bombardment are displayed in tabular form, e.g. the date of the bombing, exact location, the number and type of aircraft in the sortie, bombing load and ordinance type, the nature of the intended target, and bomb damage assessment (BDA), (…on) Cambodia's 13,000 villages; the 115,000 sites targeted in 231,000 U.S. bombing sorties flown over Cambodia in 1965-75, dropping 2.75 million tons of munitions; 158 prisons run by Pol Pot's Khmer Rouge regime during 1975-1979, and 309 mass grave sites with an estimated total of 19,000 grave pits; and 76 sites of post-1979 memorials to victims of the Khmer Rouge." The director of the Genocide Center, Ben Kiernan, with a perversity seldom equaled in academia, fails to include the US murder and maiming of millions of Cambodians in his discussion of genocide—he focuses only on Pol Pot's regime. On the basis of that selective view of genocide, he secured a tenure position at Yale University, his center won a distinguished award and the generous financing of George Soros and the Coca Cola Corporation.

7   On Korea see John Gittings and Martin Kettle, "US and S Korea Accused of War Atrocities", *Guardian*, January 18, 2000; Bruce Cummings, *The Origins of the Korean War, Vol.I, Vol II*, Princeton University Press, Princeton, NJ, 1981, 1990. According to figures published in the Soviet Union, 11.1 percent of the total population of North Korea (1,130,000 people) were killed by US air and ground forces. In all of Korea, over 2.5-3 million people were killed, more than eighty percent of the industrial and public facilities and transportation works, three quarters of the government offices and one-half of the houses were destroyed. Between June 1950 to May 1953, US Generals Eisenhower and McArthur, Presidents Truman and Eisenhower, and the Joint Chiefs of Staff (Military Command) considered or recommended the use of nuclear weapons against

Korea. According to Gittings and Kettle, apart from the thousands of refugees murdered by US military officials, *"many more Korean civilians were killed by US bombing later in the war, particularly during the saturation bombing of Pyongyang (Capital of North Korea) in 1952."*

8   See http://www.samarthbharat.com/bengalholocaust.htm

9   Caused by commencing the process with the removal of price controls—except on natural resources—and then a precipitate unprepared privatization.The US Treasury, IMF, USAID and Harvard University played a large advisory role in policies undertaken in great haste, which proved consistently "erroneous" in managing a successful transition [but highly successful in terms of bringing Russia to its economic knees], effecting a devastation in industrial capacity greater than that suffered in WWII, see Joseph Stiglitz, *Globalization and Its Discontents*, W.W. Norton, 2002.

10   Richard Hovannisian (ed)., *The Armenian Genocide: History, Politics, Ethics*, St. Martin's Press, New York, 1992; Richard Hovannisian, ed., *Remembrance and Denial: The Case of the Armenian Genocide*, Wayne State University Press, Detroit, 1999.

11   Patrick Bell et al., *State Violence in Guatemala 1960-96*, AAAS, Washington DC 1999; *Amnesty International Report: Guatemala* (1982, 1983, 1984) London; Thomas Melville, *Through a Glass Darkly: US Holocaust in Central America*, Xlibris Corporation 2005; Kent Ashabranner, *Children of Maya*, Dodd Mead, New York, 1986; *Guatemala Nunca Mas: 4 Tomos*, Officina de Derechos Humanos Arzbipado 1998.

12   Gilbert Burnham, Riyadh Lafta, Shannon Doocy et al., "Mortality After the 2003 invasion of Iraq: A Cross-Sectional Cluster Sample Survey," *The Lancet*, Oct. 29, 2006, 368(9545):1421-1429.

13   Daniel Goldhagan, *Hitler's Willing Executioners: Ordinary Germans and the Holocaust,* Knopf, New York, 1996.

14   See Thomas Childer, *The Nazi Voter: The Social Foundations of Fascism in Germany 1919-1933,* University of North Carolina Press, Chapel Hill, NC, 1983, especially pp. 264-266.

15   In the November 1932 elections, the Nazis received 33.1 percent of the vote, the Communist and Socialists received 37.3 percent, see Thomas Childer, *supra.*

16   See Richard Rhodes, *Masters of Death: The SS Ensatzgruppen and the Invention of the Holocaust*, Alfred A. Knopf, New York, 2002. Rhodes shows that Hitler and Himmler intended the Jews to be only their first victims; their plan was to open up Russia to German colonization by destroying more than 30 million Slavs and members of other ethnic groups.

17   The Israeli-Palestinian genocide is well documented by Edward Said, *Politics of Dispossession: The Struggle for Palestinian Self-Determination,* Vintage, New York, 1995; Benny Morris, *The Birth of the Palestinian Refugee Problem: 1947-49,* Cambridge University Press, Cambridge, 1987; Felicia Langer, *With My Own Eyes*, Ithaca Press, Ithaca, 1975; Naseer Hasan Aruri, *Palestinian Refugees*, Pluto Press, London, 2001; Ilan Pappe, *Israel/Palestine Question: Rewriting History,* Routledge, London, 1999; Edward Said, *The Question of Palestine*, Vintage Press, New York,1979; Maxine Rodinson, *Israel: A Colonial Settler State*, Monad Press, New York, 1973; Walid Khalidi, ed., *All That Remains*, Institute of Palestine Studies. The major Zionist lobbies in the US, the Conference of Presidents of the Major Jewish Organizations and AIPAC, are unconditional supporters of the Israeli-Palestinian genocide, totally back the blockade and the daily killings of Palestinian civilians by Israeli special forces.

18   See Richard Rhodes, *supra.*

19   Iris Chang, *The Rape of Nanking*, Penguin, London, 1997.

20   According to the US Pentagon, there were 54,246 US war deaths in the Korean War and 8,142 US personnel were listed as 'Missing in Action'.

21   During the Korean War, Douglas McArthur ordered the US Air Force to "destroy every means of communication, every installation, factory, city and village",

south of the Yalu River boundary with China. Quoted in http://www.brianwillson.com/awol/koreacl.html

[22] See Benny Morris, supra. According to Edward Said, supra, four million Palestinians have been turned into refugees and nearly two million are under Israeli military occupation. According to Palestinian Human Rights Monitors, since the Second Intifada over 300 Israeli military assaults in the Occupied Territories occurred weekly resulting in scores of killings, hundreds of injuries and prisoners, the demolition of over 10,000 homes and the destruction of thousands of acres of farm land. Subsequent to the democratic elections in Palestine in 2006, Israel imposed a total blockade of food, health and emergency goods on the Occupied Territories, jeopardizing the lives of over 2.5 million Palestinians.

[23] James Petras, Henry Veltmeyer, Luciano Vasapollo and Mauro Casadio, *Empire with Imperialism*, Zed Press, London, 2005.

[24] Richard Hovanassian, ed., *Armenian People from Ancient to Modern Times*, St. Martin's Press, New York, 2004.

[25] Said, *Politics of Dispossession*, supra.

[26] James Petras, *The Power of Israel in the United States*, supra.

[27] Damien Kingsbury, *The Politics of Indonesia*, Melbourne, Oxford, 1998, p. 57.

[28] See the Israeli English language daily *Haaretz* between February and June 2006 on the Israeli blockade policies and its catastrophic effects on Palestinian health and nutrition.

[29] See Ilan Pappe, *Israel/Palestine Question: Rewriting History*; E. Said, *Politics of Dispossession,* supra.

[30] In "Sanctions in Iraq Hurt the Innocent," *Seattle Post-Intelligencer*, August 3, 2007, Bert Sachs wrote: "Richard Garfield, a health specialist at Columbia University, is cited as an expert on these statistics. A year ago, he told us his low estimate of children's deaths was 400,000. If one extrapolates the excess death rate for Iraqi children from a 1992 *New England Journal of Medicine* report, there would now be more than 800,000 dead Iraqi children." On the US-Iraq genocide see *Lancet*, supra; Anthony Arnove (ed), *Iraq Under Siege: The Deadly Impact of Sanctions and War*, South End Press, Boston, 2002; Alex Cockburn and Jeffery St. Clair, *Imperial Crusades*, Counterpunch, California, 2004.

[31] Public knowledge throughout the world of US systematic use of torture and mass murder to conquer Iraq is a result of reporting by a vast network of websites and even some of the mass media. See, for example, the English language websites: informationclearinghouse.info; commondreams.org, counterpunch.org, axisoflogic.com, dissidentvoice.com, among others.

[32] Turkey does, however, face the issue of the Armenian genocide in deflection of its effort to join the European Union, and indeed Armenian genocide denial has now taken its place as an indictable offense in countries such as Switzerland and France.

[33] James Petras, *The Power of Israel in the United States*, supra.

Chapter 7: THE GLOBAL RULING CLASS: BILLIONAIRES AND HOW THEY "MADE IT"

[1] The primary data for this essay is drawn from *Forbes Magazine*'s "List of the World's Billionaires" published March 8, 2007.

[2] In particular, Andrei Shleifer and Jeffrey Sachs. Schleifer, an advisor to Chubais, subsequently "faced damages of up to $104 million for conspiring to defraud the government while advising a U.S.-funded program to privatize the Russian economy in the 1990s." However, in the end, Harvard University itself paid $26.5 million in settlement of the conflict of interest suit launched against it by USAID. See Zachary M. Sewart, "Harvard to Pay $26.5 million in HIID suit", *Harvard Crimson*, July 29, 2005.

PART II: ZIONIST POWER IN THE UNITED STATES

Chapter 8: NO EXIT: THE JEWISH LOBBY SINKS THE IRAQ STUDY GROUP

1   *Financial Times,* November 16, 2006, p.1.
2   *Newsweek,* November 20, 2006, pp. 40-43.
3   BBC, November 23, 2006.
4   *Financial Times,* November 15, 2006, p. 8.
5   Id.
6   BBC, November 25, 2006.
7   *Novartis,* November 4, 2006.
8   *Jewish Telegraph Agency,* November 20, 2006.
9   Amy Tiebel, "Israeli Official: Strike on Iran Possible", Associated Press, November 10, 2006.
10   *Haaretz,* November 14, 2006.
11   For a discussion of the immediately preceding history of the US confrontation of Iran over its effort to exercise its legitimate rights as a signatory to the Nuclear Non-Proliferation Treaty, see James Petras, *The Power of Israel in the United States,* supra.
12   *Forward,* November 17, 2006.
13   *Maariv* Israeli Daily Newspaper, November 14, 2006.
14   Id.
15   Nathan Guttman, "Groups Mum on Iraq Despite Anti-War Tide," *Forward,* March 2, 2007.
16   *Haaretz,* November 20, 2006.
17   *Jewish Telegraph Agency,* November 14, 2006.
18   *Jewish Telegraph Agency,* November 11, 2006.
19   *Guardian,* November 15, 2006.
20   *Daily Alert,* November 22, 2006.
21   *Wall Street Journal,* November 22, 2006.
22   *The Financial Times,* November 18, 2006, p.11.
23   November 24, 2006.
24   Reuters/*Haaretz,* November 21, 2006.
25   November 18-19, 2006 p.6.
26   Ilan Pappe,The Ethnic Cleansing of Palestine, Oneworld Publishers, Oxford, 2007, pp.10-28.
27   aljazeera, November 26, 2006.
28   *New York Times,* November 27, 2006.
29   *The New Yorker,* November 27, 2006.

Chapter 9: FACING DOWN THE FACTS: THE LOBBY AND THE MEDIA ON LEBANON

1   James Petras, *The Power of Israel in the United States,* supra.
2   See Associated Press, "Israel Strike Destroys UN Post, Kills 3: Fourth Observer Feared Dead, Annan Condemns Attack", July 25, 2006. The article quotes Annan as saying Israel appeared to have struck the site deliberately.
3   On casualties during and after Israel's 'cluster bomb' invasion of Lebanon, see aljazeera, August 20, 2006; Robert Fisk, *The Independent,* August 13, 2006; *Haaretz,* August 15, 2006; *Financial Times,* September 20, 2006. On cluster bomb deaths and injuries one month after the 'ceasefire' amounted to 98 killed and wounded, see *New York Times,* October 6, 2006 and BBC, October 19, 2006.
4   Alan Cooperman, "Jewish Charities Seek $300 Million For Israel", *Washington Post,* August 3, 2006.
5   "Israel-Hizbullah conflict: Victims of rocket attacks and IDF casualties: July-August 2006" Israeli Ministry of Foreign Affairs, http://www.mfa.gov.il/MFA/Terrorism-+Obstacle+to+Peace/Terrorism+from+Lebanon-+Hizbullah/Israel-Hizbullah+conflict-+Victims+of+rocket+attacks+and+IDF+casualties+July-Aug+2006.htm

6   "No Shelters, Sirens for Israel's Arab Citizens," August 14, 2006, Democracy Now, see http://www.democracynow.org/article.pl?sid=06/08/14/1358258. In fact, as Oxfam further reported, "During Hezbollah rocket attacks this summer, government offices in northern Israel that distribute welfare benefits have been closed. Compensation schemes and other alternative arrangements have been put in place by the government but the information and application forms are only in Hebrew." See http://www.oxfam.co.uk/what_we_do/emergencies/country/middleeast/latest.htm

7   See *Jerusalem Post* online posting of Casualties of War, http://info.jpost.com/C002/Supplements/CasualtiesOfWar/leb2.html

8   *Haaretz,* August 15, 2006.

9   A *Guardian* op-ed article cites Jonathan Cook as writing: "Several Israeli armaments factories and storage depots have been built close by Arab communities in the north of Israel, possibly in the hope that by locating them there Arab regimes will be deterred from attacking Israel's enormous armory. In other words, the inhabitants of several of Israel's Arab towns and villages have been turned into collective human shields protection for Israel's war machine. Before the strike close to Nazareth late on Sunday night, several Arab villages in the north had been hit by Hezbollah rockets trying to reach these factories. No one at the BBC saw the need to mention these attacks nor the fact that "mostly Muslim" villages had been hit. So why did the strike against Nazareth and its mistaken Christian status become part of the story for the BBC?" See http://commentisfree.guardian.co.uk/david_hirst/2006/07/post_237.html

10   United Nations Office for the Coordination of Humanitarian Affairs, August 26, 2006

11   *Haaretz,* August 27, 2006.

12   See S. Hersh, *The New Yorker,* August 21, 2006.

13   *Forbes,* July 12, 2006.

14   AFP, July 12, 2006.

15   *Asia Times,* July 15, 2006.

16   Cornel Uguhart in Tel Aviv, "Israel planned for Lebanon War Months in Advance, PM Says," *The Guardian,* March 9, 2007.

17   *Jerusalem Post,* August 21, 2006.

18   *Jerusalem Post,* August 25, 2006.

19   *Jerusalem Post,* August 25, 2006.

20   *Times-Bloomberg Poll,* July 25-August 1, 2006, published in the *Jewish Telegraph Agency,* August 15, 2006

Chapter 10: US EMPIRE AND THE MIDDLE EAST: ZIONISM, PUPPET REGIMES AND POLITICAL ALLIES

1   See "The Spy Trial: A Political Bombshell," in James Petras, *The Power of Israel in the United States,* supra.

2   See *Forward,* supra.

3   *Financial Times,* March 23, 2007, p. 5.

4   aljazeera, March 31, 2007.

5   According to Jeremy Scahill, "There are 100,000 private contractors in Iraq. We know from the Government Accountability Office that there are 48,000 employees of private military firms, mercenary companies operating in Iraq. 180 separate firms are registered operating in Iraq, Blackwater sort of being the industry leader." "Blackwater: The Rise of the World's Most Powerful Mercenary Army," interview on DemocracyNow.com, March 27, 2007.

6   On the compatibility of state-owned oil and gas companies and high rates of profitability of private oil companies, see Francisco Guerrera and Carola Hoyos "Hidden Value: How Unlisted Companies Are Eclipsing the Public Equity Market", *Financial Times,* December 15, 2006, p.11.

7   Edward Tivnan, *The Lobby,* Simon and Schuster, New York, 1987, p. 180.

PART III: THE POSSIBILITY OF RESISTANCE

Chapter 11: PAST, PRESENT AND FUTURE OF CHINA: FROM SEMI-COLONY TO WORLD POWER?

1   On the growth of inequalities in China, which by some estimates is greater than that in the US, see *Financial Times,* February 28, 2006.

2   See Chapter 1, "Who Rules America?" herein.

3   Foreign penetration of the Chinese economy has extended to almost all strategic sectors. See Japanese penetration of manufacturing, transport sectors (*Financial Times*, April 5, 2007, p.3); Citigroup doubled its banking outlets in China in 2007 (*Financial Times*, March 3, 2007 p. l9); Intel dominates semiconductor (*Financial Times*, March 17, 2007 p.20); takeover of beer sector by Anhauser-Busch (*Financial Times*, April 4, 2007, p.18); Agribusiness moves into agriculture (id., p.9); Exxon into oil (BBC, March 30, 2007). Seung-Wook Baek, "Does China Follow the East Asian Development Model", *Journal of Contemporary Asia,* Vol. 35, No. 4 (2005): the ratio of China's intra-regional trade with Asia is very high (52.3 percent of exports and 64.5 percent of imports in 2002).

4   See the following publications by the OECD: OECD, *Review of Agricultural Policies: China,* France, 2005; OECD, *Economic Survey of China 2005*, France, 16 Sept. 2005; OECD, *China in the Global Economy: Governance in China*, 2005.

5   FIE (foreign investment enterprises) account for half of China's international trade (50.85% in 2001) investing mainly in labor-intensive industries...with growing role of FIE; degree of dependence of China on foreign trade has doubled from 23.1% in 1985 to 44% in 2001 (since China joined WTO this has accelerated). SOE (State-owned enterprises) 60.9% of total assets of large enterprises in 2002. State sector a major part in heavy industry, high percentage of gross domestic-fixed capital formation, gross output value, and number of employees. Hundreds of other foreign MNCs are moving rapidly and extensively into China's lucrative market, pension funds and local savings. Over 70 banks are now active in China *Financial Times*, March 19, 2007, p. 19.

6   Demonstrations, protests and unrest in China in response to illegal state seizures of peasant lands for developers, real estate speculators. See reports in *Financial Times* on January 21, 2006, p.5; February 23, 2006, p.5; March 9, 2006, p.3; August 8, 2006, p.14.

Chapter 12: US-LATIN AMERICAN RELATIONS: RUPTURES, REACTION AND THE ILLUSIONS OF TIMES PAST

1   In Spanish, the acronym is ACLA, *Área de Libre Comercio de las Américas.*

2   Information Clearing House, May 6, 2007. The count of US wounded comes from the Iraq Coalition Casualty Count website at http://icasualties.org/oif/, but the figure is from February, 2007.

3   Information Clearing House, May 6, 2007.

Chapter 13: NEW WINDS FROM THE LEFT OR HOT AIR FROM A NEW RIGHT

1   James Petras, *Brasil: Ano Zero*, Furb 2004.

2   Under the previous Center-Right President Cardoso regime, 48,000 families received land each year compared to 25,000 per year under Lula, leaving over 200,000 families camped by highways under plastic tents and 4.5 million landless families with no hope.

Chapter 14: FOREIGN INVESTMENT IN LATIN AMERICA: SOCIAL COSTS AND POLITICAL RISKS

1   *Boletin: Cedada da Divida,* No 12, May 31, 2005, p. 2.

2   Id, pp. 2-3.

3   Id.
4   Cited in *Boletin*, p. 6.
5   *La Jornada,* June 7, 2005.
6   Tanushree Mazumdar, "Capital Flows into India", *Economic and Political Weekly*, Vol XL No 21, p. p2183-2189
7   See James Petras and Henry Veltmeyer, *Social Movements and State Power* Pluto, London, 2005.

INDEX